D1484439

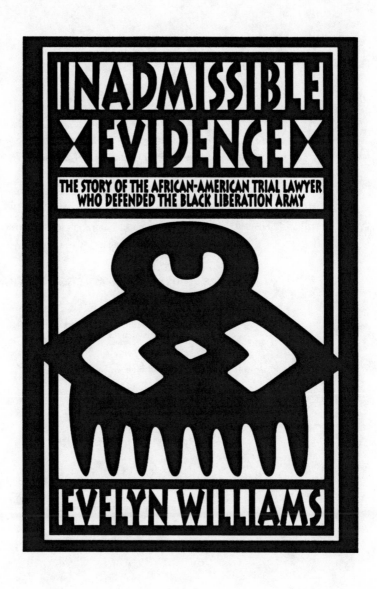

INADMISSIBLE EVIDENCE

THE STORY OF THE AFRICAN-AMERICAN TRIAL LAWYER WHO DEFENDED THE BLACK LIBERATION ARMY

EVELYN WILLIAMS

AN AUTHORS GUILD BACKINPRINT.COM EDITION

Inadmissible Evidence:

The Story of the African-American Trial Lawyer Who Defended the Black Liberation Army

All Rights Reserved © 1993, 2000 by Evelyn Williams

No part of this book may be reproduced or transmitted in any form
or by any means, graphic, electronic, or mechanical, including photocopying,
recording, taping, or by any information storage or retrieval system,
without the permission in writing from the publisher.

AN AUTHORS GUILD BACKINPRINT.COM EDITION
Published by iUniverse.com, Inc.

For information address:
iUniverse.com, Inc.
620 North 48th Street, Suite 201
Lincoln, NE 68504-3467
www.iuniverse.com

Originally published by Lawrence Hill Books

ISBN: 0-595-14170-6

Printed in the United States of America

Dedicated to my African ancestors, my grandparents, my parents, my sister, and my nieces, all of whom have waged their own struggles against the multiple facets of racism that continue to structure the world.

And to all political prisoners, wherever they are confined within the mirrored noon of the dead.

Т he great W. E. B. Du Bois once observed that one ever feels one's "twoness," being both Black and American. How much more the dilemma must be compounded when one is also both female and a lawyer. The barriers for entry into the profession for African Americans is a matter of clear historical record. The new Republic was more than a half century into its existence before Macon B. Allen gained admission to the bar in the 1840s. It was not until 1872 that, overcoming all obstacles, the first African American woman lawyer, Charlotte Ray, emerged. Evelyn Williams is in that brave, proud tradition. In this remarkable book she tells the story of her life—of becoming a lawyer and of using her considerable skills in the service of change. It is at once a window into a life and an insightful view of the turbulent times in which that life has been led.

Like most African Americans Williams has deep southern roots. Hers is, in part, an American family saga, as her parents follow the Great Migration out of their native North Carolina, seeking a better life for their children and themselves in the teeming metropolitan areas of the North. The South is a place to escape from, while at the same time a source of nurturing family strength. It is a sanctuary to retreat to in times of trouble—especially when, as with Williams's family, one comes from Black landowning stock that has managed to keep the homestead intact.

Evelyn Williams's Queens, New York, lower-middle-class upbringing is not unlike that of many other gifted African Americans. Despite the rigors of the Great Depression, her parents fight not only to survive and to improve their status but to give their talented daughter every advantage of which they are capable. They also provide her with the tools of dignity and strength to meet the inevitable American racism against which neither her intelligence nor her middle-class station is a shield.

This fine autobiography details the difficulties in becoming an African American female lawyer in an age when to do so was still a great rarity. Working full time, struggling to survive, and simultaneously going to law school is part of the success story of many outstanding members of the profession, but the added dimensions of also being both Black and female are set out in bold relief by Williams's account. She also lets us know that the difficulties flowing from race and gender do not somehow magically melt away upon admission to the bar. Becoming a lawyer is only the end of the beginning. Growth, development, finding mentors, honing one's skills, and directing one's fire all come afterward.

This book is not just about Evelyn Williams becoming a lawyer. It is about the kind of lawyer Evelyn Williams becomes. Mr. Justice Oliver Wendell Holmes once declared that life is action and passion and that one must share the actions and passions of one's times or be deemed not to have lived. Judged by this standard, Evelyn Williams has lived and lived greatly. She has lived her life as a lawyer committed not just to law but, with fierce determination, to justice as well. This is evident at every juncture of her illustrious career.

The loss of Black land in the South through economic hardship or unscrupulous white greed has been an ongoing phenomenon for some time. Evelyn Williams has to confront it when her beloved family land in North Carolina is put in jeopardy. What develops is a classic struggle of a young lawyer against injustice and against the odds. Her role as a legal pioneer and crusader for justice is further played out as she becomes one of the earliest female African American teachers at New York University School of Law. We see her dedication to her community and to the fight for change as she directs the neighborhood legal services office in Harlem, in her opening her own neighborhood practice, and in the way she serves those desperately in need who walk through her door. It is evident, as well, in her fearless representation of unpopular and controversial clients who have dared to risk all in the interest of deliverance of African American people.

Nowhere do the personal Williams and the political Williams become more illuminated than in her descriptions of her relationship with her famous/infamous niece, the alleged Black Liberation Army leader Assata Shakur (JoAnne Chesimard)— Williams's "Joey," who in Williams's words "became more my child than my niece." Williams describes all the expected excitement generated by Assata's exploits and the state's repressive response to her alleged activities. She provides powerful insights into the workings of the police, the prosecutors, the judges, and the judicial system. Assata looms large as a heroic figure committed to the liberation of her people in the Harriet Tubman tradition. Her capture, multiple trials, imprisonment, escape, and Cuban exile are the stuff of high drama.

However, Williams's book does what no other has done in humanizing Assata, breaking her loose from the stereotypical portraits arising out of mass media demonology. She presents Assata as a full human being in all her dimensions—a niece, a daughter, a new mother birthing in prison. This is an important and valuable contribution to our understanding of just who Assata is as a person, removing her from the realm of either archvillain or idealized heroine.

A treatment such as this is unprecedented and unparalleled in the literature dealing with the defense of political activists. But then this relationship is unprecedented and unparalleled in the annals of social activism. There has been no comparable situation in which a major radical activist had as her major legal defender a close blood relative. From these basic ingredients Evelyn Williams brings forth an account of the textured complexity of the surrogate mother/daughter, aunt/niece, attorney/client interconnection. And in the telling she reveals a great deal about both of them—how they learned from each other and grew; how Evelyn Williams had to come to accept the political judgments of her "Joey" who was now Assata; and how, all other limiting, defining labels aside, their relationship was nurtured by the mutual respect and deep love of two strong, uncompromising African American women.

Evelyn Williams fought hard for Assata. So much so that her zeal wound her up in jail from the inside looking out. Her single-minded commitment was attributable, at least in part, to familial devotion. But transcending personal ties and loyalties is Evelyn Williams's unstinting commitment to justice and the liberation of African peoples in these United States. Because of this, she surely would have defended Assata even if she had not been her niece. But she was, and from their history of closeness they were able to start off at a different place than most accused and their attorneys.

x   These memoirs are a true reflection of a Black woman legal warrior who asks for and gives little quarter—an implacable foe of injustice. Her opinions about issues and characterizations of persons will not win universal assent. Certain targets will want and doubtless will deserve some rebuttal time.

In the end Williams is forced to confront what she really believes about law and race and society, and about a criminal justice system that is all too often more criminal than it is just—one in which, in her view, all Black prisoners are political prisoners, one whose corruptions and perversions she had witnessed as a social worker even before she entered law school. While still able to hold out a grand vision for a better and changed society, Williams comes to some quite sobering conclusions about the limits of law as an instrument for social change, speaking in a voice not unlike Assata's. We should listen.

Haywood Burns
March 1993

Part One

Chapter 1

Police sirens twisted around the corners of the night. Menacing. Searching. Chasing. Hunting down JoAnne Chesimard, my only sister's first child. Whom they called cop killer, bank robber, and a member of a terrorist gang of criminals, the Black Liberation Army (the BLA). Who was known to militants by her African name, Assata Shakur, and whom I called Joey.

It was the spring of 1973 and for the last two years the nationwide dragnet for her capture had intensified each time a young African American identified as a member of the BLA was arrested or wounded or killed. The Joint Terrorist Task Force, made up of the FBI and local police agencies across the country, issued daily bulletins predicting her imminent apprehension each time another bank had been robbed or another cop had been killed. Whenever there was a lull in such occurrences, they leaked information, allegedly classified as "confidential," to the media, repeating past accusations and flashing her face across television screens and newspapers with heartbeat regularity, lest the public forget.

For the first time in its history, the New York City Police Department equipped patrol cars with shotguns. More police were added to the force. Revised guidelines were issued: travel only with a backup team and use caution in the chase. Special training programs in urban guerrilla warfare became mandatory, and printed instructions were distributed detailing the degree of care to be used when stopping suspicious-looking Black men in vehicles or on the street, whether alone or in a crowd.

Between January 1971 and February 1973, the FBI claimed that BLA members had attacked twenty-two policemen in cities across the country, from San Francisco to New York, including Atlanta, Houston, St. Louis, and New Orleans, and had robbed innumerable banks to finance their primary goal, which, according to FBI intelligence, was to ambush and kill cops. The first

4 incident that was catapulted into national prominence occurred in Manhattan on May 19, 1971, Malcolm X's birthday and six days after the Panther 21, members of the Black Panther Party, were acquitted on charges of conspiracy. The two-year trial for attempting to bomb the Statue of Liberty, the longest trial in the history of New York State, had resulted in the acquittal after one hour of jury deliberation.

On May 19, at about 9:00 P M , machine gun blasts were fired from a car traveling in the wrong direction on Riverside Drive into a patrol car in which policemen Thomas Curry and Nicholas Binetti were riding. The attempted murder took place near the home of District Attorney Frank Hogan, the prosecutor in the Panther 21 trial. While seriously injured, both police officers survived, and two days later an envelope containing a live 45-caliber cartridge, a license plate purportedly belonging to the car from which the shots were fired, and a letter was delivered to *The New York Times*. The letter stated:

> May 19, 1971.
> All power to the people.
> Here are the license plates sought after by the fascist state pig police.
> We send them in order to exhibit the potential power of oppressed peoples to acquire revolutionary justice. The armed goons of this racist government will again meet the guns of oppressed Third World Peoples as long as they occupy our community and murder our brothers and sisters in the name of American law and order. The domestic armed forces of racism and oppression will be confronted with the guns of the Black Liberation Army, who will mete out in the tradition of Malcolm and all true revolutionaries, real justice We are revolutionary justice

JoAnne Chesimard and others were wanted for questioning.

On August 23, 1971, a Queens, New York, bank was robbed. Joey and others were wanted for questioning, and the bank surveillance photo became a permanent fixture in every teller's window in every bank in the city. It was enlarged and mounted on the walls of subway stations. The poster displayed three rows of alleged bank robbers, six photographs to a line. The only woman in this lineup wore thick-rimmed black glasses beneath a high hairdo pulled tightly above her head, and she held a firmly pointed gun. While the names of none of the others were given, this strange-

looking person was identified in large print as JoAnne Chesimard.
The same poster was used in full-page ads, prominently inserted between important newspaper stories and paid for by the New York Clearing House Association, a bank conglomerate.

On December 20, 1971, two policemen in a patrol car were chasing three men and a woman in a stolen car in Maspeth, Queens, when the patrol car was demolished by a grenade thrown from the car. Both police officers escaped serious injury. A witness to the attack identified the woman in the car, from photographs, as JoAnne Chesimard.

On January 26, 1972, a cop whose name was never released was wounded as he tried to serve a traffic summons in Brooklyn. JoAnne Chesimard and others were wanted for questioning.

On January 27, 1972, patrolman Gregory Foster and Rocco Laurie were shot to death in the East Village as they were walking their beat. JoAnne Chesimard and others were wanted for questioning.

On March 1, 1972, a Brooklyn bank was robbed of $89,000. A woman was reported to have been driving the getaway car. The New York *Daily News* boldly headlined the question of the day under the Queens bank surveillance picture: "Was That JoAnne?"

On September 1, 1972, JoAnne Chesimard and others were wanted for questioning concerning a Bronx bank robbery.

On September 9, 1972, a New Orleans bank was robbed of $129,707 in cash and $29,375 in bonds. The Secret Service issued a bulletin circulated throughout police departments in every state calling for the arrest of JoAnne Chesimard.

On December 28, 1972, a Brooklyn drug dealer was kidnapped. JoAnne Chesimard and others were wanted for questioning.

On January 2, 1973, a Brooklyn drug dealer was murdered. JoAnne Chesimard and others were wanted for questioning.

On January 15, 1973, an automatic weapon shattered a police radio car windshield, wounding both patrolmen before the police car escaped. JoAnne Chesimard and others were wanted for questioning.

On January 28, 1973, JoAnne Chesimard and others were wanted for questioning in the attempted ambush murder of two Queens policemen, Michael O'Reilly and Roy Pollina.

In all of these incidents, the police subsequently changed

the designation "wanted for questioning" to "wanted." The former category is used for a person who the police believe has information about an unsolved crime. The latter designates a person who allegedly has committed a crime and for whom an arrest warrant has been issued. In either case the whereabouts of the person are usually unknown. One of the purposes of releasing the names to the public is to facilitate the person's apprehension, from information provided by either families or informants.

Throughout the two years of alleged BLA activity, New York City Police Commissioner Vincent Murphy intentionally released previously unreported information to coincide with the trials of captured militants. His actions were designed to enhance the hysteria being generated by Murphy's media expert, Robert Daley, deputy commissioner of the New York City Police Department in charge of public relations. In the February 12, 1973, issue of *New York* magazine, Daley wrote an article entitled "Target Blue" in which he pompously delineated his version of the organizational operations, goals, and activities of the BLA, converting hypothesis into fact through the magic of questionable police department information. He wrote, "Many of the assassins and assailants are killed or caught; others remain at large, principally Andrew Jackson, Twyman Myers, Herman Bell and Joanne Chesimard—who may in fact be their leader—a City College girl who was once shot in the stomach during a stick-up and who later said she was glad she had been shot because now she no longer feared police bullets." (Daley was referring to April 5, 1971, when Joey was shot in the stomach by a drug dealer she was trying to set up. She was then arrested while escaping from the Hilton Hotel in New York City.)

Daley's article attributed various acts to Joey, stating that on one occasion she had brought to a Bronx safe house a badly wounded and bleeding Robert Vickers, an alleged member of the BLA, who was being sought for questioning along with her. Daley described Joey as "the final wanted fugitive, and soul of the gang, the mother hen who kept them together, kept them moving, kept them shooting." Kenneth Walton, the New York division chief of the FBI, stated that his career would not be fulfilled until the day he cornered JoAnne Chesimard, woke her from her sleep with a gun pointed at her head, and said "Gotcha."

For two years I had spent my nights monitoring the radio

news stations. In the early hours, before eventful news breaks were reported, dead spots were filled in with rumors of what militants called "Assata sightings." She was reported to have been seen in different states. On the West Coast. Conducting a training camp in the use of weapons and guerrilla warfare on a farm in Georgia. Hiding out in a Brooklyn armory. Leisurely walking along East 23rd Street in New York City, flanked by serious-looking Black men who inspired such fear in the observing policemen that they refused to apprehend her without a platoon backup.

It was March 1973, and I was staring at the canvas she had painted for me on my birthday in 1969. It hung on the wall opposite my desk in Vanderbilt Hall at New York University Law School, where I had been teaching since 1968. Three young Black faces erupted from the Jackson Pollock–like background: passionate, intense, compelling. She had never identified them or told me, in fact, if they were portraits of anyone she knew. But they resembled three of the defendants in the Panther 21 trial, two men and a woman, fixed in triangular unity, their eyes directed both inward and outward, the black, green, and red of the background merging and separating at the same time. Were they among the hunted?

Although recently I had not seen Joey as frequently as I had before she joined the Black Panther Party, we still kept in touch easily and without special appointments and, as she had since she was a child, when she needed help or just plain talk, she called.

In 1967, when she was arrested, along with one hundred other students at Manhattan Community College on charges of trespassing after they had chained and locked the entrance to a building to protest curriculum deficiencies in the Black Studies program and the lack of Black faculty, she had called.

I had seen her fairly frequently in 1968, both before and after her marriage to Louis Chesimard, a CCNY student, and I remembered their pleasure as they installed the specially designed wooden shutters I had had made for the many windows in their attractive apartment on a hill overlooking CCNY.

In February 1970, when Judge John M. Murtagh arbitrarily revoked bail for Afeni Shakur and Joan Bird, the two women on trial in the Panther 21 case, she had called. Characteristically, Joey communicated the urgency of her concern without giving

many details, confident that I would help. It was a short conversation, as if squeezed between appointments, as if her time was
too valuable for her to linger over mundanities. I filed a writ of
habeas corpus, an application to the court for reinstatement of
bail, and Joan Bird was released. I was shocked to learn, many
years later, that neither had known of Joey's quiet intervention
or of our relationship.

When she attended the Revolutionary People's Constitutional Convention, held in Philadelphia later that year despite an
injunction banning it, she didn't call but she came directly from
Philadelphia to join her family vacationing at Freeman's Beach
in Wilmington, North Carolina. She came without luggage, her
hair braided and her one pair of jeans and a blouse wrinkled and
still dusty from the several days she had spent sleeping on
tabletops and sitting on the floors of rooms crowded with other
young people who had arrived from across the country. She
came to North Carolina to discuss her decision to join the Black
Panther Party, but while she posed the possibility, it was clear
that she had charted her course and that this was just a courtesy
stop. I had no opposition. Although my concept of the party was
limited to what I had read, I viewed it as a correct, domestic
response to the untenable conditions facing Black people. Joey
talked in terms of global parameters, Africa, and the politics
needed to ensure permanent change in the United States. As
always, her vision encompassed more than the immediate, while
mine was rooted in alleviating the source of imminent disaster.

After she joined the Black Panther Party she came to ask for
help in obtaining community donations for the party's summer
school, where she taught.

And in 1971, after she was shot in the Hilton Hotel, she
called me from French Hospital, where the police had brought
her after her arrest and asked me to represent her on the felony
charges.

But now, for more than two years, I had heard nothing from
her. I knew the danger to her was real, whether the reason for it
was fabrication or fact. And I also knew she would not risk
making a telephone call to me. But I kept repeating to myself,
"Find a way!"

Joey and I had a special bond that began before she was
born. Her mother, Doris, a year and nine months older than I,

had always been my closest friend. But Doris was sickly, even as a small child, and suffered exaggerated reactions to the usual childhood diseases that most children recover from after a few days. When she squeezed a teenage pimple alongside her eyebrow, she became infected and was hospitalized for two days with hourly hot and cold compresses applied by nurses in that pre-penicillin era. The doctor called her recovery a miracle. And when her menstrual cycle began, the pain was so severe that she had to stay in bed for each week of its duration. As she moved into late adolescence, the family doctor warned her against having children, explaining that she had an inoperable uterine malformation that could result in death during childbirth.

So her first pregnancy filled my parents and me with nine months of unrelieved fear. At that time I was not yet married and lived at home in Queens. Doris and her husband, a World War II veteran, had bought a house near my parents' on the GI Bill, but they separated a few months before the baby was born and Doris moved back home. During those months I rushed home from work every day to walk with her the mile prescribed by the doctor.

JoAnne was born at 4:00 A.M. in Women's Hospital in Brooklyn on July 16, 1947. Despite our desperate pleas, Doris's doctor refused to let my parents and me remain in the hospital during the long, difficult labor but promised to call us as soon as birth seemed imminent or complications arose. When the doctor finally did call, my father drove through the quiet night streets from Queens to Brooklyn as if it were he who was about to give birth. We arrived just as the baby was being carried to the nursery, but it was not until several hours later, when Doris was wheeled from the delivery room and greeted us with "I can finally see my feet," that we relaxed.

Doris was bedridden for about a month after she returned home from the hospital. Although the bassinet was in her room, which was next to mine, I always heard Joey cry at night and, to keep her from waking my sister, I would race in, pick her up, change her, carry her downstairs to the kitchen, warm her formula, and feed and rock her back to sleep. She became more my child than my niece. And I gave vent to that sense of proprietorship, inappropriately but quite characteristically, when she was about a year old and my sister and her husband had reconciled. His mother was caring for Joey while Doris was completing graduate school. One day, during one of our frequent visits to see the baby, my mother and I saw her standing in a corner of her crib, her large eyes filled with tears that spilled down her cheeks. She was crying hysterically without making a sound. I picked her up and told my mother that in no way was Joey going to remain for one more minute in that house with that person—someone who so frightened her that she dare not cry out loud. My mother got Joey's clothes and later that day we told Doris why the baby was with us. Soon afterward, she and her husband separated permanently and Doris and Joey moved in with us again.

Joey was stubborn, even at crib age. When she refused to eat, I was required to do somersaults and other gymnastic feats before she would reward my efforts with a laughing open mouth, which I quickly filled with a spoonful of food. As she grew older, we all centered our attention on this fatherless miracle, especially me. Joey's talent in art and story writing was so much like mine as a child and she was so eagerly curious and precocious that, at a very early age, I began to take her to museums, parks, unusual restaurants, theaters, and all of my other special places. Nothing was too strange to her, including the architectural design of the Guggenheim Museum, or too mundane, like a walk through Central Park.

When she was thirteen, she ran away from home and came to live with me. Her emerging personality amazed me, although then, as now, she voiced her uncompromising opinions in soft, unhurried tones. I had not classified it as a generation gap, but in junior high school I had never challenged the educational system as Joey did. She criticized the Spanish course because Castilian Spanish was taught rather than the Spanish her friends spoke; she refused, for instance, to accept the Castilian pronunciation of the letter c as "th" rather than as "s." And she absolutely disagreed with the grammatical correctness of my speech, preferring the idiomatic phrases used by many African Americans because she felt they had just as much legitimacy in communicating thought as "proper English" and certainly were more colorful. We had many heated arguments about language until, reluctantly, she agreed to speak both.

Joey wrote poetry in blank verse, discounting rhyme as too artificial, and at fourteen was reading my Hart Crane and T. S. Eliot collections. She considered Latin a dead language, useless

in the real world, and chafed at the necessity to learn it. And she
had no patience with education for the sake of education,
whereas I thought (and still do) that it is important to know
about subjects that serve no specific purpose in the foreseeable
future. Despite my strong objections, Joey quit high school in
her senior year because it was "an exercise in futility," her
generation's most quoted observation. While I helped her find a
job, I breathed a sigh of relief when she decided to give the
educational process another chance and enrolled in college.
During her late adolescence she had returned to live with her
mother, but our time together through the "terrible teens," while
difficult, further cemented our bond.

Between 1971 and 1973, the possibility that she would be
shot to death filled my every waking moment and broke my sleep
at night. I had no way of knowing whether I was dealing with
manipulated media coverage or untainted reality. I lived in
constant fear that an informant's tip would tighten the net
around her and that she, like so many other Black Panthers,
would be cornered and killed in a shoot-out. I again saw photographs of the bodies of Fred Hampton and Mark Clark, two Black
Panthers, as they lay dead on their beds in a Chicago apartment.
They had been killed in their sleep in the predawn of December
23, 1969, when police fired eighty-two bullets into their apartment. More recently, on January 22, 1973, the New York City
Police Department received a tip that two alleged members of the
BLA were in a Brooklyn tavern. Eight heavily armed detectives
were dispatched to ambush them, and as Woody Green and
Anthony White sat at the bar quietly watching a heavyweight
fight on television, the squad, guns blazing, crashed into the
tavern and shotgunned them both to death.

The years of anticipating Joey's capture or death drained
the family in different ways. Since there was no communication
from her, we were adrift in continuously swelling tidal waves of
official misinformation. There was no direction or clarity or
truth. Because my telephone was tapped, conversations with my
parents, who lived in Wilmington, North Carolina, were limited
to health and weather conditions. We had to speak as if the most
important fact of our lives did not exist. My sister and I never
referred to Joey on the telephone, in our apartments, or on the
street. We walked outdoors and small-talked until we entered
certain spaces that appeared to provide some protection from

the surveillance we believed to be omnipresent. I had just one old and trusted friend, Doe (Isadora Robinson Burke), to whom I revealed my terror. Like a well-trained long-distance runner whose body had entered the pain zone, only the discipline of my legal training kept my mind moving.

My parents refused to believe any of the news reports. They could offer no explanation for the intensive search or for the charges leveled against Joey. In my parents' world, no respectable person was hunted or arrested for no reason. So they provided their own: the police were vicious liars. Their granddaughter was incapable of the horrendous acts of which she was accused. Although newspaper coverage of the BLA and the nationwide dragnet for Joey was not a daily or even a weekly event in Wilmington, a friend of theirs reminded them of the nearby presence of the Delta Force, the specially trained counterintelligence government agency, telling them to warn Joey not to come to North Carolina. Until the day my mother died she believed that her grandchild was a victim and defied anyone to tell her differently. She believed that Joey would be exonerated.

My sister vacillated between fear for her child's life and fear for her own. Imperiled by a situation about which she had no information except from the newspapers and television, she avoided both. Previously known to her friends and colleagues as a conventional elementary school teacher in the New York City public school system, a tournament bridge player, and a friendly, if occasional, party giver, she was now considered the mother of a cop killer and a bank robber. Her friends were questioned by the FBI. Their telephones were tapped. My sister's situation threatened their hard-earned positions, if not their safety.

Doris had taught school since her graduation from Hunter College. While married and teaching, she had obtained a master's degree and completed all of the course requirements for a Ph.D. Although she had received many awards for innovative teaching techniques and for successfully working with so-called unteachable students, she began to have difficulties at her school. Her methods were scrutinized. Her daily school plans were questioned and disapproved. After years of teaching, she was subjected to classroom monitoring by either the principal or a supervisor from the Board of Education. Plans were set in motion to fire her. While that effort failed, the tenuousness of her civil service status, always believed to be permanent, as well as

the ineffective assistance she received from the United Federa-
tion of Teachers, her union, made her vulnerable for the first
time in her working life to the fear of economic insecurity, that
singular nightmare for children of the Great Depression. She was
no longer sure she would be permitted to retire at the usual age
of sixty-five with a decent, livable pension.

In addition to the withdrawal of all but her closest friends,
the pattern of her life changed dramatically. Telephone calls
with strange messages or menacing silences persisted even after
she changed her phone number and had it unlisted. And her
apprehension of shadowy figures following her, not always imagined, permanently altered her life. It was difficult to believe that
mere coincidence accounted for the fact that each apartment
surrounding hers in the thirty-three-floor high rise, including the
apartment beneath, remained empty for years at the height of a
buyer's market. Electric eyes were installed both in an empty
apartment next to hers and at the end of the hall facing the door
of her apartment. When she returned home from a visit to my
parents one summer, her apartment had been broken into
through the terrace window, but nothing had been stolen. Apart
from the glass fragments on the floor and the broken window-
pane, the only indication of intrusion was the black fingerprint-
ing powder left on door frames, on clothes in her closet, and on
other personal items.

After that, asthmatic attacks and allergic reactions to sub-
stances that her doctor could not pinpoint constantly afflicted
her. She canceled summer plans to travel to Europe or the
Caribbean because of her anticipated need for emergency medical treatment and her belief that traveling outside the country
increased her vulnerability, but primarily because she would not
be available in the event Joey was captured. I'm sure there were
many times when she asked the same question asked by other
families whose children were hunted as members of the BLA:
Why my child? Why me?

Joey's sister, Bevvie, five years younger, was defiantly angry
and loyal. Joey had been her mentor and best friend, patiently
accompanying her through the mysteries of adolescence, giving
her books to read about the conditions of Africans living in
America, elevating her political awareness. Bevvie was nineteen
in 1971 when Joey's name first appeared in newspaper headlines. She believed none of what she read about her sister. One

day Joey was there, teasing her, being responsible for her, listening to her, sharing secrets with her. And then suddenly she was gone, without warning or explanation. And Bevvie's memory of her slim, soft-voiced, popular, humorous, dance-loving, pretty sister was replaced by a mug shot of a swollen-faced stranger who stared ominously at her from newspapers and subway posters. "Wanted, dead or alive," was no longer a cliché from old western movies. It meant her sister.

I was better able to withstand the barrage of publicity than my family because I was a criminal trial lawyer. After years of representing Black and poor defendants hopelessly mired in the "system" I had long ago ceased referring to as the criminal justice system, I was suspect of the airtight public indictment against Joey. I screened every newspaper accusation for loopholes, photocopied reports, compared them, and filed them for future reference in the event she was captured alive. I taped radio reports and transcribed them. I evaluated every fragment of information leaked by the police department or the FBI for inconsistencies, unintentionally revealed clues, or suspect sources.

I became aware of the police department's efforts to both generate and maintain public support for any unauthorized police action that might result in the apprehension of those suspected of being BLA members. To keep public sentiment on their side, however, the police first had to prepare the public for the possibility that the killings of police not only would continue but were the acts of a gang of terrorists. It was critical to their plan to portray the BLA as vicious thugs and to carefully avoid making public any information given them by the BLA that suggested purpose and structure to their alleged random activities.

It was not until the deaths of policemen Gregory Foster and Rocco Laurie in January 1972 that the New York City police decided to make public the fact that, in their opinion, there did exist a nationwide, organized conspiracy to assassinate police officers. In 1971 department officials had asked *The New York Times* not to publish a letter the newspaper had received from the BLA claiming responsibility for the May 19 Riverside Drive attack. Nor did the media report Robert Daley's press conference, held a few days later, in which he announced, "There is a conspiracy of black extremists who are responsible for the cop killings. Always in the past the police have been quiet about this conspiracy because of fear of accusations of racism. But it isn't

the black community that is doing this, it is a few dozen black
criminal thugs, and it just has to be said."

But by early 1972, the police department was forced to
confront the wide discrepancy between its official policy and the
public face it had put on its policy. The day after the Foster and
Laurie murders, on January 28, United Press International
received a letter signed by "The George Jackson Squad of the
BLA," claiming: "This is about the pigs wiped out in Lower
Manhattan last night. No longer will Black people tolerate Attica
and oppression and exploitation and rape of our Black community. This is the start of our spring offensive. There is more to
come. We also dealt with the pigs in Brooklyn." Anticipating the
public reaction of fear combined with outrage at the impotence
of the police department to arrest those responsible, police
officials reached an agreement with the media to withhold the
letter until the police could demonstrate containment of the
threat and thus dilute its importance in the public's mind. Police
Commissioner Murphy huddled with his top command, especially his public relations adviser, Daley, to produce the correct
official posture. Ten days after the murders, he designated Albert
Seedman, chief of detectives, to deliver his analysis of the BLA
and to release the names of nine suspects, including JoAnne
Chesimard, who he claimed were responsible for the crime. This
cooperative venture between Murphy and the media resulted in
extensive live television coverage of Seedman's press conference
and assurance that the story would appear on the front page of
every New York newspaper the next day.

Following the press conference, Queens District Attorney
Thomas Mackell, concerned about the effects of pretrial publicity, criticized the public disclosure of the names of the suspects
and the extensive revelation about the backgrounds of four of
them because "it might hinder efforts at a fair trial for any of the
group if ever arrested."

During the press conference, Seedman had added:

> This group and a handful of others have been responsi-
> ble for killings and assaults on policemen, both black and
> white; holdups and assaults against ordinary citizens and
> businessmen, both black and white. This small group has
> labeled itself the Black Liberation Army. There is no evidence
> to connect these people to others who have used similar
> names such as Black Liberation Party or Black Liberation

Front, etc. This is a handful of people who have taken it upon themselves to assault and kill police officers and who finance their activities by committing holdups and other crimes.

What is the Black Liberation Army? It is composed of this small group of militants who do not have an organizational base, and who would like to give some semblance of legitimacy to their homicidal acts. Certainly it does not represent the thinking of the black community, since, as a matter of fact, these assaults have brought blacks closer to their police than ever before in an effort to combat a common enemy.

This multifaceted approach was carefully constructed to assuage the fears of the general public, to appeal to the peaceful, law-abiding instincts of African Americans, and to provide them with an acceptable rationale for rejecting the BLA.

But it was not until 1975, when Senator Frank Church's committee released the results of its investigation of government surveillance practices, that I learned of the FBI's secret plan called COINTELPRO, a "covert action program" initiated in 1967 "to disrupt and 'neutralize' organizations which the Bureau characterized as 'Black Nationalist Hate Groups.' "[*]

The FBI memorandum explaining COINTELPRO described its goals as follows:

1. Prevent a coalition of militant black nationalist groups . . . .

2. Prevent the rise of a messiah who could unify and electrify the militant nationalist movement . . . Martin Luther King, Stokely Carmichael and Elijah Muhammad all aspire to this position. . . .

3. Prevent violence on the part of black nationalist groups . . . .

4. Prevent militant black nationalist groups and leaders from gaining respectability by discrediting them. . . .

5. . . . prevent the long-range growth of militant black nationalist organizations, especially among youth.

While the Black Panther Party was targeted for FBI infiltration, other, nonmilitant organizations were also disrupted and

[*]U.S Senate, *The Final Report and the Staff Report of the Select Committee to Study Governmental Operations with respect to Intelligence Activities,* Books II and III (Washington, D C GPO, 1975). The report is popularly known as the Church Committee Report

destroyed by the FBI, which planted agents and created dissen-
sion through media-supplied lies. Supporters and members were
discouraged and discredited in a cooperative campaign between
the FBI and local police departments in every state. There were
warrantless telephone taps on Black militant groups as well as
surveillance of civil rights rallies, marches, and demonstrations.
Included in the FBI's plot was every Black organization of
national or local significance, including the NAACP, the Urban
League, the Congress for Racial Equality (CORE), the Nation of
Islam, the Southern Christian Leadership Conference (SCLC),
Black student unions, the Revolutionary Action Movement
(RAM), Black Libya, and the Republic of New Afrika. When the
BLA drew national attention and caused media hysteria begin-
ning in 1971, it became one of the prime targets of COIN-
TELPRO.

The Church Committee Report also revealed that in 1970 a
"Key Black Extremist" list was created identifying Black militants for concentrated investigation and COINTELPRO actions
as well as placement in the top-priority category of the Security
Index, a list compiled jointly by the Department of Justice and
the FBI based on the department's plan to detain "dangerous
individuals" in the event of a national emergency. The variety of
illegal and extralegal actions committed by the government
against Black nationalists ranged from arresting them "on every
possible charge until they could no longer make bail" (Exhibit O
attached to the Church Committee Report) to declaring that
"the most effective countermeasure against extremist activity is
criminal prosecution" (Exhibit P).

The report's most chilling revelation, however, was that the
FBI, in cooperation with state law enforcement authorities, had
not only fabricated criminal charges against militants but had
relentlessly prosecuted them. The Congressional Summary of
FBI activity contained in Book III notes the instrumental role
that the FBI played in planning and preparing the Chicago police
for the raid that resulted in the 1969 murders of Fred Hampton
and Mark Clark.

Once the Church Committee Report was made public,
convicted Black Panthers requested the release of their FBI files
through the Freedom of Information Act. Despite the bureau's
severe censoring of material, they documented the fact that the
FBI and local police had manufactured evidence against them,

18   had forced witnesses to give perjured testimony during their trials, and had withheld evidence that would have exonerated them.

But, as I said, none of this was known until 1975. As of 1973, all I knew was that police authorities believed that BLA members were former Panthers who had split from the party because of their more militant stance and that Joey was among them. I did not know then that the BLA was absorbing the full attention of COINTELPRO, and so I could not foresee the danger that was to come.

Chapter 2

My parents were both born in the first year of the twentieth century in Wilmington, North Carolina, on the Atlantic coast. Wilmington was divided in several ways: post–Civil War segregation had separated whites from Blacks and post–Civil War slave-class structures had separated plantation Blacks who relocated to the city from Black country folk who lived near the ocean in a section called Seabreeze. My mother's father, Robert Bruce Freeman, had escaped from the Cherokee Indian reservation in North Carolina, fled to Seabreeze, and, with financial backing from unknown but suspect sources, purchased large tracts of farm, forest, and beach property. He died shortly after my mother's birth, leaving eleven children: six boys from his first wife and two boys and three girls from his second wife, who died when my mother was nine. There was a wide age difference between the first and second set of children, and, with one exception, the older ones were notorious for their clannishness, hard drinking, and economic independence derived from fishing, farming, and operating illegal moonshine stills. All the children had inherited large homestead tracts on which they lived, reciprocating the disdain in which they were held by Blacks in the city.

The exception was my mother's second oldest half-brother. He had moved to Philadelphia, finished college, and was teaching school there when my mother's mother died. He brought my mother to live with his very proper wife and their three children. Nine years later, when my mother returned to Seabreeze after completing high school, she found herself removed from the other Freemans by more than absence. She resented their undisciplined ways and the stigma of being a Freeman that the city people attached to her. To white people, however, the Freemans were entrepreneurs and huge landholders from whom they purchased granite, clay, timber, and valuable beach property.

My father was born and raised in the city. He was a sophisticate: brown-skinned, tall, and flamboyantly handsome. His father had achieved social position in the community by virtue of his status as chauffeur for a wealthy former slave-owning family, the Sprunts. I remember Papa Link as a straight-backed, quiet man who reflected all of the dignified and "gentle-manly" qualities considered typical of the perfect house servant. Atypical was that his dignity and his respect for his own family came first in his life: unlike many others, he never shed his "respectable" behavior when he came home from work. His deep voice and available lap always reassured me during our summer trips South, whether I had fallen off the front porch swing or just wanted to be hugged.

My grandmother, Momma Jessie, who had given birth to thirteen children, was a tall, vibrant, strong-minded, determined woman who demanded, and received, a larger house from the Sprunts when the size of her family grew. It was the house in which my father was born, and it became the center of social activities, primarily because my grandmother was relentless in her aspiration that her children live on the same social level, with the same advantages, as the Black professionals who lived in Wilmington. She indulged all of her children and spent every penny my grandfather earned to realize her ambitions for them. In the same way that she refused to permit the Sprunt family to extend their influence over her family, she refused to submit to segregation and, rather than ride in the backs of buses, walked downtown to shop or pay bills. She was a fierce and marvelous person. Both my grandparents welcomed my mother into the family. My father's sisters and brothers, however, whose only claim to superiority was the fragile and illusory world with which my grandmother had surrounded them, never accepted her as their equal.

My parents were as opposite in appearance as they were in personality. My mother's temper, combined with the color of her hair, which had earned her the nickname "Red" as a child, flashed without warning, searing all objects before it, and re-mained undiminished throughout her life. My older sister, Doris, and I always heard her voice raised in loud disagreement with my father whenever family matters were discussed, and we assumed she made the decisions that resulted. My father never raised his voice and we never heard his quiet commands to her.

But his dominance over my mother was as complete as it was subtle. It was his decision to move to New York after the birth of my sister, when both my parents were twenty years old. It was his decision to give me violin lessons when I was four, and it was his decision to redirect our religious training away from my mother's Baptist upbringing to Catholicism, his mother's religion.

Like Europeans flooding New York City in search of a better life, my parents fled from the escalating atrocities of the Ku Klux Klan, from legalized racial segregation, and from the limitations imposed by both job discrimination and the types of jobs available to Black people in the South. They immigrated North, to life, to refuge, and to potential employment opportunities.

They were extravagantly adventurous, never doubting that my mother's high school education and my father's two years of college would generate the security that steady wages would provide. And for a time the expectations were borne out. While my mother stayed home to care for my sister in a furnished room in Brooklyn, my father searched for a job. He had learned to drive at the age of twelve along untraveled dirt back roads, as was true of many southern children, and it was his driving ability that enabled him to get hired as a truck driver again and again after being repeatedly fired, usually after only one day's mistakes because he was unfamiliar with New York City streets. Undaunted, he kept trying. But the country was in a post–World War I boom and, by the time I was born, two years after their move, he had obtained a permanent job as a truck driver and automobile mechanic, among the few occupations still available to Blacks in the North. He worked the two jobs and attended a school for dental technicians between shifts, never relinquishing his dream of owning his own business.

When I was four, my mother received a small inheritance from her father's estate, and my parents bought a one-family house in Merrick Park, Queens, an island separated from South Jamaica's Black lower class by Merrick Road and isolated from white middle-class St. Albans geographically by a large park and economically by redlining. Two years later, when the stock market crashed, my father, along with millions of the working class, became instantly unemployed.

I was six then, but I vividly remember the changes in our lives. My father could find work for only one day at a time, with no promise that he would be rehired for a second day. Widespread joblessness spawned riots by white people competing for the same jobs and widened the gap between opportunities available to white and Black laborers.

Small needs required major decisions. Was money to be spent looking for a job in the city or on repairing the soles of my father's shoes so that he could walk the long distances between prospective employers once he arrived there? He had completed the course in dental technology and had built a small laboratory in the basement of our house in the hope that establishing his own business would solve our economic crisis. But neither white nor Black dentists would give him an opportunity to prove his skills, even when he offered to make initial dentures free of charge.

My mother found work in a dress factory. She battled to specialize in hemming only men's pants because that work paid the most per piece. At a time when there were few Black factory workers in the garment industry and when the International Ladies' Garment Workers Union had yet to organize Blacks, she was hired because she was believed to be other than Black. She ate half-hour lunches brought from home, worked in windowless rooms crammed with hot, sweaty workers toiling over aisle-to-aisle machines roaring at a frantic pace, and then returned home to fix dinner for two small, noisy children and a still hopeful but intermittently employed husband. And always my parents feared the imminent loss of their house. When a mortgage payment was overdue, they were assailed by bill collectors who came to the house and yelled from the street to hurriedly locked doors and bolted windows, "Hill, Hill, pay your bill." Over and over. And over again.

My parents survived the Depression years by taking in roomers and by not allowing their love for each other to degenerate into blame over circumstances for which they bore no responsibility. Cheap food could be found, such as two-day-old bread sold in special locations established by the large bread companies. Fish peddlers hawked bargains on Wednesdays and Fridays, and on weekends my mother baked cornbread and rolls and cake. There were outlets where sample shoes, not in every size or width, could be purchased at less than half price, and my mother made all our clothes, including winter coats. We saved on electricity. And we saved on coal. Money was spent for nothing that was not absolutely essential to survival, and it helped that neither of my parents smoked or drank. Somehow they managed to maintain all the outward appearances of economic stability. My father painted the window frames of our brick and stucco house every year, clipped the front hedges, mowed the lawn, and made all household repairs himself. My mother, a compulsive cleaner, waxed the large living and dining room hardwood floors once a month.

My parents adhered to each other tightly, almost desperately, rarely spending time alone and always sharing social activities. The one exception was my mother's neighborhood bridge club that met every other week. I was aware of my father's deep resentment of my mother's outside interest when he sarcastically appraised her bridge partners, but he was wise enough not to openly express his displeasure. Unfazed, my mother continued playing bridge, her one passion (which she taught my sister and me when we were very young, "to keep her in practice between games") until late in her life when she was no longer able to concentrate.

Outside of having the Baptist minister to dinner once a month, my parents' diversions were confined to the Sundays we spent at Jones Beach on Long Island, where the parking was free and we didn't need much gas to travel in the tin lizzie, purchased when the family still had money. We would spend an entire day, arriving at seven and not leaving until after the traffic congestion subsided in the evening. My mother taught us to swim, and my sister and I played Ping-Pong, handball, and shuffleboard on the free courts. And we played bridge after eating the fried chicken, rolls, potato salad, and chocolate layer cake that my mother had prepared, while my father spent the day sitting under the umbrella reading the Sunday papers, never going near the water because he said it was too cold.

Except for the successful musicians and other professionals who had moved to Merrick Park at the same time we had, our poverty was the same as everyone else's. All the children played together, and differences in economic status were never mentioned. I later married the son of Clarence Williams, the musician and composer who wrote "Royal Garden Blues" and "Baby, Won't You Please Come Home," who owned a record company with offices in the Brill Building on Broadway, and whose wife, Eva Taylor, was a successful radio singer. Rich and famous in those days, they had a chauffeur, hunted wild ducks with

tians, sent their three children to private schools, and
oned in Hot Springs, Arkansas, every winter. But their
....ce, surpassing that of St. Albans's middle-class whites, did
not unlock the invisible doors that the white society shut in their
faces.

While I lived in a relatively insulated community, my
parents did not permit my sister and me the luxury of being
oblivious to the world surrounding us. There was no television,
but after dinner we sat in the living room listening to the radio,
discussing the reports about the Black Shirts, who were organized to deprive Black workers of jobs; the Ku Klux Klan, who,
together with policemen, destroyed vans containing the furniture of Black families trying to move into the Sojourner Truth
Homes in Detroit, the federally built houses for those working in
defense factories; the mass lynchings of Black people that white
people called race riots; the uprising in Harlem sparked when a
white policeman brutalized a Black woman during an unjustified
arrest; the Cranbury, New Jersey, case in which a gang of
handkerchief-masked white men, believed to be government
officials, invaded a camp of Black migrant workers in the middle
of the night, pistol-whipped them, threatened them with genital
mutilation and rape, poured white enamel paint over them, and
chased them in a southern direction, "back to where they came
from." My parents told us about segregated Black soldiers who
were conscripted to fight a war for freedom in Europe, and I will
never forget my mother's face as she described the sudden
appearance of white-hooded men emerging ghoulishly and
threateningly at night from the trees surrounding her family's
farmhouse in Seabreeze when she was a child.

My father read us stories of the slave revolts of Nat Turner,
Denmark Vesey, and Toussaint L'Ouverture and talked about
Marcus Garvey's "Back to Africa" movement, which advocated
economic independence under Black nationalism. We sat word-
less with wonder as he read the miracle of Hannibal's army of
elephants crossing the Alps and told us that Hannibal, an
African, was the greatest general in the history of the world.

My parents provided my sister and me with a formula for
survival with dignity. They taught us from the earliest age never
to lower our eyes when we spoke to white people, and they
carefully avoided exposing us to the media-generated stereotypical behavior of Black people so negatively portrayed in every-

thing created allegedly to entertain us: the shuffling Stepin Fetchit, the servile mammy roles of Hattie McDaniels, and the sly connivance of Amos and Andy that never quite reached the level of cleverness. Every Christmas my father scoured the city to find Black dolls to put under the tree. The *n* word was never used in our house, under any circumstances, either humorously or accusatorily. It was not necessary to know the etymology of the word. It was only necessary to understand that white people used the word "nigger" to denigrate Black people. To this day, when I hear it hurled across streets among young Black people, I cringe.

My parents taught us to maneuver adroitly along the tiny cracks of opportunity the United States of America reluctantly opened to its Black citizens, while at the same time teaching us to expect sudden, unexplained, and undeserved closures. Above all, they tried to help us maintain sanity as we balanced the two polarities of ambition and opportunity, and they were always clear that when we tried we bore no responsibility for defeat. They did not teach us that we could be president of the United States, nor did they teach us to make the sick adjustment of loving America.

From our earliest years, my parents had drilled a special reality into my sister and me: that only by being superior to white people could we approach their success. But embodied in that paradigm was a painful, ultimate reality—only some occupations guaranteed economic security, no matter how superior we were. So while college after high school was as inevitable as day after night, my parents discouraged us from even dreaming of attaining superiority in the exotic professions, with their implicit insecurities and concealed discrimination. It was clear to them that the jobs that had survived the Depression were in civil service—teaching, fire fighting, law enforcement. And although only a few Black people were employed in these kinds of jobs, the hope of appointment was at least a realistic one, provided that one could achieve a high enough grade on the required examination. As a result, my parents ignored my talent in art and writing and refused to permit me to attend the High School of Music and Art even after the district school superintendent came to our house and pleaded with them to send me (their pretense being the unacceptable distance I would have to travel from Queens).

In the early 1940s, my father was able to begin earning more money than the family required, thanks to the efforts of A. Philip Randolph, the Black president of the Brotherhood of Sleeping Car Porters. In 1941, Randolph threatened a massive march on Washington to protest discrimination in defense industries commissioned to produce war products for the government. Before the march could take place, President Franklin Roosevelt was pressured into signing Executive Order 8802, which established the Fair Employment Practices Commission and abolished discrimination in defense industries and in the federal government.

Almost immediately my father found work at Todd Shipyards in New Jersey, where he crawled into navy ship boilers and repaired them with an acetylene torch. When the United States entered World War II, he worked as many hours overtime as his body would allow. My mother's income in the factories, now making uniforms for the armed forces, quadrupled. The Depression was over. When the war ended, my father started a successful automobile repair business, hiring seven people, and my mother stopped working. But their frugal lifestyle didn't change. They saved their money in anticipation of the next depression.

As a child I was taller than any friends my age, male or female. I was so skinny that when my mother made skirts for my sister and me, she had to attach mine to a vestlike top to hold them up. My sister's shapely body did not add to my confidence. I wore glasses from age five and suffered through various unflattering nicknames, like "stringbean" and "four eyes." I was clumsy and shy, except with the boys in the neighborhood: I played marbles and stickball, hitched my sled and bicycle to the backs of buses, dared them to climb up to the highest branches of the tall trees on our block, and raced them the three miles to Alley Pond Park where, if we arrived before eight, we could swim for free. I was the classic example of overcompensatory behavior.

I have no doubt, however, that one of the factors that contributed to my early withdrawal into contemplative inspection of the world in which I lived was the fact that I was Black in America. I am always amused, as well as outraged, when Black people deny that they ever experienced racism as children. Some extend the lie to include their adulthood. But I believe that there has never been a Black person in this country whose pores have not been contaminated with the fumes of hatred to which they have always been exposed. Like the effects of Agent Orange, people's reaction to racism is occasionally dormant, but never absent. It is somehow fashionable today to equate understanding and forgiveness of racism with a civilized condition.

I had my share of experiences that show one how Black people are perceived by white people. My first remembered experience took a subtle form. I was about seven when, one Sunday morning, my mother sent me to the store to buy some Karo syrup and return quickly before the pancakes were done. I asked the white store owner for Karo *surrp*. He didn't know what I meant. I explained it was *surrp* to pour over pancakes and it was made by Karo. He didn't know what *surrp* was, he said, repeating my pronunciation. Vainly, almost in tears, I kept telling him what I wanted. My mother was waiting, and so was her temper. The merchant finally gave in to his need to make the sale. He said, "Oh, you must mean *syrup*," emphasizing each syllable. My humiliation at the moment was secondary to my need to get home with it before the pancakes were ready. But I promised that never again would I give a white person a reason to ridicule me for improper pronunciation. I got my father's dictionary and from that day, throughout my childhood, I practiced pronunciation from it, whispering words over and over in the downstairs bathroom. I didn't call that man's treatment of me racism then, but I learned that a white person's hatred could be so intense that he was capable of venting it on a seven-year-old.

Another memorable occasion was when I was in the sixth grade. There was a citywide contest for the best essay about Theodore Roosevelt, and one contestant was to be chosen from each class in the sixth through eighth grades. Those students would recite their essays in front of a school assembly and a winner would be chosen. When my teacher picked a white girl to represent my class, I protested. When he didn't change his selection, I went to the principal. I didn't tell my parents; I was saving them for backup. But the principal read my essay, listened to me recite it, and directed my teacher to add me to the group of contestants. Mine was the only class with two contestants. I won for the school, and my father proudly took me to the citywide ceremony held at the Museum of Natural History.

As a child I had to find my own methods of emotional survival. Initially I employed infantile and demeaning devices: white people's skin was blue-lined paste; their thin lips were undefined slash holes in a flat white wall; they were not interesting looking and definitely not sexy. I watched them on trains and buses on my way to school and I realized that they were not like the fake images I saw in movie magazines or motion pictures. As a matter of fact, they were decidedly unattractive. Having fortified myself with this analysis rather early in life, and having always been smarter and more accomplished than most of the whites I knew, I easily dismissed the myth of their "natural superiority."

I was a superachiever no matter what I did. At ages twelve and thirteen, before I began working during the summers, I was the New York City playground tennis champion. I was valedictorian at P.S. 116, a member of the academic achievement society at Jamaica High School, in the top one percent on the first SAT given for admittance to Brooklyn College, and I was readily accepted into the master's degree program in psychology at the New School for Social Research. While my parents successfully deflected my chosen career goals, my interest in the arts continued and I fully participated in the cultural diversity of New York City during my college years, the most carefree period of my life.

It was the time when I rummaged through basement and second-story used-book stores for out-of-print treasures, like the slim, navy blue, leather-bound edition of Aristotle's *Poetics* and inexpensive Caruso records. It was the time when we of the intelligentsia met in the Sunken Garden on the campus of Brooklyn College and debated Sartre's existentialism and Marx's evolutionary development from Kierkegaard. When I sat on the stone steps of the great outdoor CCNY Guggenheim amphitheater and listened to La Bohème and other operas sounding across the sky. When I purchased season tickets for the Philharmonic Symphony at Town Hall with summer and after-school earnings. When I frequented the jazz clubs on 52nd Street where, for the price of admission, I could listen to the genius of improvisational technique while standing at the bar drinking a club soda. When I leaned my chin over the felt-covered platform at the Columbus Circle Dance Repertory and watched a barefoot Pearl Primus perform authentic African dances. When I studied with Alain Locke, the great African American philosopher at the New School for Social Research. When I attended every Wednesday amateur night at the Apollo Theater in Harlem and was there the night Sass, Sarah Vaughan, won the contest with her rendition of

"Body and Soul" (and, I am proud to say, she later became my
friend, along with another classic jazz artist, Carmen McRae).
When I regularly walked through the city's many museums and
spent Saturday mornings in 57th Street art galleries that pre-
viewed new, avant-garde work. When I spent Saturday nights
dancing at the Savoy Ballroom and Sunday afternoons watching
the Harlem Globetrotters at the Renaissance Ballroom in Harlem. When I sat on bare wooden floors in student-artist
Greenwich Village apartments when rent was cheap and it really
was a haven for struggling artists, and I listened to Schönberg's
classical innovations as we solemnly read each other our latest
poetic creations. When my favorite quiet time was spent in the
reading room of the 42nd Street library, where I wrote my first
novel at twenty and dreamed of being both a writer and a painter.
When I lived an exciting, experientially eclectic existence that
would never be repeated.

Chapter 3

Just before the end of World War II, immediately after I graduated from Brooklyn College, I passed the civil service examination for social investigator for the Department of Welfare. Political favoritism had not yet corrupted civil service. Appointments were made in order of placement on the test, and I had come in first. Caseloads were assigned to investigators according to their religion, not their race, and since there were few Black Catholics, the mothers and children I supervised under the Aid to Dependent Children program were primarily white.

My job was to determine whether or not the poor families were poor enough to be entitled to financial assistance; whether or not they were sick enough to be entitled to free medical care; and whether or not they were hiding assets received from a contributing boyfriend or an absent, impoverished, but occasionally lucky husband who helped with food or rent or clothes for the children. On home visits I refused to notice signs of extra income like a pair of cheap shoes on the feet of small children or to make the required inspection of the refrigerator that might have revealed an extra dozen eggs or two bottles of milk instead of one.

My first assignment was the Lower East Side. When I climbed over drunken white men lining the narrow hallways to reach the apartment of the family I was to visit; when I saw the tiny cold-water flats with one bathroom to a floor, inhabited by seven or eight people, the walls marred by stained, peeling paint, rats scampering at my entrance; when I forced myself to perch on the edge of soiled sofas with escaped stuffing and crawling roaches and listened to pleas for help, I saw unredeemed, abject submission to poverty for the first time in my life. There was no uncombed hair in my childhood. No unwashed bodies. No baggy-eyed babies. Although my mother urged me to quit after my first day when she saw me sitting halfway up the stairs of our house crying in disbelief, I stayed. I was determined to somehow forge a difference. And I did. But only on a case-by-case basis, and after four years I realized that I would never make a significantly positive impact on this pathologically destructive agency. I took the civil service examination for probation officer in New York City Children's Court, a job that paid the same but held out the promise of greater satisfaction. I came out number one on the list and was hired in 1950.

But I didn't realize then that I had only substituted one imperfect arena for social change with another. The endless stream of petitions that alleged the same kinds of neglect—abusive parents, incapable parents, alcoholic parents, all poor and all defeated by the mere process of existing in a society that had failed to touch their lives except with rejecting hands—made it impossible for me to feel any gratification from the small results I was able to achieve. Frequently I could not recommend that children remain at home with their parents, but at the same time available institutional space was dwindling, and relatives, overwhelmed by their own problems, were unable to accept additional children into their homes. After two years I could no longer delude myself that I could stop the cycle of crises on which their lives revolved; in an attempt to center my life with a career that would sustain it in a meaningful way, I applied for admission to St. John's University Law School. St. John's was a logical choice for me because it was a block away from the Children's Court in Brooklyn where I had been assigned, and it was one of the few law schools that offered night classes toward a degree. Despite the fact that I was twenty-nine years old, I plunged into this new direction of hope, a career in law, without a second thought.

But law school was very demanding. St. John's method for determining eligibility for admission, whether in the day or evening session, was to weigh both the LSAT score and college grades. To continue in the program and ultimately to graduate, you had to place in the top two-thirds each year or be dropped from the school. My entering class of 500 was prepared at orientation for failure, and the school delivered on its promise: only 154 students from my class graduated, including only two Blacks, a man and me.

The difficulty of functioning competently in both law school and my job was compounded in 1954 when I was appointed to investigate a petition of neglect filed on behalf of the children of Julius and Ethel Rosenberg, who had been found guilty of conspiracy to commit espionage during World War II, sentenced to death, and executed. The large rallies in support of the Rosenbergs prior to their execution, the many appeals from the controversial sentence imposed by the Jewish federal judge, Irving Kaufman, and the international attention given the case were still fresh in my mind as I read the petition, filed by the New York Society for the Prevention of Cruelty to Children, based on the allegations of the commissioner of welfare.

Before the Rosenbergs were arrested in August 1950, the children, Michael and Robert, ages ten and six, had been living with their maternal grandmother, Tessie Greenglass, in New York City. While the parents were facing charges of treason, they voluntarily committed the children to the custody of the Department of Welfare, which placed them in the Hebrew Children's Home. On March 29, 1951, the parents were found guilty and four months later the boys were released to the permanent custody of their paternal grandmother, Sophie Rosenberg. The petition alleged that, contrary to an agreement between the Department of Welfare and Sophie Rosenberg, she permitted the children to leave the state of New York with their parents' attorney, Emanuel Bloch, and to live with a family in Toms River, New Jersey. After Ethel and Julius Rosenberg were executed, on June 19, 1953, the Department of Welfare learned that the children were in New Jersey and demanded that Bloch return them to New York, which he refused to do. Following his death in January 1954, the children lived with Abel and Anne Meeropol on Riverside Drive in New York City.

The petition charged the Meeropols with "retaining the children without legal right and contrary to law" because "no legal guardian had been appointed by a court of competent jurisdiction." The petition further alleged that since the children had been removed from their grandmother's custody they had been "exploited and made subjects of propaganda by persons seeking to raise funds" and that "in their present environment they are further exposed to such exploitation."

I was chosen to investigate the case on the recommendation of my supervisor, Gertrude O'Connor, and because my designated religion and my race were both considered politically neutral qualities during the Red scare perpetrated by Senator Joseph McCarthy and J. Edgar Hoover. On February 17, 1954, the day the petition was filed, Judge Jacob Panken ordered that the children be placed in the Jewish Child Care Association's Pleasantville School in upstate New York. They remained there until the following day when their attorney appealed Panken's decision and the Supreme Court of the State of New York reversed the ruling and released the children to Sophie Rosenberg, pending the findings of Children's Court concerning the allegations in the neglect petition.

Panken, a short, scraggy, white-haired man, unexpectedly found himself in the middle of a jurisdictional as well as a personal dispute. He joined forces with the Jewish Board of Guardians, whom he had appointed the children's temporary guardian and who had pressured me from the beginning of my investigation to recommend institutionalization. Before my investigation was complete Panken called me into his chambers and threatened to fire me if I did not follow that recommendation. I made a choice: to base my decision concerning my future recommendations for the children solely on my own investigative findings and the hell with the job.

I reviewed all of the information available to me, visited Sophie Rosenberg, and responded positively to her genuine display of love for the children. I visited the Meeropols (Abel, a freelance Hollywood writer who composed the song "The House I Live In," and Anne, a former New York City schoolteacher and director of a California nursery school), and I was convinced that their only concern was what was best for the children. I spent a long time with both children in their grandmother's small, clean apartment and found Michael to be as talkative as Robert was reticent. I found both boys to be talented, exceptionally intelligent, and lacking any discernible behavior disorders. I found only excellent school reports, religious involvement, and no evidence of "hostile, alien or treasonable influences." I was determined to ensure that they remain with their grandmother. I believed that the Meeropols were equally qualified to provide them with love, which was the most important ingredient they needed, having been torn from both parents in the most brutal of permanent separations, but I also knew that the best chance of avoiding institutional placement was to recommend that they remain with a relative. And I knew that the Meeropols would continue to be an important factor in the children's lives if they were permitted to remain with their grandmother. I had seen too many children delivered to the confines of institutional indifference, and I hoped I would be able to support my conviction that they, like all children, should live with loving relatives. But I was careful. The investigation had to provide an objective foundation to support my recommendation, and I strove to achieve that.

When I saw Gloria Agrin, the children's attorney, in the tiny courthouse elevator, we carefully avoided each other's eyes, neither acknowledging that I would make the critical evaluation she was waiting to challenge. I did recommend that the children remain with their grandmother, but before Panken had an opportunity to act on it, the commissioner of welfare, the petitioner, unwilling to allow my report to be the basis for the court's decision, withdrew his petition of neglect. Jurisdiction over custody of the children then became the sole province of the Supreme Court of the State of New York and Justice James McNally borrowed me from Children's Court to conduct his investigation.

But the state had not yet relinquished its determination to remove the children from their grandmother's care and institutionalize them. Within days after it had withdrawn its petition from Children's Court, the state filed a new one in Surrogate's Court asking that the Jewish Child Care Association be appointed as the children's legal guardian as well as their guardian for administering a trust fund established for them by Bloch and left to them in his will. The legal question to be resolved was whether the trust fund was the children's property or Bloch's. But however that question was decided, the tactic of filing such a joint petition in Surrogate's Court, which administered estates, served the state's primary purpose—to remove the resolution of the custody from the Supreme Court and thereby nullify the recommendation I had made to Judge McNally.

The three courts, Children's, Supreme, and Surrogate's, reached an agreement whereby all custody questions would be decided by Surrogate's Court and the other two courts would abide by its decisions. Each court had its own probation officers and I wondered how the one who would be chosen in Surrogate's Court would respond to the challenge he or she would face. I imagined all kinds of behind-the-scene deals being made to implement the state's plan. Among the many instructions that had been given to me by the Children's Court director of probation were two mandates: I was not to discuss the case with anyone and I was to be impartial and free of any emotional entanglements. But in light of the frightening and well-structured political maneuvers I was witnessing, compliance with both directives became increasingly difficult. So I spent hours in Gertrude O'Connor's office giving vent to an anguish intensified by my helplessness and fear about what I felt was a foregone conclusion.

To my amazement, Surrogate's Court Judge William Collins called me into his chambers and asked if I would accept the responsibility for conducting his investigation about custody of the children. I was not just overjoyed. I was grateful to Ms. O'Connor because, although she had never mentioned it, there was no question in my mind that she had been instrumental in his choice. I slept even fewer hours than I normally did as I went to law school and maintained my other cases in Children's Court. I worked late into the night visiting suburban relatives who were employed and unavailable during the day and rushed to meet the deadline for completion of my report.

When I submitted the report to Judge Collins he asked me to be present in the courtroom on the day he rendered his decision. The court was packed with the press, lawyers, and a curious public. He read his decision into the record, awarding custody to the grandmother, Sophie Rosenberg, with whom the children would live, and appointed as co-guardian the dean of the New York School of Social Work, Kenneth D. Johnson. Judge Collins said that he had rejected institutional care because it could not substitute "for the warm and sympathetic atmosphere of a private home." Next to parental care, he said, came the "devotion and interest of close relatives who could shield the children from taunts and shadows of the past as well as the darts of the present. Mrs. Rosenberg loves the children and the children love her."

He praised the objectivity and thoroughness of my investigation, and I was given a meritorious award by the New York State Department of Social Work for my performance on the case. In a very brief space of time the children had become central to my life, their destinies almost an obsession, but after the decision I never saw them again.

The Rosenberg case was my first direct experience of the

complicity between the judiciary and official government agencies that can result in manipulation of the fairness principle, a danger to which the judicial system is allegedly immune. And it was the first time I was exposed to the way in which lives, especially those that have been the focus of national attention and fall within judicial jurisdiction, can be permanently altered by prejudice and arbitrary decisions.

The experience had prepared me, however, to walk through the corridors of justice with open eyes when I became a lawyer.

Chapter 4

On a hot and humid day in August 1959, surrounded by white faces, I sat alongside my family at the swearing-in ceremony for admission to the bar and listened to the presiding judge of the Court of Appeals project a future in which all graduates would participate. His words were brilliant with promise, bathed with the benediction of commitment to the ideals of the oath we took to uphold the Constitution of the United States and the legal canon of ethics. He passed a clear mandate to the chosen—all of us—to march forward, to carry the banner of our profession high, to redress legal injustices, to meet the challenge of our times, and so forth. I was, however, less than impressed because all of his lofty hopes did not apply to me.

I watched my parents beam with the same pride radiating from the faces of the white parents. To them, I was now a lawyer and, therefore, guaranteed a successful future. How could they know that the number of Black lawyers was so few that no effort would be made to count them until 1965, when it was learned that of the 65,000 current law students, only 700 were Black and that of those, by statistical projection, only 10 percent would pass the bar and enter the profession? They had no way of knowing that, in addition to a law degree, other qualifications were needed to guarantee success: graduation from a prestigious law school; selection to law review, in which a chosen few top students were invited to publish their research on arcane aspects of the law; clerkship with a U.S. Supreme Court justice or, at the very least, with a federal judge (who accepted only those who had been on law review at a prestigious school); and being white and male. Absent all of the above, employment by a large law firm was impossible and, without such an association, success was strictly accidental. The significance of that reality for me was to strengthen the choice I had already made.

While I managed to get through St. John's Law School, I was

not on law review nor did I graduate at the top of my class. I did, however, make one effort to reach the apex of intellectual achievement. Since only day students were eligible for law review, I transferred from night school after my first year. To supplement the limited evening courses allowed, I accelerated my credits by attending four hours of classes in the morning and four at night. And between the hours that day classes ended and night classes began, I worked as a clerk at the Jay Thorpe department store on Fifth Avenue. The part-time job enabled me, after covering my rent, to pay carfare and buy food at the Automat on a strict budget of one dollar a day. After a year, I weighed less than one hundred pounds and was close to a complete physical breakdown. I relinquished the prospect of writing great legal theorems for the law review and returned to my job as a probation officer and to law school at night.

Because there were no school loans available in those days, to pay tuition and buy books I borrowed from banks and Beneficial Finance, repaying them on the installment plan by the end of each year so that I could borrow money for the next. After I passed the bar examination, I continued to work as a probation officer for another two years to complete paying my debts and to save enough money to meet expenses for at least one year without working. I had made my choice. I was going to be a criminal trial lawyer, with my own office, free from political pressures that would compromise my representation of those charged with criminal offenses.

Gertrude O'Connor, my supervisor in Family Court, believed I had made the wrong decision, pointing out that with the law degree I could attain the highest position possible in the department, that of chief probation officer. I appreciated her advice, but nothing she said swayed me.

My decision to become a criminal trial lawyer was encouraged by Eugene Kinkle Jones, himself a criminal trial lawyer. I had met Gene in 1955 when I had taken a one-year leave of absence from Family Court to participate in an experimental program in the Court of General Sessions, at that time the criminal division of the New York State Supreme Court. The pilot project was designed to reduce recidivism of first-time offenders between the ages of nineteen and twenty-one who were also substance abusers by expanding probation to include psychiatric counseling, job referrals, and other rehabilitative ef-

forts. Caseloads were very small and probationers were seen
frequently. The program had excited me as an alternative to
prison and, with a little help from Ms. O'Connor, I was allowed
the one-year sabbatical.

I met Gene when he came to my office in General Sessions
Court to discuss the progress of one of his clients whom I was
supervising. He was one of the few lawyers who bothered to
discuss their clients' progress once sentence had been imposed
and their fees had terminated. We became close friends. Gene
also became my legal mentor, and at every possible occasion I
would watch his courtroom performances from the spectator
row behind the front bench marked "For Lawyers Only," anticipating the day when I, too, would sit there.

Those were the days when the poor were represented by the
Legal Aid Society in exceptionally few cases, when there was no
state or federally funded groups of lawyers assigned to indigent
defendants (now called 18B panels), and when disheveled white
lawyers roamed the corridors of the Criminal Court building
approaching bewildered-looking Black people to find out
whether they had a case in court and needed a lawyer. These
lawyers took any small amount of money such people had, filed
a notice of appearance in court, and pleaded them guilty. Legal
representation was a shabby and indifferent process. And defendants, mostly Black, demanded nothing more than an acceptable
plea bargain or, at least, one that had the appearance of something they could live with. A trial, for these lawyers, was a waste
of time. They were as ignorant of trial practice as the assistant
district attorneys, many of whom spent their entire careers
without ever trying a single case. The few who did were vigorously prosecutorial and politically active in their pursuit of
judgeships or high elected office. But for the majority, a judge's
favorable ruling subsidized their careers, on whichever end of
the counsel table they sat.

Gene was different. With gray eyes, a narrow face, and a
sardonic mouth that seldom smiled, he viewed both assistant
district attorneys and defense lawyers with the same dispassion-
ate contempt. He was one of the first Black lawyers who made a
living from his practice in the criminal courts. Regarded as a
genius by white lawyers, he blazed the trail for other Black
lawyers and had no heroes. The presence of his tall, well-tailored,
slender body and narrow-brimmed hat discouraged familiarity. He

was a loner. But I was one of the few exceptions. We remained close friends until he died on October 18, 1973, just a few years after his son's fatal crash over Long Island Sound while testing an air force jet plane. He was my teacher in those early years, and I was fortunate to be able to reciprocate his support by supplementing his trial preparation with legal research and analysis that he felt was secondary in importance to the trial itself and for which I accepted no monetary compensation.

To gain experience, I appeared during arraignments every day, including weekends, and offered to represent defendants free of charge. I placed my name on a list provided by the court for volunteer private lawyers, and judges quickly recognized me as a golden resource, despite their frequent irritation with my multiple motions and refusal to enter into plea bargains. I read all new U.S. Supreme Court decisions and applied them to the cases I handled. One of my proudest moments was when I aided Judge Hyman Barshay, later to become the ultimate authority on hearings to suppress illegally obtained evidence. In 1961, when the U.S. Supreme Court rendered its decision in *Mapp v. Ohio*, few judges and even fewer criminal trial lawyers understood how the ruling was to be applied. When would the motion to suppress illegally obtained evidence be made? Should a hearing on the motion be held before the trial or during the trial, just before the evidence was to be offered? Should the motion be oral or written? Before the full implications of the Supreme Court decision were understood, I represented one of the first applications of the landmark decision before Judge Barshay. We decided on a course of action: the motion would be written and the hearing would be held before trial. If the motion was granted, the evidence would be excluded. And if that evidence constituted the sole evidence to prove the prosecutor's case, the indictment would be dismissed. When the indictment of the defendant I represented was dismissed, I shared this major victory with Gene. Thereafter, I became his consultant on exclusionary pretrial motion practice, which the decisions of the Supreme Court were rapidly expanding.

By the end of my first year I had gained valuable experience. I learned to discount protestations of innocence and instead depended on investigation to determine whether the allegations of the complaint or indictment could be proved. I went to the crime scene and made notes of obvious inconsistencies with the

accusatory document. I found witnesses and obtained statements from them. I filed motions to dismiss indictments, an
unheard of practice in those days. My resources were meager,
but each time I went to trial I established that the prosecution
either could not prove its case or had no case. The defendants I
represented, many of whom were facing a jury for the first time
in their lives, believed in me. By the end of my first year I felt
confident enough to try a murder case.

A case was assigned to me by the court. The defendant not
only was poor, alcoholic, and unknown, but was indicted for
murdering another poor, unknown person. I will never forget
this man's unfocused, bleary-eyed attempts to convince me of
his innocence. He was accused of strangling a female drinking
companion by fracturing her cricoid cartilage, which resulted in
death by suffocation. In addition to interviewing all persons who
might have some information, evaluating their credibility in the
event they would be used as witnesses, and making the usual
pretrial motions, I spent hours in the medical libraries across the
city learning about the structure of the throat and the cricoid
cartilage, about which I had never heard. After reading the
medical examiner's report, I was as convinced that my client was
telling me the truth as I was convinced that the prosecutor could
not prove that death was intentional.

My client insisted on going to trial, rejecting the many offers
I relayed to him from the district attorney's office of a reduced
sentence in exchange for a guilty plea. He told me he would
rather go to jail than confess to a crime he didn't commit. I had
never before borne the responsibility of defending a person faced
with a sentence of twenty-five years to life, but his faith that I
would make the right decisions carried me over every hurdle.
Together we would win, whether or not we could.

The most incriminating evidence against him was the
medical examiner's testimony. I cross-examined him for three
days. At the end of the prosecutor's case I moved for dismissal of
the indictment because the prosecutor had failed to produce any
evidence to establish the fact that the deceased had died from
strangulation or, in fact, that a homicide had been committed.

The judge recessed to consider my motion. I assumed when
he did not make the decision instantly, as was the usual case,
that he had called a recess just for a cigarette break. The first
time his clerk came to me with an offer of a reduced charge, I was

stunned. But the process continued all day. The offer was reduced from murder to manslaughter one to manslaughter two to assault as a felony to assault as a misdemeanor with credit given for time already served. The last offer meant that my client would be released immediately. He refused each offer, but I was not so sure he was making the right decision. I held my breath as I communicated the last "no" to the clerk and the two of us waited for the judge's decision.

It was at the end of the day by now, but the usual courtroom observers, retired people who spent their days watching trials in Criminal Court and who considered themselves experts in predicting a jury's verdict, having learned of this unusual situation, had collected from the various courtrooms in the building and congregated in the hall discussing possible alternatives for the judge. When the motion was granted and the indictment dismissed, the spectators roared with approval.

Together, my client and I walked through the revolving doors of the Criminal Court building. He saw the sun setting from outside prison walls for the first time in over a year. His eyes were clear now and sparkled with the strange sensation of hope.

I remember his name to this day, although I've never seen him since. Except for a few lines in the *Amsterdam News*, there was no newspaper report of the dismissal. But I keep that short paragraph as the most positive punctuation my first year of practice could have produced. I had proven my ability as a criminal defense trial lawyer. Now I needed to make a living from it.

Chapter 5

By the end of my first year, judges no longer directed me to leave the well of the courtroom when I entered to check the calendar or file a notice of appearance; court officers no longer ordered me from the first bench reserved for lawyers; court clerks no longer asked me what law firm I was filing papers for; and assistant district attorneys initiated negotiations with me for disposition of cases. I had met the challenge of being Black, female, and a criminal trial lawyer.

Historically, lawyers have been classified by the clients who retain them. The average criminal lawyer defends poor, Black, alcoholic, or drug-related transgressors, and the contempt society holds for the powerless is transferred to the lawyers who represent them. The corporate criminal is charged with "white-collar crime" and is usually represented by former U.S. attorneys who cash in on their expertise in the manipulation of evidence and other dirty tricks learned on the federal payroll. But they are perceived as respectable and smart. Their clients always have a shot at beating the system. When we criminal trial lawyers win, it is indeed against all odds.

As my reputation grew, I began to make enough money to establish an office that would reflect the respect I held for my clients. Despite the tentative steps I took in that direction, I made no change in my personal living arrangements; I remained in the large, unpretentious, pleasant one-room apartment with kitchen, bath, and backyard that I had lived in for the last eight years. It was near Central Park and convenient to every means of transportation. Suburban life, with the endless waits for buses to get to crowded subways to get to school or jobs in the city, was as tedious as the long, boring hours spent as a child watering the lawn with a hose before the age of automatic sprinklers. Completely free of envy, I watched the stream of cars making their daily escape routes across bridges and through tunnels into and out of the city from and to the suburbs.

My first office, in 1959, was located in the rear of a greeting card store on Reid Avenue in Brooklyn. From there I moved to an office that I shared with a female lawyer friend, also Black, across the street from the Brooklyn Criminal Court building on Schermerhorn Street; to lawyers' row on Court Street in Brooklyn; to 55 Liberty Street in the Wall Street area near the office of Carson De Witt Baker, a Black lawyer most remembered for his defense of Hulan Jack, the first Black Manhattan borough president, on charges of corruption. When I signed the Liberty Street lease the space was restructured to meet my personally requested dimensions. Bookcases were concealed, the paint was in soft earth tones, and the furniture, which I bought, was made of modern Scandinavian wood.

My office was immense, but the floor-to-ceiling windows, covered with drawn curtains, created a confidential and friendly atmosphere. The secretary's office was designed for efficiency, and I hired an excellent man who not only was proficient in shorthand and typing but kept track of my court and appointment schedules, placated irate clients when I was delayed in court, and watched over me with protective concern.

I joined bar associations and volunteered to conduct a legal clinic in the office of Mark Southall, a maverick Harlem political leader who had stretched the power of his office to help his constituents. I helped consumers who had been given default judgments for failure to appear in court for alleged nonpayment of debts, often because a summons was not served and the consumers were unaware of a court date. I devised short forms they could use to reopen their cases and three times a week held classes in self-representation in Landlord Tenant Court. When evictions were threatened and the cases became more complicated, I appeared in court myself.

I rarely shopped or ate at home, except for coffee, because my large meal for the day was at lunchtime with Gene. Sometimes at the end of the day, we shared frustrations for an hour or so over martinis. During the summer, when the courts practically closed down, I spent days at Atlantic City or on Fire Island. On weekends I hung out at favorite Harlem bars where my friends met—the Red Rooster, Jock's Place, Facts, or Carl's Corner—and I ate breakfast on Sunday mornings with Romare Bearden at Frank's Restaurant. My lifestyle changed dramatically, however, when Joey came to live with me and my new responsibilities left me with little extra time.

The next five years, from 1960 to 1965, were an economic roller coaster, hurtling me unpredictably either upward or downward, depending on whether my clients paid me. Unlike large law firms, whose yearly retainers from businesses cushion them during lean years, when I was not paid I had no extra resources to tide me over. Clients seemed to be ignorant of the fact that the expenses necessary to maintain a law office were the same as those needed by their doctors and dentists.

But when the relatives or friends of loved ones who had just been arrested called me in panicked desperation to represent them, I could not say no. Unlike other contractual arrangements, once a lawyer files a notice of appearance with the court declaring that he or she has been privately retained by the defendant, it cannot be withdrawn without approval of the court. And because I accepted small retainers toward the larger fee, which was seldom paid, I had a plethora of clients, a paucity of funds, and a pyramid of work.

Large law firms not only demand that an entire fee be paid before they accept a case, but their attorneys also chair important committees in national bar associations (which only recently admitted Black attorneys as members) and set the ethical standards for the legal community. When such associations, in their annual statements on legal representation for the poor, urge corporate lawyers to volunteer some small part of their time to represent the needy, called "pro bono" work, they aren't speaking to the Black single practitioner or the small Black law firm. For us, pro bono is a way of life.

In addition, the types of cases available to Black lawyers were limited. Few of us were personal injury specialists because Black victims of accidents, with rare exceptions, chose white lawyers to handle their claims. And, of course, so did white victims. Black lawyers who made a living either handled real estate transactions, were beneficiaries of the political patronage system, or were affiliated with churches with large congregations, a ready-made source of clientele. And then there were the criminal lawyers, who depended in large part on referrals from bondsmen, numbers bankers, or narcotics dealers.

On one occasion I was approached by a numbers banker to

represent all the runners on his payroll who were arrested. These cases, with the exception of loitering violations, which included prostitution, constituted the majority of arrests in the lower criminal court system. The prospect of a steady source of paying clients was tempting. But that terminated as quickly as it began.

The fabrication of "dropsy" evidence by the arresting officer was a familiar device used to make arrests and obtain convictions. In a typical case, a police officer would testify that he had made the arrest after he had observed a numbers transaction (usually from a distance through binoculars). The officer would further testify that when he approached the participants, they dropped policy slips on the ground, in clear view of the officer, who then picked them up and considered the recovery justification for a search of the parties, on whom more slips would be found. The officer would then make the arrest. The cop's testimony was sufficient to convict, and a plea of guilty was therefore usually entered. This scenario, with its obvious illegalities, was familiar to both judges and assistant district attorneys. Credibility was always afforded the arresting officer. But in the early sixties Supreme Court decisions were changing the standards of admissibility of evidence resulting from searches and seizures, and "dropsy" evidence was becoming more and more suspect.

I used every tactic and new decision available to force the prosecution to prove its case beyond a reasonable doubt, and I usually won acquittals. What I didn't know, however, was that a deal had been struck between the banker who approached me and the police. Their agreement was that the banker would choose a few runners periodically, usually those with minor previous convictions, and give them up to an officer to enable him to meet his monthly quota of arrests, in exchange for money and protection of the banker's major business. The deal was that the runner would plead guilty and pay a small fine or serve a limited jail sentence. Legal representation was a mere formality, but it was necessary to lend legitimacy to the deal.

As I began my usual preparation in defense of one particular defendant, the banker directed me to plead him guilty. When I pointed out the weakness of the prosecution's case, the situation was explained to me. Small-fry runners were regularly sacrificed for the survival of the organization. If I wanted the steady income promised, I would follow the banker's instructions. As I said, that potential business relationship ended before it began. I was not willing to mouthpiece my way to economic security. And supplying my legal expertise to the Black death peddlers of the narcotics trade was out of the question.

Somewhere during this stretch of economic suicide I decided to give up private practice and get a job. Perhaps had the only consideration been my own survival I might have continued the struggle, but I was responsible for Joey, and my financial ability to support both of us and a law practice was diminishing with frightening rapidity. I applied to the NAACP Legal Defense Fund, but nothing was available. I was, however, hired by Legal Aid, but I quit after a week. Despite my extensive trial experience in felony cases, involving many jury trials, the Legal Aid people insisted that I learn to represent clients from their perspective and from the ground up. I began their training program by sitting in on arraignments. I walked out during a class conducted by a Legal Aid attorney who had never tried a case, in the middle of his pedantic explanation of the difference between a complaint and an indictment.

So in January 1965, when Livingston Wingate, the executive director of HARYOU (Harlem Youth Opportunities Unlimited), the Harlem antipoverty agency, asked me to establish guidelines for a Legal Services to the Poor program for Harlem, I closed my office without regret and leaped at the opportunity to join a different battle to ensure legal justice for the disenfranchised.

HARYOU, spearheaded by Adam Clayton Powell, Jr., the congressman from Harlem and the pastor of Abyssinian Baptist Church, was established in 1964 when President Lyndon Johnson signed the Economic Opportunity Act and launched his "war on poverty." The Harlem community, like every Black ghetto across the country, had been destroyed by white opportunism. As whites left the surrounding inner cities, emerging middle-class inner-city Blacks followed, leaving a great void for those who could neither leave nor regenerate the few remaining institutions necessary for minimal existence. A debilitating immobilization spawned apathy, distrust, hostility, and hopelessness and provided the fuel that police brutality sparked, producing the 1964 Harlem and Rochester, New York, uprisings, harbingers of the 1965 Watts, Los Angeles, conflagration.

In January 1965, 232,000 people lived in central Harlem.

Thirty-one percent were under the age of twenty-one, with a disproportionate rate of juvenile delinquency, narcotics addiction, venereal disease, and welfare assistance. Housing units had been intentionally permitted to deteriorate under an urban renewal projection of a white occupied Harlem planned by white politicians in City Hall. As a result, only 10 percent of new housing constructed in the city since 1929 was built in Harlem. More than 80 percent of youngsters were below grade level in reading comprehension by sixth grade and 55 percent were high school dropouts. More than two-thirds of the adults were under-employed laborers earning below the annual $4,000 poverty level. And there were no statistics to reflect the number of residents victimized by illegal installment contracts, evictions, and denial of welfare and social security benefits because they were ignorant of their legal rights.

I immersed myself in the task of establishing the legal services program. I attended meetings in Washington with Office of Economic Opportunity officials, structured budgets, and developed a workable format with relative ease. But the job posed challenges for me I had never before encountered: I was required to fulfill the mandate of the act "to establish community action programs with maximum feasible participation of the residents in the area."

I was a technician, accustomed to evolving strategies within the framework of my own creativity and perceptions, uncluttered by other people's intrusive suggestions and unsolicited opinions. I was inflexible to the demands of situations outside those small parameters, and I rejected carelessly presented opposition. I was not used to consulting anyone in making decisions to pursue a course of action or in altering those decisions, once made, to accommodate political expediency. Now, in charge of devising a program that demanded "maximum participation of the residents in the area," I needed other qualifications. I needed to be a conduit for the plans submitted by others, superior to mine because of their very genesis, advanced by those who would be affected by any decision made. I was called on to be a conciliator of competing interests and duplicate programs proposed by antagonistic groups with identical goals. The major question became who would get a piece of the antipoverty pie being baked in Washington. Additionally, because I had never lived in central Harlem, my credentials were suspect. And my personality, at ease in a courtroom before a hostile judge or a reluctant jury, was on uncertain ground when confronted with the various community groups who, justifiably, demanded input.

In addition to Wingate, two other geniuses were involved in community relations in Harlem: George Broadfield and Evelyn Payne. With their help I learned to listen, to compromise, and to alter my decisions when convinced they needed revision. But my ultimate proposal was challenged by Paul Chevigny, a 1960 Harvard Law School graduate and former Wall Street lawyer whose only credentials for understanding the legal needs of the poor was his participation in a Mississippi summer project in 1964 and who was rewarded by being appointed the director of a neighborhood law office in 1965. He proposed that the supervisory structure for the projected neighborhood law offices in Harlem be provided by the ACLU instead of the Harlem Lawyers Association, which I had recommended. My rejection of his proposal was uncompromising.

And later in 1965, when Jean Cahn, employed by the Office of Economic Opportunity to approve funding for proposals for legal services to the poor, came to Harlem to evaluate my proposal and insisted that I include affiliation with Columbia University Law School, I became instantly apoplectic. Her claim to expertise rested on an article she and her white husband had written for the 1964 *Yale Law Review*, titled "The War on Poverty: A Civilian Perspective," which had received national acclaim.

I admired the article but disagreed strongly with their conclusions that the neighborhood law office needed the inclusion and participation of a major law school to aid in its supervision, to provide law student interns who would use the program as a laboratory, to conduct seminars for recruiting and training indigenous community leaders, and to increase self-awareness and comprehension of larger community problems for students who were preparing for leadership roles in the war on poverty.

While I understood Cahn's focus on the urban university's potential role, no law school had been accommodating so far, and certainly not Columbia, located in the heart of Harlem. I understood her compulsion because her article had grown out of a two-year study of a neighborhood social services program in

50   New Haven, Connecticut, funded by Yale Law School, for the purpose of producing the law review article as well as of breaking new ground in the analysis of President Johnson's War on Poverty. I did understand. But I was not to be convinced, moved, or otherwise directed. When my proposal was accepted by the HARYOU board of directors, my sense of achievement was both professional and personal.

But Adam Clayton Powell, the driving force behind HAR-YOU, who had held his congressional committee meetings in the streets of Harlem, was charged with the misuse of government funds in 1967 and stripped of his twenty-two years of seniority, including his chairmanship of the congressional subcommittee that funded and administered the program. HARYOU, under siege, faltered, and my Legal Services to the Poor proposal was never implemented. By March 1966, the extinction of HARYOU's bright promise became inevitable. So when my parents called to tell me that they had been betrayed by the lawyers they had hired to establish their claim to the beach lands my mother's father had owned and asked me to come to North Carolina to help them, I felt free to do so. And the fact that Joey had left high school and was now working made my decision easier.

Chapter 6

I went to North Carolina reluctantly, not believing I could reverse the legal misfortunes inflicted on my parents by a racist judicial system, corrupt judges, corrupt surveyors, corrupt clerks of court, and corrupt lawyers, all of whom had collaborated with real estate land barons to steal the Freeman beach lands. After all, exploitation of minorities in this country had a long history and had never been restricted to African American and immigrant labor. It had its genesis in the theft of the land owned by Native Americans. I also hesitated because I had no experience in either real estate transactions or real estate law and was totally ignorant of North Carolina practice. But all of these legitimate considerations vanished when I realized the enormity of the business and legal fraud that had denied the Freeman heirs their rightful ownership of Freeman's Beach, and I ended up spending most of the next year and a half in North Carolina trying to undo the wrong.

Each year, from as early in my life as I can remember, my parents had made the southern pilgrimage to Wilmington, North Carolina, and a major part of our holiday had been spent at Freeman's Beach and Seabreeze, home of the Freeman clan. In addition to crabbing, oyster and clam gathering, and fishing in the waters of Myrtle Grove Sound, the eastern border of the Freemans' mainland property, we spent time at Freeman's Beach. To reach it we had to drive through segregated Carolina Beach. Black people were not permitted to swim in the ocean fronting Carolina Beach and, with the exception of the Freeman family, whom the whites called Indians and whose ownership of the beach north of Carolina Beach was grudgingly admitted, were not even permitted to drive on the only road leading to Freeman's Beach. We would park on the silky white sand and I remember how proud I felt as I gazed at "our beach"—as far as I could see, the last remaining large expanse of beach property owned by African Americans in the United States—and listened to my parents plan to someday develop it for Black people.

The land had been in my mother's family since 1876, when Robert Bruce Freeman, my mother's father, purchased 2,800 acres, some of it on the beach and some on the adjacent mainland. His entire family—six children and their families from his first marriage and five from his second—lived on four hundred acres of the mainland property, which he called the Freeman Homestead. My grandfather had purchased the property for personal, philanthropic, and investment purposes. He gave the state of North Carolina one acre for a public school, and he gave acreage to St. Stephen's Church and the local African Methodist Episcopal churches. He also leased the rights to some of the land for timber cutting and gravel and clay excavating.

He bequeathed to the children from his first marriage the fifty-seven-acre plot of land on which each of them had lived during his lifetime, and the same acreage to his second wife, my mother's mother. The remainder of the property was divided equally among all his children from both marriages. After his death, in 1902, my mother's brothers and sisters continued to live on the homestead, reaping the profits from the timber, clay, and gravel leasing on their other mainland properties and basically ignoring the beach property. At the time it held neither monetary nor practical value for them.

As a result, when Ellis Freeman, my grandfather's oldest son and the executor of his will, legally partitioned the homestead tract in 1914, he never divided the beachlands described in Grant 97 issued in 1776 by the state of North Carolina. On June 12, 1940, Ellis orchestrated the sale of the beach, but it was not until two decades later, after I had analyzed many court documents, that I realized that he, in cahoots with a real estate developer, had fraudulently extracted his siblings' consent (with the exception of my mother and four others) to sell the land and had misrepresented the amount of property conveyed. The effect of the deed was to extend the boundaries of Carolina Beach north for 3,500 feet into Freeman's Beach, and immediately after the sale to Home Real Estate Realty Company in 1940, summer homes, small hotels, and condominiums sprang up along this previously undeveloped land.

So when the 1940 deed proclaimed its artificial boundaries as being those of Grant 97, my parents assumed the deed's description was correct and, in 1945, while still in New York, hired a North Carolina lawyer to partition the beach among the remaining Freeman heirs and Home Real Estate. It should have been the simplest of all legal actions, and had it not been for the clever, illegal manipulations of the white lawyers they hired, it would have been. Unfortunately the one Black lawyer in Wilmington was not willing to accept their case.

During the next six years it became necessary to hire and fire three different Wilmington lawyers because they refused to tangle with the real estate interests on whom their own practices depended. But in 1951, despite the fact that the litigation was still unresolved, my parents sold their house and business in Queens, New York, and returned to Wilmington to pursue my father's dream of building a business on the beach.

When my father applied for a building permit it was denied because, he was told, he had no proof that the portion of the beach on which he wanted to build belonged to the Freeman heirs. He realized then that Grant 97, a document he had never seen, would have to be located and surveyed. His new lawyers refused to research the court records for the grant, and he discovered it only through the painstaking efforts of Thomas Jervay, publisher of the African American weekly newspaper his father had founded, and brother of Willie Jervay, who had been best man at my father's wedding.

He then brought the grant to John Foard, a North Carolina historian and land surveyor, who certified that the land in Grant 97 was indeed Freeman heir property and also extended into the portion being fraudulently sold by Home Real Estate and its 1947 grantee, Resort Development Company. Once he showed the officials the grant and Foard's map, he was issued the building permit.

The building was completed on July 4, 1951. My parents proclaimed that day Robert Bruce Freeman Day and celebrated it for many years afterward. The building was large, even grandiose compared with many of the Carolina Beach structures, and was situated three thousand feet from the ocean, its white cement facade gleaming above the dunes. There was a dining area (which doubled as a dance floor at night), a long counter for take-out orders, a locker room, bathrooms, shower rooms, and two bedrooms in the back for the family. A local muralist painted the entire interior with brightly colored seascapes, and my father built a hard red clay road from 17th Avenue to the parking lot adjacent to the building claimed by the Town of Carolina Beach to be its northern boundary. My mother, with help from workers in Wilmington, kept the restaurant as spotlessly clean as she did her own house, and her clam fritters were as famous as Mc-Donald's hamburgers are now. Black people came to the beach from all over the country and my parents were instantly success-ful. Surprisingly, many whites vacationing in Carolina Beach also frequented the restaurant and danced without incident both in the building and on the pavilion my father had built a short distance into the ocean.

Now determined more than ever not only to establish the specific boundaries of the parcel surrounding the restaurant, to expand the development of the beach, and to sell oceanfront property to Black people, but also to have a court determination of the actual location of the boundaries of Grant 97, my parents reactivated their dormant legal action. In April 1953, they retained John Bright Hill, another white real estate lawyer from Wilmington, and he engineered the disaster that inflicted inju-ries from which they would never recover.

Hill's first treacherous act was to bring a new action for partition, this time allegedly for a division of all the land described in Grant 97, but intentionally misrepresenting the description by setting forth as the grant's entire acreage only its southern half, where Resort Development Company was illegally building. He omitted the northern half of Grant 97 that Resort's predecessors had actually purchased from the other Freeman heirs. Resort denied that it was a tenant-in-common with the Freeman heirs and claimed sole ownership of the land described in Hill's petition. And, indeed, it was not a tenant-in-common. Resort owned no property at all in the southern half of the grant. But my parents, relying on their lawyer and unaware of the trickery of conveyance nomenclature, did not recognize Hill's malevolent conversion and waited with great anticipation for the case to reach the trial calendar.

In the meantime, in August 1954, hurricane Hazel, one of the most destructive hurricanes to hit the eastern coast of the United States in over a century, ripped across the Carolinas, leveling property from Cape Hatteras to Myrtle Beach, but aimed primarily at Carolina Beach. The morning after the hurricane passed, my parents rushed to the beach to assess the damage and

saw nothing except smooth sand still being washed over by the   55
ocean where their building had stood the day before. My fatalis-
tic mother's reaction was stoic, and she directed her energies to
the care of my father, who collapsed and was bedridden for
several weeks. The loss was compounded by their having been
unable to obtain a bank loan to build, and so a large part of their
savings was washed away with their business. Nor did their
insurance cover water and wind damage. Nevertheless, my
father rebuilt, pulling concrete block after concrete block from
the sand where the remnants of the demolished building lay.
Having learned about the force of hurricanes, he positioned the
new structure farther back from the ocean and purchased
insurance for wind and water damage from the only company
that offered it, Lloyds of London. But the new building, too, was
flattened when hurricane Connie stormed ashore in August
1955. Again my father rebuilt, and my parents reopened their
business as they waited for their case to be tried.

It was not until 1956, when they pressed Hill to explain the
delay in bringing the case to trial, that they learned that the case
had been stricken from the trial calendar on October 30, 1955.
When it was eventually restored, on October 20, 1956, Judge
Clifton L. Moore stated that he had inadvertently removed the
case from the calendar because "the original papers could not be
found and were not before the court." Hill denied having any
prior knowledge of Moore's action, and Lois Ward, the clerk of
court in charge of civil trial scheduling and responsible for all
pleadings filed in the court, had no excuse for the "error." She
was, however, to continue to play a major role in the catastro-
phes that followed.

I had finished law school and was studying for the bar
examination when my parents called to tell me that their case
had finally been scheduled for trial on February 18, 1957. I flew
to Wilmington and, after reading the petition, Resort's answer,
the description of the 1940 deed, and the grant, I recognized
Hill's betrayal. I begged them to withdraw the case from the
calendar and retain a new lawyer from outside of Wilmington
who would represent them honestly. I knew that their case
would be summarily dismissed once proof was offered that there
was no joint ownership of the lands they sought to divide.

My mother agreed with me and joined my efforts to dissuade my father from proceeding further. But the trial was only

a few days away and his impatience to begin the development of the beach blinded him to the obvious obstacle to its realization. He stubbornly refused to accept my opinion, and for the first time I questioned my father's judgment. But then again, it was the first time that his judgment was impaired by denial.

The one-day trial was held before Judge Malcolm Paul. Foard testified that he had located the boundaries of Grant 97, testified to its location as reflected on the map that he had introduced into evidence, but admitted that he had not physically surveyed the land, a fatal omission in establishing boundaries. My parents could not have been expected to know that they needed a surveyor's appraisal, but Hill, a leading real estate lawyer, obviously did. Clearly he had not asked Foard to conduct the physical survey in preparation for the trial to ensure the defeat of my parents' action.

Every day for the next five months my father, no longer willing to rely on Hill, went to the courthouse and asked Lois Ward whether or not a decision had been rendered, and every day she told him no. I made my annual visit to Wilmington on the Fourth of July and, on July 9, went to the court and searched the Judgment Roll (the public document on which decisions are recorded), only to discover that Moore's judgment had been entered that day. It stated: "The petitioners [my parents], having failed to show that they have good record title to the lands described in the petition or any part thereof, are not entitled to recover the lands described in the petition or any part thereof."

My parents immediately hired Herman Taylor and Samuel Mitchell, Black law partners in Raleigh, North Carolina, to appeal the decision. On July 10, when Taylor attempted to file an appeal with Ward, whose authority included the setting of appeal bonds, she refused, stating that the judgment had been rendered on June 18, not July 9, and that the ten-day statutory period for filing an appeal had expired.

Taylor appealed the decision to the Superior Court in Wilmington, and, during the hearing held before Judge Moore, Ward testified that she "could not satisfactorily explain the time-lapse between the signing of the judgment and its entry into the Judgment Roll." She also admitted that she had lied to my father about the status of his case. My father, in turn, testified that his lawyer, Hill, had never advised him that the judgment had been signed. But Moore responded that that didn't matter because my father had a lawyer from whom he could have obtained the information. Taylor's last witness, Dwight McEwen, the court reporter during the trial who had been present in Judge Paul's courtroom on June 18, put the final piece into place. He testified that Hill had prepared the judgment and, together with Resort's lawyer, had presented it to Paul who, after signing it, directed him to write into the minute book the fact that both attorneys had written on a carbon copy of the judgment that it was satisfactory. Paul had further directed that in the event my parents appealed, the carbon copy was to become a substitute for the original, filed judgment, which neither attorney had written his approval. Paul's intentions were clear: to reflect the fact that my parents' lawyer had prepared the judgment and had knowledge of the date on which it had been signed, thereby imputing this information to them and binding them to it.

Taylor appealed Moore's decision, but the Supreme Court of North Carolina refused to accept the case for review. Two years later, on March 5, 1959, Resort pursued its advantage and brought an action to evict my parents from their business on the beach, citing Paul's judgment. Taylor answered the eviction petition and Joseph Parker, Superior Court judge, conducted the hearing. He ruled against my parents, stating that "While Judge Paul's judgment did not specifically pass title to Resort," he did find that my parents were "not entitled to recover the lands described in the petition nor any part thereof"; that the judgment operated as a legal prohibition against any claim my parents had in relation to that property; and that "since they had not appealed Judge Paul's judgment, they cannot now impeach it." He gave them ten days to vacate the property or be removed by the sheriff, and they were ordered to pay all of Resort's costs.

Taylor leaped at the new opportunity to attack Paul's judgment, and had he not been my parents' attorney, I hesitate to predict how either of them would have responded. He appealed to the Supreme Court of North Carolina, which reversed Parker's decision, ruling that while Paul had decreed that my parents did not own the southern half of Grant 97, he had not determined that Resort was the owner. Resort therefore had no legal right to evict my parents.

A year later, on August 15, 1960, Resort tried to evict my parents again, this time demanding that the court grant the development company a writ of possession, claiming Paul's judgment as the basis for its suit. The doctrine of res judicata, based on the Supreme Court determination, could have been interposed to defeat Resort's complaint, but Taylor seized the opportunity to reopen the issue of the ownership of Grant 97, asserting that the land on which my parents' building was located was within the grant. Simultaneously, my parents hired Robert McHenry and Gerritt Greer, highly qualified surveyors from Leakesville, North Carolina, to physically survey Grant 97 and to testify in court. My father walked every mile of the land with them, and their physical survey established, as had Foard's projection, that the southern boundary of the grant was in Carolina Beach.

On May 31, 1961, the trial began before the same judge who had ruled against my parents in 1957, Judge Malcolm Paul. After one day of testimony presented by Resort, Paul's guilt about his past actions in the case surfaced. He forced Resort to enter into a consent order signed by both attorneys and my parents, directing Resort to begin a new action by December 1, 1961, in which it would "set out and seek to establish its title to all lands claimed by it in Federal Point Township [where Carolina Beach was located], or . . . to establish the boundaries to the lands claimed by it." Further, my parents would set forth their own claims to the land.

The consent order swept the slate clean, nullifying all past judgments and giving my parents another opportunity to have the court determine the boundaries of Grant 97 and to discredit Resort's claim that it owned the southern half of the grant. It was a rare victory, but one that my parents were unable to take advantage of.

On May 1, 1962, Resort filed a complaint demanding that the court determine that it was the sole owner of two tracts of beach land extending north from Carolina Beach and terminating just short of the southern boundary of the 1940 deed, declaring that the land thus described was "entirely without Grant 97." In this action Resort also claimed to own the property by "adverse possession." While Taylor denied Resort's ownership and maintained that both tracts were within the boundaries of Grant 97, he mistakenly alleged that Resort was a tenant-in-common with the Freeman heirs in all of Grant 97 and failed to state that the Freeman heirs were the sole owners of the property Resort described. My only explanation for the error was that, unknown to my parents, Taylor was at the same time defending his license to practice law against the North Carolina Bar Association's charges of misconduct in previous cases, a common device used to discredit lawyers who vigilantly represent unpopular causes, and the focus of his attention was diverted. He was disbarred in 1963, and I have no doubt that the charges were manufactured in direct response to his efforts on my parents' behalf. Samuel Mitchell, his partner, continued to represent my parents in his absence.

In August 1962, hurricane Diane struck Carolina Beach, ripping the building from its foundations as effectively as if it had been Resort's accomplice. This time, burdened with legal expenses, threatened by future court actions, and unwilling to again make the major investment needed to rebuild, my parents took the Lloyds of London insurance money and opened a restaurant specializing in my mother's famous seafood cuisine on Red Cross Street in Wilmington. It was the beginning of the Vietnam War, and Black soldiers stationed at nearby Fort Bragg crowded the restaurant. They also flocked to an adjacent building in which my parents had created a recreation center for teenagers during the week and a dance hall for the soldiers on weekends. Business thrived until 1967 when the South's implementation of desegregation laws began, and the soldiers, as well as other Wilmington residents, integrated their money into the cash registers of white establishments. The resultant dwindling business forced my parents to close the restaurant.

There had been no hurricane for five years, and my father applied for a permit to conduct a business on the beach. Not only was it denied, but this time the town of Carolina Beach declared that the beach had been condemned because of high tides and erosion. He was told that no buildings could be constructed on the beach, despite the fact that two condominiums had been erected adjacent to where the original buildings had been. The town even denied him a permit to sell refreshments from a portable stand.

Samuel Mitchell had replaced Taylor as my parents' attorney until 1966, when he failed to appear at several pretrial hearings scheduled by Resort to take depositions from four witnesses that it planned to call at the trial. In January and February of that year Mitchell had also failed to appear for two successive court hearings. Anticipating another betrayal, my parents became so frightened and desperate that they asked me to come to Wilmington. At first I believed I could be most helpful in obtaining counsel to replace Mitchell, but when I examined the file he released to me I was appalled to learn that the foundation of our case, establishing Grant 97's chain of title, had not been researched, nor had a title search been conducted of each deed from which Resort now claimed its title.

I realized we were not ready for trial and persuaded Robert Bond to ask the court that I be allowed to practice in North Carolina for this one case. I also requested that Bond be my co-counsel. He agreed, provided I did all the research, and I plunged into the archives in the basement of the courthouse, grateful for every day of research afforded me by Resort's reluctance to move the case forward on the trial calendar. For obvious reasons, the task of establishing the chains of title of both Resort and Grant 97 could not be referred to a North Carolina title search company. I could rely only on myself to prove our title and disprove Resort's. After seven months of daily examination of ancient maps and fading handwritten deeds bound in heavy tomes that I had to lift from the shelves on which they had been stored, I uncovered and traced the chains of title for Grant 97.

Using my research as a basis, I made a motion to amend Taylor's answer: to delete the cross-claim in which he alleged the Freeman heirs were tenants-in-common with Resort and to substitute the allegation that the Freeman heirs were the sole owners of the land Resort claimed. The motion was denied, and I took exception to each ruling to preserve the error on appeal. In the meantime, I contacted McHenry and Greer, who had sur-veyed Grant 97 in 1960, to alert them that I felt the case would soon reach the trial calendar and to arrange a meeting with them to discuss their testimony. They told me, without apology, that they would not testify in our behalf, and a further search for North Carolina surveyors who were willing to take on the job was fruitless. Through my friend Doe's association with surveyors in Richmond, Virginia, we retained the firm of Foster and Miller, who qualified in North Carolina, to conduct a physical and aerial survey of Grant 97 in 1966.

After the restaurant closed in 1967, with no money coming in and my parents' savings depleted, my father took the only job available to him: supervisor of the bell captains at the Blockade

Runner, a large hotel in Wrightsville Beach, a few miles north of Carolina Beach. Nor were my parents able to continue giving me the small amount I required for my rent in New York. But satisfied that I was ready for trial, I obtained a job as a supervisor in the graduate VISTA (Volunteers in Service to America) program at New York University Law School in January 1968. I researched North Carolina law at the New York County Lawyers Association and was able to fly to North Carolina as I was needed. I was fortunate that spring breaks, holidays, and summer vacations at NYU allowed me to hold a job and continue to work out my parents' legal problems.

On September 18, 1968, the case was scheduled for trial before William T. Bundy. On his own motion, the judge removed it from the trial calendar and ordered a "compulsory reference," stating that because of the complicated boundary dispute, a referee should decide all of the issues involved. He directed both parties to split the referee's initial costs of $400.

Bond and I appealed the order, arguing that the compulsory reference deprived poor people of the constitutional right to pursue their legal claims because they incurred litigation costs they could not afford and that it also denied the right to a jury trial. The Court of Appeals affirmed Bundy's order, stating that neither of our claims had merit and required no consideration.

When the case was returned to Leon Corbett he appointed a Wilmington surveyor, Henry Von Oesen, to survey both contentions and plot them on a map to be used by the referee during his hearing. Von Oesen refused to survey Grant 97, claiming that he could not locate the boundaries, despite the fact that Miller, our surveyor, had shown him his own map resulting from his physical survey. We brought a motion to have Von Oesen removed as the court surveyor, which Corbett denied.

The hearing was held on March 17, 1969, in a small conference room in the courthouse. Resort tried to prove its ownership by claiming title through a 1858 grant issued to James Adkins by the state of North Carolina. That grant was clearly south of Grant 97 as well as the property on which Resort had been building. Von Oesen testified that although he did not survey the Adkins grant, he "had enough information" to plot its location on the court survey map and offered no explanation for his inability to similarly plot Grant 97. Our surveyor and the aerial photographer testified for us, and strangely enough Resort's lawyer did not cross-examine either of them but routinely objected to every one of my questions, and Corbett routinely sustained the objections. Additionally, the transcript of the hearing omitted substantial rulings made by Corbett as well as my objections to them, information that would have been necessary for an appeal.

Before he rendered his decision Corbett required payment of another two thousand dollars. His judgment, filed on June 30, 1969, concluded that despite the fact that the "beginning corner of the Adkins' Grant cannot be located on the ground," Resort had shown title and possession to the lands it claimed and that my parents had failed to show title to the lands described in their answer.

Bond and I filed a list of written objections and demanded a jury trial, which was heard by Judge Albert W. Cowper on February 9, 1970. The only similarity to a jury trial was the choosing of a jury of six. No oral testimony was given by the witnesses. The only evidence presented to the jury was the truncated, defective transcript of the hearing, which was read to them by the court reporter and on which they were supposed to render a verdict. But after one day, Cowper relieved the jury of even this responsibility; he dismissed them and rendered a verdict in favor of Resort. His judgment stated that Resort owned the property described in their complaint; that they were not within the boundaries of Grant 97; and that "defendants have no right, title or interest in the lands described."

Soon after the decision Robert Bond died of a heart attack, and we retained the law firm of Pearson, Malone, Johnson, and DeJarmon to file an appeal. The intermediary appellate court, the Court of Appeals, affirmed Cowper's judgment and we pursued the appeal to the highest court, the Supreme Court of North Carolina, which rendered its decision on February 10, 1971.

To our objection that we had been denied a jury trial, the court said, "A compulsory reference does not deprive either party of his constitutional right to a jury trial of the issues of fact arising on the pleadings, but such trial is only upon the written evidence taken before the referee." Only one of the three judges, Sharp, concurred with the majority opinion but dissented on the issue of a jury trial, stating that "the credibility of the witnesses and the weight of the evidence is for determination by the jury."

The court upheld the lower appellate court's ruling that we had no interest in the lands claimed by Resort but reversed the finding that Resort owned any of the land it had described in its complaint. While we were mildly comforted by the court's decision that Resort owned none of the land it claimed, it was of small solace because we were bound by the decision that we did not own the southern half of Grant 97, unless we were able to achieve a reversal from the U.S. Supreme Court.

Because I had never argued a case before the U.S. Supreme Court, I retained a New York law firm with extensive experience in the Court to file a writ of certiorari requesting the Court's permission to appeal. Shortly thereafter, one of the law partners apologetically advised me that he had failed to file the writ within ten days following the North Carolina decision and that his motion for an extension of time had been denied by the Chief Justice. I was heartbroken, but my parents accepted the news without blaming me, reassuring me over and over that I had done everything I could. But the bitterness of this southern brand of American justice never left them and remained with me as I later confronted it in the North.

Chapter 7

In 1968 I had sent my résumé to New York University's Urban Affairs and Poverty Law Program, which had advertised its need for supervising attorneys. After several interviews by the search committee, headed by Leroy Clark, a Black full-time professor and the chairman of the program, I was hired along with two others to supervise one of three teams of fifteen lawyers each. The teams would be assigned as house counsel for various community organizations that had requested legal assistance but had no funds to provide their own. The goals of the program as outlined to me were impressive. The university was attempting to fulfill its responsibility as an urban center of knowledge by sharing its expertise with needy communities through young lawyers who had volunteered under the auspices of Volunteers in Service to America (VISTA) in exchange for credit toward a graduate degree. A list of organizations, each with specific legal needs, had been provided from which the VISTA volunteers chose their assignments, ranging from forming not-for-profit corporations to bringing class action suits. I noticed that, with few exceptions, the organizations, many of which were familiar to me, were located in Black areas of the city. The job seemed to be a logical extension of my abstract experience at HARYOU. The work promised to be challenging, and the salary was good.

But my eager anticipation came to an abrupt halt on the first day of orientation when I met the VISTA volunteers. They were all white. No one had prepared me for that. They were not only white; they were rich. Long-haired and casually dressed, they joked throughout the two-week orientation. I wondered if they could coexist with the problems of the poor and disenfranchised. Was it even possible? I was determined to understand the reasons that were sufficiently compelling to force the reluctant powerful to aid the powerless. And I did.

Prior to that time I had had no direct experience with

prestigious law schools or with their universities' undergraduate divisions, for that matter. But within a few months, I had put all of the pieces of NYU's program and its participants into place. And the prototype was alarming.

Academia rapidly descends from its lofty perch of intellectual and exclusionary purity when offered large sums of money, called bribes by ordinary people. And New York University Law School was no exception. By 1968 the government and all those who had a stake in maintaining the political status quo came together to prevent a repetition of the urban riots that had occurred across the country in the mid-sixties. Conditions seemed to be as ripe for major urban violence in 1968 as they had been in 1967, when the Kerner Commission, appointed by President Johnson on July 27 of that year to study the causes of the two-week Newark and Detroit riots during the summer of 1967, concluded that "our nation is moving toward two societies, one black, one white, separate and unequal," and warned that, next time, white America "would not escape."* In response, the government and academia were creating innovative, preventive programs with significant amounts of money made available for this purpose.

Despite the commission's findings that societal inequalities were essentially responsible for the 1967 riots, it nevertheless reached the conclusion, quite unexplainable and unsupported by any data, that the riots were caused by "militant organizations, local and national, and individual agitators, who repeatedly forecast and called for violence in the spring and summer of 1967." The commission further called for increased surveillance and intervention in the affairs of organizations and individuals considered by this august body to be "militant." That recommendation justified intensification of the atrocities later committed by the FBI's counterintelligence program (COINTELPRO) initiated in August 1967 to penetrate and destroy Black organizations.

The commission further intoned, "In the summer of 1967

---

*The study, conducted by the National Advisory Commission on Civil Disorders, is commonly called the Kerner Commission Report because its chairman was Otto Kerner, then governor of Illinois. The report was funded by the Ford Foundation and the composition of the commission was so conservative that Dr. Martin Luther King, Jr., was rejected as a member because he was not considered a "bona fide moderate."

66   we have seen in our cities a chain reaction of racial violence. If we are heedless, none of us shall escape the consequences." It urged "investigations of organized activity" to be continued "at all levels of government, including committees of Congress. These investigations relate not only to the disorders of 1967, but also to the actions of groups and individuals, particularly in schools and colleges during this last fall and winter. The Commission has cooperated in these investigations. They should continue." It is significant that these words mirrored the stated COINTELPRO goals.

As a result, federal and private funds were quickly made available to every institutional mainstay, including universities, to quell the possibility of another "long, hot summer." And in 1968, an additional ingredient fostering potential societal eruption was factored into the already explosive equation: resistance to the Vietnam War.

Using federal funds siphoned from those allocated to VISTA, New York University Law School had put its shoulder to the wheel and established the Urban Affairs and Poverty Law Program, which was designed to absorb and deflect militant opposition to the Vietnam War by offering young lawyers automatic exemption from the draft, which by then had peaked to over 475,000 and was increasing every day. The motivation of the VISTA volunteers for personal survival was shared equally by the poor and the Black, but survival was afforded only to the rich and the white, for whom the country had established legitimate escape routes.

To further extend the policy of containment, major private contributors guaranteed increased law school enrollment of Black students at NYU by establishing funds to be used expressly for their tuition and other expenses. Among the contributors were the Carnegie Foundation (responsible for the funding of the 1944 study of race relations in the United States called *An American Dilemma: The Negro Problem in the United States*, authored by Gunnar Myrdal), which contributed a $100,000 scholarship grant for each of the three years beginning in 1968; the Samuel Rubin Foundation, which donated $25,000 a year for ten years, terminating in 1974; and the Strook Scholarship, which guaranteed $5,000 a year for five years, from 1968 to 1972. In addition, between 1967 and 1969, New York University Law School alumni donated $10,000.

A credible facade of racial inclusion was constructed by appointing Leroy Clark, the only full-time Black professor at the law school, albeit untenured, to chair the Urban Affairs Program. The school protected itself against possible charges of either racial or sex discrimination by hiring me. And so the package was complete.

But as in so many instances when political architects construct their careful plans to contain specific activities, the designers' intentions are not always followed. Within several months the program exceeded the parameters set by the administration and it was forced to give reluctant permission to the VISTA volunteers' involvement with "undesirable" organizations like Fight Back, which used a grassroots approach to end job discrimination, and community groups such as the parents of Ocean Hill–Brownsville, who were demanding community control of their schools. VISTA volunteers assigned to my team worked with both groups. We spent many weekends locked inside an Ocean Hill–Brownsville school with parents and other community members, writing their positions on legal pads, fashioning them into memoranda and briefs, rushing to get them typed, serving them on the Board of Education, and filing them in court. When the motions were argued, the community petitioners were there, asserting their ultimatums. We were a part of the settlements forged, and we shared in the few victories hammered out.

I must say that some of the VISTA volunteers met the challenge they faced in worthy fashion. Despite their frank admission that when the Vietnam War was over they would cut their hair and exchange their jeans for Wall Street attire, the experience permanently altered the career directions of many. One in particular, Andrew Loeb, the nephew of the founder of and major contributor to the Loeb Student Center at New York University, joined a California legal services agency representing migrant farm workers when the program ended.

When the VISTA program was terminated in 1969, Robert McKay, the dean of the law school, appointed me his assistant as minority student adviser and gave me the opportunity to design and teach a clinical course in juvenile delinquency for third-year and graduate law students. Bob was careful to impress on me the exact nature of my appointment. I was the assistant *to* the dean, not the assistant dean, an immeasurable difference. But the essential significance to me of my position was that I was adviser to the minority students, with no need to pretend that my concern included all students.

One of my assignments was service on the law school's admissions committee. Although I reviewed white applications also, my main role was to recommend acceptance of minority students. A gigantic problem arose, however, when I differed with Daniel Kimball, who was in charge of the admissions standards, over the meaning of "minority" applicants. He wanted to include all white foreigners in that category, thereby diluting representation by Blacks in the thirty spots designated by the Carnegie Foundation for disadvantaged minorities who because of racism had been denied equal education in the United States. I was specifically opposed to the inclusion of self-exiled Cuban students who, under the Batista regime, had enjoyed every advantage their society had to offer and continued to benefit from U.S. largess after they arrived here. But because of low LSAT scores and grade point averages, they competed unfavorably with the 5,000 white students applying for the 350 slots in the freshman class. I argued against Kimball's concept of "minority" ad nauseam, bringing my complaints to the full admissions committee. I pointed out that, if his interpretation prevailed, the two-fifths of the population who earned 65 percent of the national income, also a "minority," would be entitled to Carnegie scholarships. Kimball's position was so transparently specious it would have been ludicrous and dismissed without comment had he not been so insistent. Our fights were endless. But I persisted, and no Cubans became law students through the Carnegie program while I was at NYU.

Only the Black Allied Law Students Association (BALSA) and the relaxed environment of Greenwich Village surrounding NYU relieved the social and emotional isolation of the minority students, most of whom were Black. The expressed reason given by the white students for their pervasive hostility was their perception that the minority students had been accepted into the law school only because their tuition was guaranteed by the Carnegie Foundation grant, thereby depriving whites of thirty spaces in the entering classes for the years 1969 through 1971. While, admittedly, applications for admission had climbed to more than five thousand a year, competition was fierce in law schools across the country, and LSAT minority scores were not

as high as those of white students admitted, the whites ignored
the special advantages given them through the Root-Tilden
scholarships, a two-million-dollar working capital fund, which
provided full tuition and other expenses as well as an additional
$1,500 yearly stipend. And those scholarships were not based on
need. They also overlooked the fact that few, if any, graduates
fulfilled their promise to enter public service in exchange for the
scholarships and the fact that the LSAT scores for the Root-
Tilden recipients were far below those of the average white
student admitted and that throughout its history only two
Root-Tilden recipients had been Black.

It didn't matter to the white students, resentful of the 10
percent minority set-aside for entering classes, that only 1
percent of lawyers in the United States were African Americans
or that this minuscule number, excluded from bar associations
and corporate law practice, was hardly a threat to their privileged positions, economically or otherwise. They still insisted
that the standards used for the "affirmative action" Root-Tilden
scholarships given to undeserving white students were unconscionable, unfair, and downright "reverse discrimination" when
applied to deserving Black students. The BALSA members venti-
lated their bitter feelings to me during our evening meetings, but
while I could try to ease some situations, I could provide no real,
permanent window in the brick wall they faced daily.

And there were other battles. At the end of the first year, the
credentials committee recommended that many Black students
be dropped because their grades fell below a set minimum. In
this situation, Bob McKay came to my aid, using his influence to
retain every minority student in academic trouble. I prepared a
statistical analysis demonstrating the wide differences between
the financial resources of minority and white families and
supporting my contention that almost no white students worked
because their loans were supplemented by their families and that
90 percent of minority students worked because their families
had no resources with which to help them, despite the school's
prohibition of any employment during the first year. I argued
that the school had an obligation to provide remediation for
students it had admitted with lower LSAT scores and GPA and
that it could not accept Carnegie Foundation money, designed
for just such students, and then allow them to fail after one year

of difficulties compounded by employment and exclusion from campus life.

As a result, no Black student during my years at NYU flunked out. Of the several who were permitted to continue with lower grades beyond the first year, one is a New York State Supreme Court judge. I don't know what most of the others are doing now, but I am especially proud of John Walker, who moved to the state of Mississippi to practice law on behalf of Blacks dispossessed of their human rights, and of Henrietta Turnquist, who bravely began her own private practice in Atlanta, Georgia.

I was expected to attend faculty meetings, at which I dutifully appeared whenever I could find no satisfactory excuse for my absence, but I soon lost interest in the faculty's clever articulations and lofty posturings, which barely concealed their hidden agendas and infightings. They considered me too unimportant to be looked at directly and, even if I was sitting between two faculty members who were being addressed by another across the room, the speaker would look from one to the other without his eyes ever crossing my face. An amazing feat. I usually spent the time scratching out tic-tac-toe games with an imaginary opponent. Only when matters of importance to minority students arose did I lift my voice and demand eye-to-eye confrontation. Apart from Bob and Leroy, only Norman Dorsen, director of the Hays Civil Liberties Program at the university, talked to me.

My involvement with the Black undergraduate students at the university was unexpected. Because they considered Roscoe Brown, the head of the Black Studies Department, a part of the "system," unwilling to jeopardize his own ambitions to support their positions, they asked me to be their unofficial faculty representative. I met with them regularly at the Martin Luther King, Jr., Center on campus and gave whatever advice I could. After forty-six of them occupied the chancellor's office in the law school for twenty-two hours in 1970, demanding an increase in the Martin Luther King Scholarships (a federally funded program) to absorb increased dormitory and tuition costs, I represented them when they were arrested for trespass, to the dismay of Bob McKay and the disgust of Leroy Clark. On October 25, 1971, after almost a year of preliminary hearings and trials, criminal complaints against twenty-four were dismissed outright and those against the remaining twenty-two were dismissed on

condition that they create no disturbances for a period of three
months.

My primary responsibility was the clinical course I conducted in juvenile delinquency. It was an elective, open only to
third-year or graduate students, and required a great deal of
preparation. In addition to the weekly seminar, the class was
divided into two sections, one assigned to the Legal Aid Law
Guardian Unit in Family Court to defend accused juveniles, the
other to the Corporation Counsel's Office to represent those who
made the complaints against the juveniles. I prepared the students for the court appearances, for which special permission
had been obtained from the Appellate Division of the Supreme
Court, helped them investigate the charges and research legal
questions, and frequently appeared in court with them, although
they were supervised day to day by the agencies to which they
had been assigned. Each course continued over two semesters
and students made four visits each semester to institutions for
delinquent children, as close to the university as Spofford in the
Bronx and as far away as Warwick in upper New York State. The
course was innovative, one of the few clinical opportunities
provided in any law school in the country.

During the years 1971 and 1972, Bob chaired the New York
State special commission on the Attica Prison uprising of September 13, 1971, the bloodiest prison revolt in the history of the
country. New York state police, on direct orders from Governor
Nelson A. Rockefeller, had killed thirty-two inmates and ten
hostages in an assault on the prison. McKay chose the panel and
named Haywood Burns, later the head of the National Conference of Black Lawyers, as a member. The McKay Commission
report criticized Rockefeller for not personally going to the
prison when requested to do so by the inmates before ordering
the armed assault as well as state prison officials for not having
nonlethal weapons.

Since 1970, when I became the dean's assistant, I had met
with McKay frequently to discuss law school matters relating to
the minority students. He discussed a little of the commission's
activities and progress, but he never referred to the nationwide
search for Joey, although certainly the FBI and the police had
talked to him about her and our family relationship. The FBI had
been to my apartment on at least four occasions when I was at
work, and agents James Murby, Al Genkinger, Pete Malley, and

John Jimerson had slipped notes under the door asking that I contact them, which I refused to do. In 1972, three agents stopped me in the hallway leading to my apartment and demanded that I talk to them. The conversation terminated quickly. I told them that I was Joey's lawyer and that I had no comment to make. Since then they had not communicated with me directly, but telephone surveillance continued without interruption and the surveillance of my person never ceased.

I don't know if all my nonstop activity was merely type A mania or whether it was an intentional device to crowd out my fear for Joey's life and to keep dampened the flames of anguish that frequently interrupted my thoughts. I never went to sleep. I simply fell asleep as I rested my head on the table for a minute while writing or changing from an uncomfortable reading position. But at night the radio was always tuned to the news station.

Throughout these years I wrestled with my own feelings about the BLA, its reported crimes, and its reported justifications. My extensive study of the European slave trade of Africans throughout the world and of African American history, as well as my own fifty years of living within the racist context of America, had made it impossible for me to reject the BLA's philosophy out of hand. When I read the accounts of the shipments of necklocked and ankle-ironed Africans delivered to slave blocks in the Americas, where they were auctioned off to the highest bidder, I was there. I made the journey for unshackled liberation along with them when the armed resistance to our slave revolts terminated in our deaths. I mourned the lives we lost fighting in the Revolutionary War only to learn that the freedom that was promised in the Declaration of Independence or the Constitution was not ours.

I supported our abolitionists who printed newspapers and circulated pamphlets and led organizations that peacefully demanded the end of slavery, Jim Crow laws, and the Fugitive Slave Act and peacefully penetrated into life-threatening territory again and again to rescue our people from bondage. We insisted on joining the Union Army in a war we were told was a war for our freedom, only to learn that the Emancipation Proclamation did not guarantee our freedom and that the Thirteenth Amendment to the Constitution of the United States was required to end the constitutional protection of slavery. The proclamation was promptly nullified by the sneering Black codes of the southern states and was never fully implemented even after two additional constitutional amendments had been enacted. I watched helplessly as Ku Klux Klan night riders crisscrossed the country burning our Black bodies on their white crosses.

I suffered as the murders continued into the 1950s and 1960s, cutting down the young civil rights workers who had joined Dr. Martin Luther King's marches through the South as they fought for desegregation and voting rights, remaining steadfastly nonviolent and nonretaliatory despite the vitriolic attacks on them, and as the KKK punctuated its contempt for their passivity by assassinating white civil rights workers who had joined the movement for freedom. And I agonized as more civil rights legislation was passed, checked, and checkmated.

In 1963 as I walked with King through the streets of Washington, D.C., I listened to him urge his dream of equality upon white America and realized that his words did not change the poverty-ridden and unequal lives of African Americans or prevent the bomb-murder of four Black children as they prayed in a Birmingham, Alabama, church one month later. I heard Malcolm X's forceful analysis cry out against King's nonviolent strategy when bulldogs and firehoses were turned loose on thousands of Black people as they marched from Selma to Montgomery to register to vote singing "We Shall Overcome."

I despaired with the Student Nonviolent Coordinating Committee when political activities could not redesign the political process so that Black voters could legitimately compete for participatory roles in political parties once the poll tax, literacy tests, and other legalized impediments to free elections had been declared unconstitutional.

I understood when a new generation of African Americans grew impatient with years of theoretical progress, heralded when change occurred and discredited when no change resulted. I was not surprised when the Black Panther Party rejected King's dream that guilt-ridden white Americans would share the benefits they had realized from institutional racism and when the party urged California Blacks to arm themselves for self-defense against continued police assault.

I thought about the racism that had eroded the socialization process for African Americans, a process that is essential for all humans because it provides the structure within which all behavior is fashioned. When the social order provides rewards for compliance with its rules, compliance is voluntary. When the equation is fair, hard work and the achievement of educational or vocational goals will translate into jobs that will enable physical survival for the individual and the family. When a person is excluded from the equation, there is no need to comply with the rules, and the struggle for a different social order will emerge by necessity.

In 1973, I thought about the one thousand African Americans who had been killed by police on the streets of America in the previous two years and the twenty policemen who had lost their lives, allegedly from the guns of the Black Liberation Army. And, I thought, the equation did not balance. It was top-heavy with Black people, weighted down with bullet fragments and twisted nooses. The equation will never be balanced even after all the murders stop. Even then, history will report the one-sided picture of lynched Black bodies swinging from poplar trees in silent testimony.

And, I thought, whether accepted or rejected, whether approved or disapproved, as long as all of the conditions that prevent inclusion continue, the possibility exists that another and another and another Black Liberation Army will emerge, prepared to kill and to die.

These were my thoughts when I heard the news flash at about 1:30 in the morning of May 2, 1973. There had been a shoot-out on the New Jersey Turnpike involving two state troopers and three people traveling south in a white Pontiac. One passenger and one state trooper were dead. One had escaped and a woman was seriously wounded and captured. No names were given, but I knew it was Joey.

Part 2

Chapter 8

I quickly learned how to cross the distances separating Middlesex General Hospital from Middlesex Superior Court from the New Jersey state police headquarters from Roosevelt Hospital in Edison, New Jersey, from the Middlesex County Workhouse in East Brunswick. But that Wednesday morning, May 2, 1973, I didn't even know where Exit 9, the scene of the shoot-out on the New Jersey Turnpike, was. All I knew was that if I went south on the turnpike, I would reach New Brunswick, where Middlesex Hospital was located and where Joey lay in critical condition.

The information that Zayd Shakur was dead and JoAnne Chesimard was wounded and captured was not released until late that morning, after a rushed fingerprint check had identified them. An unknown third person had escaped. And my night fear had been confirmed by the time the first streaks of sun illuminated the sky. I called my sister as I dressed. She had heard the news but was too shaken to drive. I couldn't wait. I didn't own a car and I didn't drive, so I hired a cab for the day.

The next day's papers placed the story on the front page, complete with pictures of the smashed and bullet-riddled white Pontiac in which Joey had been a passenger, the state trooper cars involved, the by now familiar mug shot, and a surprising amount of information concerning the circumstances of the shoot-out. *The New York Times* reported:

> A state trooper and a former information minister for a New York faction of the Black Panthers were killed and the woman leader of the so-called Black Liberation Army was wounded and captured today in a shoot-out and chase on the New Jersey Turnpike. . . .
>
> She apparently was being taken by two male companions to a new hideout in Philadelphia when their car was stopped at about 12:45 A.M for a routine traffic check and the shooting erupted. . . .

Miss Chesimard was reported in serious condition at Middlesex General Hospital today with gunshot wounds in both arms and in a shoulder. . . .

The Panther who was fatally wounded was identified as James F. Coston, 32. . . . He also used the Islamic name Zayd Malik Shakur and was the information minister for the Black Panthers under Eldridge Cleaver. . . .

The state police superintendent, Col. David B. Kelly, said the incident began when Trooper [James] Harper observed a 1965 Pontiac LeMans with Vermont license plates exceeding the speed limit "slightly" as it headed south on the turnpike. The trooper ordered the driver to pull over about 200 yards south of the Turnpike Administration Building at exit 9, near New Brunswick.

In accordance with state police procedure, the trooper called for a back-up man and Trooper [Werner] Foerster arrived.

Trooper Harper asked the driver for his registration and, when he noticed a discrepancy, asked the man to get out of the car. The driver went to the rear of his car, where Trooper Foerster began to question him.

At this point one or more of the suspects began shooting with automatic handguns, according to Colonel Kelly.

Trooper Foerster fired four times before he fell mortally wounded in the head, according to police.

The driver of the suspects' car jumped into the vehicle and sped off as three patrol cars took up the chase and toll booths down the line were alerted.

The *Times* also had a three-column feature story entitled "Seized Woman Called Black Militants' 'Soul,' " repeating the many allegations reported in Daley's "Target Blue" *New York* magazine article. The *Daily News* captioned its feature "To Militants She's A St. Joanne." Its story began:

To the cops she was wanted in Queens and the Bronx for bank robbery and wanted for questioning in the slaying of police officers Rocco Laurie and Gregory Foster in Manhattan. But to her supporters and sympathizers, she was a black Joan of Arc. Such is the legend of JoAnne Deborah Chesimard, the asserted high priestess of the cop-hating Black Liberation Army. Word came to police investigators of the strange young woman accused of leading assorted Army members on cop attacks, bank robberies and other crimes. In a 15-month period her criminal reputation exceeded such heralded female felons as Bonnie Parker and Ma Barker. She became the most wanted woman in New York City history. Veteran cops, incensed by the murders and attacks on fellow officers, said privately that they would shoot her down on sight if given the opportunity.

Highlighting the article was the well-publicized Queens bank robbery surveillance photo, under which the caption read, "JOANNE CHESIMARD allegedly taking part in a Queens bank robbery in August, 1971."

The papers gave no clue to Joey's real condition, and I could barely contain my growing apprehension. Turnpike traffic was backed up for miles as we approached Exit 9 and when we finally made the slow, curved turnoff down the exit ramp to head toward New Brunswick, I could see the turnpike as it continued south past the state police administration building on the hill. Directly below the building on the highway were the state troopers' marked cars that were involved in the shoot-out, differentiated from the many other marked cars by their red and white rooftop lights. which continued to revolve. Although I would visit this scene many times in the future, that first inspection revealed the full terror of the night. Broken glass was everywhere as the crime scene personnel gathered evidence and reporters and television crews took photographs. Some state troopers surrounded the site while others scurried from the road to the top of the hill and into the building.

Over the next few days New Jersey officials erected an impenetrable barrier that effectively prevented me from seeing Joey. On the first day the hospital staff said that her condition was too critical to permit visitors, no matter who they were. And even if her condition was not serious, I would need to get permission from the sheriff, Joseph DeMarino. His office was located in the Middlesex County jail, but he was out. A deputy told me that, in any event, the state troopers would have to approve the visit. I went to the state police administration building, passing a security check before being permitted into the parking lot behind it, and was told that the person I needed to see was occupied. I was told to return tomorrow. Or some other time. The fact that I was Joey's lawyer meant nothing. Neither did the fact that I was a relative, of which proof would be needed. A promise was made, however, that consideration would be given the next day.

This endless charade lasted all day. I tried to learn whether Joey had survived from the radio broadcasts in the cab and the afternoon newspapers, but the information simply repeated the reports of the shoot-out and the search for the escaped driver. Telephone calls to the hospital were fruitless. The staff there would give no information. I left New Jersey and went directly to my sister's house to give her a full report. She drove me to New Jersey the next day, and our first stop was at the hospital, where we were told that Joey's condition was too critical for us to see her. I later learned that that day she had been arraigned, in her hospital room, on the felony complaint related to the turnpike incident and had not been considered "too critical" to listen to six pages of charges. We made the rounds of officialdom, and at trooper headquarters we were told to return in the afternoon when permission would be given to see Joey. When we did come back, we were told to wait because the person in charge had not yet arrived. At this point I knew that further efforts along this line would be meaningless and I went directly to the Middlesex Superior Court, where I saw the administrative judge and obtained an oral order for Joey's mother, her sister, and me to see her the following day. Our only solace was that at least there had been no report of her death.

        The several days of unconcealed hatred shown by the state troopers had not prepared me for their army force at the hospital. Joey's room was located at the end of a long corridor, which was lined on each side with uniformed troopers, hats tilted forward over their eyes, in full riot gear, with shotguns pointed at me, their fingers poised on the triggers. I counted ten of them, five on each side, spaced apart for total control of my single body proceeding between them. There comes a time when ancillary emotional reactions stop, when the body ceases to function on any level except the single one required to cope with the particular danger it faces. As I walked between the troopers all my systems shut down except for the automatic mechanism I needed to walk as firmly and as arrogantly as my tall structure permitted. I had entered the quiet world of primal survival, and I had only one object: to see my child. And all of those triggered fingers would have had to move to prevent me from doing that.

        Before I reached Joey's room, a light-brown-skinned female sheriff, who I later learned was Mildred Scott, approached and quickly guided me through a small door into a bathroom and told

me to take off all my clothes, including my underwear. Under-
standing that resistance would prevent a visit with Joey, I removed each garment carefully in slow-motion compliance, until I stood naked before her, turned around for posterior inspection, and was directed to put my clothes back on. Accompanied by the sheriff, I walked between the last two troopers and into Joey's room for the allotted ten-minute visit. I paid this same price for the next four days, until I was able to obtain a court order prohibiting the state's humiliating treatment of me.

At that first visit I walked around the five armed troopers encircling the bed to which both her ankles were shackled, and I saw Joey for the first time in more than two years. Her face was bruised and swollen. Her right arm was in a sling, and blood oozed from the bullet wound in her bandaged chest. She was much thinner than when I had last seen her, the slender body barely imprinting an outline against the sheets. Her hair was short, only about two inches long, erasing from my mind the media-generated image of her large Afro. Yet this person was no stranger to me. This was my Joey.

I gently hugged her and we whispered together, neither of us letting the tears drop. I told her I'd been given only ten minutes and asked her to tell me as quickly as she could what I needed to know about her physical condition. She said a judge had been there the day before with the prosecutor and a court reporter and had read the criminal charges against her. She said that she had repeatedly asked for me to be there but was told I couldn't be reached. I explained that I had been in New Jersey for the last two days trying to get permission to see her. She gave me the copy of the six pages of charges that had been read to her. She said the judge had told the court reporter to enter into the record "not guilty" when she refused to participate at all without my presence.

We talked about her wounds and she told me that her right arm was paralyzed and that the bullet in her chest had not been removed. I told her we would try to get permission for a private doctor to examine her. But her primary concern was the removal of the state troopers from her room—she told me they were threatening to kill her. I told her that her mother and sister were there and she smiled, tried to sit up a little, but sank back onto the bed. The troopers moved toward us, shotguns aimed. Time was up. I told her I would visit the next day and marched back through the corridor.

For me to obtain a court order to remove the twenty-four-hour-a-day guard from her room, I had to be admitted *pro hac vice* to the courts of New Jersey (permission for an out-of-state lawyer to practice in the state for one particular case), and the rules required that only a New Jersey lawyer could make the request. So each day as soon as my ten-minute visits were over I searched for a Black attorney. But each day the threats to Joey became more vicious, soon accompanied by shotgun butts jabbed into her body, nighttime storming around her bed, and the shouting of Nazi slogans by the German descendants who made up a large part of the state trooper force. Desperate in my helplessness, I asked the director of the National Conference of Black Lawyers, Haywood Burns, to call a press conference to expose the danger to which Joey was being subjected. The conference was held in the first-floor lounge of the hospital and a few hours later Joey was "medically discharged" to Roosevelt Hospital in Edison, New Jersey, where security was not as overwhelming.

Several days after the shoot-out, Sundiata Acoli (Clark Squire), the driver of the Pontiac, was captured. He wanted Charles McKinney, his lawyer in the Panther 21 trial (the only Black lawyer for the defendants in that trial), to represent him. I not only knew Charlie, but fortunately he was a close friend of Raymond Brown, a brilliant Black New Jersey criminal trial lawyer, who agreed to sponsor our admissions to the New Jersey courts to defend Assata and Sundiata. When Ray made the formal motion on May 18, C. Judson Hamlin, the prosecutor, opposed me, alleging that I had already violated the New Jersey canon of ethics by participating in the press conference. The administrative judge, Leon Gerofsky, reluctantly granted Ray's motion, however, on two conditions: that I abide by the New Jersey canon of ethics and that I make no further comments to the press about the case. He admonished me that if I breached either condition, I would be removed from the case.

While the composition of the police changed from state troopers to Middlesex County sheriffs at Roosevelt Hospital, sheriffs remained in Joey's room, guarding her still-shackled, partially paralyzed body with pointed shotguns, even during my visits, now officially classified as attorney-client conferences despite the fact that the presence of the police prevented us from discussing legal strategy. It required another court order to

remove the police during my visits, and when the media widely
reported that court decision, Joey was moved to the Middlesex
County Workhouse and placed in a wing with other pretrial
female prisoners, separated from them by double iron doors. Our
family had retained Dr. Alan Clark, a former health director for
the city of Newark, who headed a team consisting of a thoracic
expert and a neurosurgeon to examine Joey, and after a long
delay for a "credentials check" they found her health viable and
recommended against removing the bullet because of its critical
location next to her heart. Administering an electromyogram,
they determined the extent to which physical therapy could
minimize the paralysis of her right arm.

This was the first time I had represented a political prisoner, which I now define as someone who has been illegally
incarcerated because of his or her opinions or who, having been
convicted of a crime, is brutalized while in prison because of his
or her opinions or who is convicted of committing a crime for
political reasons. I believe that all African American prisoners
are political prisoners, whether or not they label themselves as
such, because of the circumstances that got them into jail as well
as the harshness of sentencing applied only to them. Joey was no
different, but for whatever reasons she was a notorious, widely
publicized political prisoner. And she had astounding support
from many segments of the Black community whose only knowledge about her came from a negative media.

Defense committees had formed in both New York and New
Jersey; college students held meetings to disseminate information
about the political aspects of the case and to urge attendance at the
trial. The most vocal group was the Black Student Congress at
Douglass College, a division of Rutgers University in New Brunswick. The New Jersey Black Assembly, a group of elected Black
state representatives, had asked the New Jersey attorney general
to remove state troopers from Joey's Middlesex Hospital room,
declaring, "Sister Chesimard should be dealt with with the same
presumption of innocence at least that the policeman Thomas
Shea, who has been charged with murdering a ten-year-old youth,
Clifford Glover, and is allowed to walk around free on a mere
$25,000 bail." Charles Grey, assistant director of the Middlesex
County Urban League, went against that conservative national
organization and urged support of Joey and Sundiata. And Angela
Davis, speaking at Princeton University, called for support "for our

Freedom Fighters." The Law Students Civil Rights Research Council, the Prisoners' Rights Organized Defense Project of the American Civil Liberties Union in New Jersey, and the Coalition of
Concerned Black Americans, an umbrella organization of eighty
community-based and professional Black organizations, in addition to many white militants, were among those supporting Joey
and Sundiata.

But being a lawyer for a political prisoner is in no way
comparable to representing the usual criminal defendant. The
orientation of political prisoners is international, global rather
than personal, philosophical, and critically analytical. They consider the legal situation in which they find themselves entrapped
after they are arrested as simply a microcosm of the larger
society's imprisonment of all of its Black citizens, and extrication
from it must be defined by stratagems of political correctness.
While occasionally they are forced to do so, they usually will not
conform to the rules of the court, to the rules of criminal or civil
procedure, or to the rules of evidence, not to mention the rules of
prescribed courtroom decorum. Political prisoners scrutinize each
motion their attorney files with an eye not for its legal competence
or consequences but for its political ramifications in the overall,
unceasing need to expose the society in its true light, not to
extricate themselves from its grip. And they refuse to be deterred
by fear of the system's retaliatory might or by the hope that
submission to its rules would benefit them.

Representing Joey required constant adjustment from my
long practiced academic and technical approach. Her assessment of our differences was partially correct. According to her,
I would not classify a forest as such until I had counted every
tree, while she would recognize the obvious immediately; I was
cerebral and legally knowledgeable, but not the political strategist that she was. So we made a pact: I would do my legal thing
and she would do her necessary thing. She never doubted the
superiority of people power over legal power any more than she
doubted that only the people, to whom she always referred as
"my people," would care enough to understand and to help her in
any way they could. I watched with fascination her smiling,
power-fisted greeting to the friends and supporters who filled
every courtroom at every trial as if they had gathered for a social
event. And sometimes, when the going was really rough, I
watched with disbelief.

Incensed by the hypocrisy of the approaching July Fourth
Independence Day, Joey decided to make a public statement to
African Americans for the first time about who she was and what
she believed in. She wrote the message with a shaky left hand
and asked me to help her record it on a tape recorder and to
release it over Black radio stations.

While I understood her urgency to communicate her love
and her political philosophy to Black people, especially to those
who considered her an embarrassment, I also felt that my
continued status as her lawyer had to be factored into her
decision about making a public statement. I feared that Gerofsky
would use the publication of Joey's taped message as an excuse
to withdraw my admission to the New Jersey courts on the
pretext that her message in some way was attributable to me and
therefore constituted my violation of the canon of ethics that
precluded me from discussing the legal aspects of the criminal
charges pending against her. And I had no doubt that the
prosecutor would quickly make a motion for my removal as soon
as the tape was played.

I believed that I could best represent Joey because, having
resigned from NYU on the day of her arrest so that I could be
available to her, I was able to devote all of my time to preparing
the necessary pretrial motions and conducting the investigations
that Ray Brown's busy schedule did not permit. And he had
agreed to sponsor Charlie and me on condition that I assume
responsibility for the bulk of the pretrial efforts. Ray's presence
was required at each court appearance during which pretrial
motions were orally argued, during jury selection, and on each
day of the trial when it began. We paid Ray a relatively small
retainer, but the vast amount of work he ended up doing
amounted to pro bono representation.

I was concerned that the prison brutality that might resur-
face would go unchallenged should I be disqualified from representing Joey. As her attorney I could visit daily and would be
made aware of such incidents immediately. My involvement was
even more important because Joey was permitted no telephone
calls, not even to her attorneys during an emergency. I was also
in the process of preparing a motion for a court order permitting
physical therapy for her paralysis. In addition, we had been
preparing a motion for a change of venue from Middlesex County
based on prejudicial pretrial publicity. We argued that the

massive negative media coverage associating Joey with the BLA and the unproven crimes alleged to have been committed by that group had so biased prospective jurors against Sundiata and Joey that a fair trial was impossible. I was concerned that her admission of association with the BLA might undermine the thrust of our motion and, in a perverse way, contribute to the court's denial of the motion.

Despite my reluctance to tape Joey's July Fourth statement, and after discussing all of my apprehensions with her, I was finally persuaded that what she considered her political responsibilities were paramount and that as much as I wanted to protect her, it was her decision to live her life as she had determined it must be lived. At this early stage of my seven-year representation of her, I relinquished her as my child and accepted her as an adult for whom I had a special responsibility, which did not include making political decisions for her, regardless of the legal consequences. I looked at her large-eyed stubborn intensity, undemanding but imploring, magnifying the fragility of her body from which hung her helpless right arm, and I held the microphone close to her mouth. From that day she became for me what her African name meant: Assata ("She Who Struggles") Olugbala ("Love for the People") Shakur ("The Grateful"), and I never called her Joey again.

Assata's statement was aired over every Black radio station in New York City and New Jersey, criticized by the white media, and published in the journal *Black Scholar*. She said:

> Black brothers, Black sisters, i want you to know that i love you and i hope that somewhere in your hearts you have love for me. My name is Assata Shakur (slave name joanne chesimard), and i am a revolutionary. A Black revolutionary. By that i mean that i have declared war on all the forces that have raped our women, castrated our men, and kept our babies empty-bellied.
>
> I have declared war on the rich who prosper on our poverty, the politicians who lie to us with smiling faces, and all the mindless, heartless robots who protect them and their property. . . .
>
> I am a Black revolutionary, and, by definition, that makes me a part of the Black Liberation Army. . . .
>
> They call us murderers, but we do not control or enforce a system of racism and oppression that systematically mur-

ders Black and Third World people. Although Black people supposedly comprise about fifteen percent of the total amerikkkan population, at least sixty percent of murder victims are Black. For every pig that is killed in the so-called line of duty, there are at least fifty Black people murdered by police. . . .

Black life expectancy is much lower than white and they do their best to kill us before we are born. We are burned alive in fire-trap tenements. Our brothers and sisters O.D. daily from heroin and methadone. Our babies die from lead poisoning. Millions of Black people have died as a result of indecent medical care. This is murder. But they have the gall to call us murderers. . . .

They call us thieves and bandits. They say we steal. But it was not we who stole millions of Black people from the continent of Africa. We were robbed of our language, of our gods, of our culture, of our human dignity, of our labor, and of our lives. They call us thieves, yet it is not we who rip off billions of dollars every year through tax evasions, illegal price fixing, embezzlement, consumer fraud, bribes, kickbacks, and swindles. They call us bandits, yet every time most Black people pick up our paychecks we are being robbed. Every time we walk into a store in our neighborhoods we are being held up. And every time we pay our rent the landlord sticks a gun in our ribs.

They call us thieves, but we did not rob and murder millions of Indians by ripping off their homeland, then call ourselves pioneers. The call us bandits, but it is not we who are robbing Africa, Asia, and Latin America of their natural resources and freedom while the people who live there are sick and starving. The rulers of this country and their flunkies have committed some of the most brutal, vicious crimes in history. They are the bandits. They are the murderers. And they should be treated as such. These maniacs are not fit to judge me, Clark, or any other Black person on trial in amerika. Black people should, and inevitably must, determine our destinies.

Every revolution in history has been accomplished by actions, although words are necessary. We must create shields that protect us and spears that penetrate our enemies. Black people must learn how to struggle by struggling. We must learn by our mistakes.

I want to apologize to you, my Black brothers and sisters, for being on the new jersey turnpike. I should have known better. The turnpike is a checkpoint where Black people are stopped, searched, harassed, and assaulted. Revolutionaries must never be in too much of a hurry or make careless decisions. He who runs when the sun is sleeping will stumble many times.

Every time a Black Freedom Fighter is murdered or captured, the pigs try to create the impression that they have quashed the movement, destroyed our forces, and put down the Black Revolution. The pigs also try to give the impression that five or ten guerrillas are responsible for every revolutionary action carried out in amerika. That is nonsense. That is absurd. Black revolutionaries do not drip from the moon. We are created by our conditions. Shaped by our oppression. We are being manufactured in droves in the ghetto streets, places like attica, san quentin, bedford hills, leavenworth, and sing sing. They are turning out thousands of us. Many jobless Black veterans and welfare mothers are joining our ranks. Brothers and sisters from all walks of life, who are tired of suffering passively, make up the BLA.

There is, and always will be, until every Black man, woman, and child is free, a Black Liberation Army. The main function of the Black Liberation Army at this time is to create good examples, to struggle for Black freedom, and to prepare for the future. We must defend ourselves and let no one disrespect us. We must gain our liberation by any means necessary.

It is our duty to fight for our freedom.

It is our duty to win.

We must love each other and support each other.

We have nothing to lose but our chains.

In the spirit of: Ronald Carter, William Christmas, Mark Clark, Mark Essex, Frank "Heavy" Fields, Woody Changa Olugbala Green, Fred Hampton, Lil' Bobby Hutton, George Jackson, Jonathan Jackson, James McClain, Harold Russell, Zayd Malik Shakur, and Anthony Jumu Olugbala White, we must fight on.

As I had anticipated, the day after the tape was played Hamlin, the prosecutor, rushed before the court with a motion to censure me and remove me from the case. In his affidavit he stated that I "acted to create sympathy for the accused and to inflame the public by her statements in the media and in the newspapers in order to deprive the state of a fair trial." Detective Harold Bott submitted an affidavit claiming that Assata and I had met "to prepare a political and revolutionary speech . . . a call to arms, a little short of a call to treason. While maintaining her legal and moral innocence, the defendant in inflammatory terms accused the authorities, charging them with murder and kidnapping . . . the broadcast was designed to affect the thinking of potential jurors and was obviously calculated to destroy the rights of the state to a fair trial." And the assistant prosecutor, Nicholas Stroumtsos, indignantly denounced the speech, stating that Assata "falsely accused law enforcement authorities of trying to lynch her" and of receiving orders "to shoot on sight and shoot to kill" prior to her arrest on the turnpike.

But it was not until August 20 that the trial judge, John E. Bachman, issued a ruling. Ray and Charlie had made brilliant presentations urging him to carefully consider any ruling that would abridge the defendant's free speech in violation of her First Amendment rights. The judge ruled that I could no longer bring a tape recorder to the prison but he did not remove me from the case. Weeks of uncertainty were over and, after a momentary pause of relief, we continued our preparation for trial.

Chapter 9

T he trial was scheduled to begin on September 6, 1973, a nightmarish impossibility because private conferences between Assata and me had been prevented by Sheriff Joseph DeMarino, whose arbitrary control over all jail facilities in Middlesex County rejected the most elementary requirement of attorney-client meetings, that of privacy. And the same was true of joint conferences held with Sundiata and Charlie McKinney to plan a common defense. Only in the first week of August, after we had made several motions, did the judge order that the doors to the conference room and to Assata's cell during my visits be closed and we were able to plan our legal strategy.

During the open-door sheriff-monitored conferences, Assata and Sundiata made the most of their temporary release from solitary confinement. They hugged each other in hilarious greetings, whispered secrets to each other, and ridiculed the entire "justice" system. Sundiata, who had been incarcerated for two years on the phony charges in the Panther 21 case when he could not make the $100,000 bail, jokingly compared down-north justice with the up-south brand. He was a theoretician, orderly in his thought processes, a mathematical analyst by profession and a cool player in the mad, untidy world of inequality into which he had been born in Texas. The permanent furrow between his young eyebrows belied his easy, unhurried manner, and if he ever ventilated anger, I never saw it. Both he and Assata had an equilibrium, an inner balance that seemed to be immune to external pressures, except to the degree they chose to define and respond to them.

Our precious time was frittered away filing motions to obtain for our defendants the most rudimentary rights bestowed on every other prisoner: for art supplies, books, and even for Assata's grandparents to be allowed to visit when they came from North Carolina to see her. Although relatives of other inmates could bring them food, my mother's marble cake which Assata so loved was considered contraband. Newspapers were banned, and Assata was considered too much of a "security risk" to eat with the other women. She could make no phone calls, even emergency calls to me as her lawyer, and Sundiata walked barefoot on the cold cement floors of his cell because socks or sneakers were considered "security risks."

Although a court order had been signed for a physical therapist, licensed in the state of New Jersey, to treat Assata at the workhouse, no therapist was willing to come to the jail, and the court refused to transport Assata to Middlesex Hospital for treatment. It took another motion from me to provide Assata with a small rubber ball to squeeze in an attempt to regenerate the severed median nerve in her right arm. Some motions were automatic, as in any felony case, such as a challenge to the indictment because legally insufficient evidence had been presented to the grand jury, a motion to suppress evidence that had been obtained by unconstitutional methods, and motions for discovery and inspection of the materials held by the prosecutor that he intended to use at trial. And some motions that we filed were peculiar to the circumstances of our case, such as a challenge to the entire array of grand jurors and petit jurors because the selection process was discriminatory and the change of venue motion to move the trial to another county because of prejudicial pretrial publicity. All of our motions, no matter how ordinary, were opposed by the prosecutor, which meant that we had to prepare and attach to them a thoroughly researched and documented memorandum of law, primarily to ensure that on appeal the proper constitutional or statutory foundation for the motion would be on record.

Because of the sensitivity of the case and my own paranoia, I researched and typed all of my motions, waited for them to be photocopied, served them on the prosecutor, and filed them with the clerk's office myself. But it was Ray's knowledge of New Jersey rules of criminal practice that carried Charlie and me through the maze of procedures that were unfamiliar to us. I had read the rules of evidence and trial procedure, but there was no substitute for the hands-on practical guidance Ray provided. In addition, his eloquent courtroom style and easy articulation of the most complex legal principles heightened the expertise of our defense team. His color, which had so startled Assata when she first saw him, believing him to be white, seemed to be an open rejection of the white privileged society which he could easily have entered had he so chosen. His thinning gray hair and slightly rumpled suits were in sharp contrast to Charlie's dapper appearance—with his polished black hair and mustache—but in no way diminished his professionalism or his stature.

The prosecutor had provided us with discovery materials of all kinds (evidence he planned to introduce during the trial). His materials were all precise, all from allegedly unimpeachable FBI laboratories in Washington, D.C., all irrefutable, all infallibly typed, and all condemning, leaving no room for a second opinion. I struggled to find a flaw in the carefully arranged smorgasbord that had been placed before me, and I couldn't. I spent months analyzing the materials, which included all of the ballistic and other evidence, such as dirt samples removed from the section of the turnpike at the scene of the shoot-out and from the area where the Pontiac had traveled afterward, from where Zayd lay dead and Assata was captured. There were blood samples removed from both troopers and from Zayd, Sundiata, and Assata and the laboratory results that matched the samples with bloodstains found at the scene and on their clothing. There were glass samples from each of the three cars, including an analysis of whether glass had been shattered by a bullet fired from inside or outside the vehicles; more than sixty-four bullets, bullet casings, and bullet fragments; and the weapons found at each of the two sites, consisting of a 9-mm Browning automatic pistol, a .380-caliber Browning automatic pistol, a 9-mm Bergmann superautomatic Llama, a .38 Special Colt revolver, and a .38 Smith and Wesson revolver. I analyzed Harper's and Assata's hospital rec- ords and the autopsy reports conducted on Foerster and Zayd, the neutron activation analysis performed on all of them to determine whether there was gunshot residue on their hands, as well as all the official trooper reports filed about the incident and the troopers' grand jury testimony. I visited the garage in West Trenton where the Pontiac had been stored, photographed it, and went with our ballistics expert to the police barracks, where each gun was fired and the results compared with the ballistic reports we had received.

But a gnawing question continued to bother me. Did the troopers know that the Pontiac and its passengers would be on the turnpike that night? Were they watching for them? And did they shoot first? I had asked Assata whether she believed the

Pontiac had been targeted, and she had dismissed even the possibility. But I was not convinced. If, as my gut told me, the troopers were waiting for them, in all likelihood the troopers fired the first shots, in which case the defense of self-defense could be considered. The prosecution held the full deck, and before I could play they had to give up some of their hidden cards.

I returned to Harper's grand jury testimony in which he gave his version of what had happened. He said that he had observed a white vehicle with Vermont license plates and a defective taillight traveling south on the turnpike. Two Black males and one Black female were riding in the car. He pulled them over, asked the driver to get out of the car, and obtained the car registration from him as they stood behind the Pontiac. He went to the front door of the car to check the vehicle registration number and saw no irregularities. Suddenly, he said, the woman seated in the front passenger seat pulled a gun from her pocketbook and shot him. He then retreated to the back of his patrol car and the woman leaped from the driver's side of the Pontiac and began shooting at him from a crouched position alongside it. He returned fire, hit her, and heard her scream. He then fired at the male passenger who had emerged from the passenger side of the backseat, shot him, heard him scream, ejected the shells from his revolver, and reloaded. In the meantime, he saw Foerster grappling with the driver at the back of the Pontiac. While his grand jury testimony stuttered to a halt at this point, when he continued he said that after he shot the male passenger he retreated two hundred yards up the hill to the administration building, reported the shoot-out, and gave a description of the car as he saw it continue south on the turnpike.

As I compared Harper's sworn testimony before the grand jury, given on May 11, with his official police report, filed on May 3, I saw contradictions, inconsistencies, and omissions between the two. The police report supplemented the grand jury testimony, providing information that Harper had followed the Pontiac for two miles, made three passes alongside it on both the driver and passenger sides, called in the identification of the passengers as two Black men and one Black female, and then pulled them over in the lighted area of Exit 9, where the administration building overlooked the highway. I questioned the three passes he had made on each side of the Pontiac in his unmarked patrol car. Was it to make certain that the passengers were the three people the police had been told to expect? Did he trail the car for two miles before making the stop to reduce risk? Is that why Commander Foster, who was manning the turnpike communications command post that night, directed two other troopers, Robert Palentchar and Werner Foerster, to provide backup for a minor violation, a broken taillight? (The trooper manual specifies no such reinforcement for troopers making stops for minor violations on the turnpike.) Did Harper's actions suggest that he expected trouble? Did he know that alleged members of the BLA would be traveling the turnpike that night, two Black men and one Black woman? And did he believe that the woman would be JoAnne Chesimard? Did he panic when he pulled the Pontiac over? And if he did, did he fire the first shot?

I knew that Trooper John Harper was the key. He was the only eyewitness the prosecutor had, and he was the only one who could establish what I needed to know. I felt that something was wrong, but I couldn't put my finger on it. I decided to obtain a court order permitting me to listen to the entire night shift radio communications, from 10:00 P M to 9:00 A.M, and record it. The transmissions had been received in the administration building on four reels, called Magnesinc tapes, and I listened to the scratchy sounds over and over again, transcribing and comparing them. Of significance to me was Palentchar's response when Harper radioed that he was making the stop. He said, "Meet you at the pass, partner" and raced north to the scene of the stop at one hundred and twenty miles an hour. Did he expect a shoot-out? Why else would he have sped to back up a stop for a violation that, on the face of it, would have generated only a summons? Palentchar never reached the administration building. Halfway there, he received a radio communication from the command center that Harper had been wounded by the occupants of the Pontiac, which was now proceeding south. He made a U-turn, spotted the Pontiac on the side of the road, emptied his gun at Sundiata's fleeing figure, and discovered Zayd lying dead in the grass near where Assata, barely alive, was captured.

These were some of the pieces, but it was not until I discovered the "Baginski tapes" that they came together. The Baginski tapes were a series of audiocassettes that recorded the investigation conducted by Detective Sergeant First Class Rich-

ard H. Kelly on the morning of May 2. The investigation was
triggered by the discovery of Foerster's body alongside his patrol
car, which was parked directly behind Harper's, well over an
hour after Harper had run from the scene and into the building to
report the shoot-out.

I called them the "Baginski tapes" because Sergeant Chester Baginski was the first one Kelly questioned and because the
package containing the four cassettes, retrieved from the basement of the administration building, was labeled "Baginski
Tapes" and did not refer to Kelly's investigation or even to the
day of May 2. Baginski had been assigned to the trooper desk at
the administration building that night. His job was to record
everything that transpired inside the building in the station log,
which the troopers called the "station bible." Neither the tapes
nor the log had been released to us with the other discovery
material and would have remained a buried secret had I not
heard a reference to Kelly's investigation on the late-morning
recording of the Magnesinc tapes. Both the Baginski tapes and
the station bible revealed that when Harper fled to the building
during the shoot-out in fear for his life, he never reported that
Foerster was at the scene, that Foerster was engaged in battle
with the occupants of the Pontiac, or that he had left Foerster
slain on the turnpike alongside his patrol car.

Kelly's voice crackled with anger as he began his interrogation of Baginski. The following is a transcript of portions of the
tapes that were admitted into evidence.

Kelly: This is the voice of Detective Sgt. First Class Richard H.
Kelly. Today's date is Tuesday, May the, correction, today's date
is Wednesday, May the second. The time is now 7:17 AM. This
recording is being made in the office of Det. Sgt. First Class
Richard H. Kelly. Present in the room is Lt. King, executive
officer of the New Jersey Police, Troop D, New Brunswick. Also
present in the room is Sgt. Chester Baginski, New Jersey State
Police, Troop D, substation New Brunswick. Sgt. Baginski, the
reason you've been asked here is to give us your interpretation of
the facts as they relate to the shooting and murder of Troopers
Harper and Foerster earlier this date here on the Turnpike. As
best you can, to the best of your recollection, and in your own
words, would you give us your account of, from the outset, as to
what developed in this incident?

Baginski: This is Sgt. Chester Baginski. I was assigned to the, on the station record at the New Brunswick Station. At about 12:59 AM, one AM, Trooper Harper entered the station and stated that he was shot as a result of a shoot-out that he had at milepost 83. He further gave information that it was a Vermont registered vehicle, color white, and one tail light was out. He stated that the vehicle was occupied by 2 colored males and one colored female. The female would be wearing a red blouse and one of the colored males would be wearing a white jacket. This information was put on the air. . . . At the time when Trooper Harper stopped at the station, he made no mention of his back-up man when they ran into the trouble. We had no knowledge, uh, on the condition of the back-up man. We knew it was 820 and Trooper Foerster was assigned to this vehicle. We attempted to reach 820 and we got no response. . . .

Kelly: Sgt., if you can recall, how long was it from the time that Trooper Harper first entered the substation to announce the fact that he had been shot and to describe his assailants and the vehicle, how long was it from that point to the point where you became, first became aware of the fact that the back-up patrol, namely Trooper Foerster, may have been in difficulty? . . .

Well, what I'm trying to get at is how long would it have been from the time that Harper came into your presence and announced the fact that he had been shot to the point, from that point, how long was it before efforts, serious efforts were made to locate Trooper Foerster?

Baginski: I really don't know the definite time lapse, but the first we were advised of it was when the, uh, radio, rather the dispatcher went down to check a car in the parking lot and was advised that Trooper Foerster may be lying out in the roadway at 83 southbound.

Kelly: Ok, at this point, how much time would have elapsed from the time that Harper came into the substation and announced he was shot and you were notified from some other individual at the substation that there was a trooper lying out on the roadway?

Baginski: (Long pause, no response)

Kelly: At this point, Sgt. Baginski requests permission to refer to the station record. Permission was granted. He's now over there to consult the station record. It would appear to this officer at

this moment that he is confused in relation to time. And as a
result, I have allowed him to refer to the station record.

Baginski: My first knowledge of Trooper Foerster being shot was at 2:05 AM. . . .

Kelly: Again, if you recall, approximately what time was it when Trooper Harper arrived at the station announcing he had been shot?

Baginski: To the best of my recollection, it was around 12:58 to 1 AM.

Kelly: So apparently one hour elapsed from the time that Harper arrived at the station & announced that he had been shot and the time that you were first aware that Foerster was in difficulty, would that be correct?

Baginski: It's about the right time. . . .

Kelly: Did Trooper Harper make you aware of that fact that he had left, for reasons best explained by Trooper Harper, that he had left Trooper Foerster at the scene? Or did he ever acknowledge that Trooper Foerster arrived at the scene?

Baginski: There was no mention made of Trooper Foerster by Trooper Harper at the time of his arrival.

Kelly: . . . Now as I understand it, to the best of your recollection, Trooper Harper never made mention of the fact to you or to Troopers Foster or O'Rourke [two other troopers at the station when Harper arrived] the fact that he had left Foerster at the scene with these other people and these people were in fact armed and shooting?

Baginski: He made no mention of Foerster. . . .

The following is part of the transcript of Kelly's interrogation of Trooper Edward O'Rourke, who was in the administration building on the morning of May 2.

O'Rourke [after he described Harper's arrival at the administration building]: . . . I was ordered by Lt. King to stay with Trooper Harper, go to the hospital with him, see to answering any questions he wasn't able to.

Kelly: There's no mention of Trooper Foerster at that conversation, or any conversation whatsoever at the station?

O'Rourke: As I recall he [Harper] just said that he had been shot and was coherent enough to give the description of the car, plate number which was given out to all interchanges and stations. . . .

Kelly: Well, to the best of your recollection, have you in detail given us the facts as you recall them relating to this incident? Or is there anything else you can now recall you would like to add to this statement?

O'Rourke: No, to the best of my knowledge. That's about how I remember it happening. I do remember standing in the hospital emergency room with Trooper Harper when a call came in for Capt. Garrett who'd just arrived at the hospital stating that Trooper Foerster had been killed. Up until that time I didn't even know Trooper Foerster was really involved in the incident at all.

Kelly: As best you can recall from the time you first encountered Trooper Harper until the time that you received information as to the fate of Trooper Foerster, as best you can now recall, Trooper Harper never mentioned to you the fact that Trooper Foerster was also at the scene of the shooting?

O'Rourke: That's correct to the best of my recollection. Trooper Foerster's name was not mentioned.

As I listened to the tape I remembered Harper's other contradictions or, at best, incomprehensible assertions. For example, he had written in his official reports that he had never seen Foerster's state patrol car although it was parked directly behind his unmarked patrol car, its overhead flashing lights revolving until it was removed the next morning, and although the state police had recovered all of the spent shells Harper had ejected from his gun directly behind it, and not behind Foerster's car as he had reported.

But all of these speculations and questions occurred before the trial, when I was unaware of just what Harper's testimony would be. What I did know, however, was that both the Middlesex General Hospital and Roosevelt Hospital records had already established the trajectory of the bullet that had entered Assata's middle right armpit, severed the median nerve, and caused instant paralysis. And I knew that our neurological and thoracic experts had established that the track of the bullet had shattered her clavicle and entered her chest—which could have occurred only had she been shot while in a seated position with both arms raised. These facts totally refuted Harper's grand jury testimony and his sworn official reports in which he claimed that he saw Assata reach into a pocketbook while she was seat[ed] the car, pull a gun from it, and shoot him. His official reports als[o] stated that he believed himself to be in danger while he was questioning Assata because Foerster had yelled to him from behind the Pontiac where he was questioning Sundiata and had held up an ammunition clip he had allegedly removed from Sundiata.

But let me add this now: at the trial he testified that he had lied both to the grand jury and in his official reports; that he had never seen a gun in Assata's hand while she was in the car; that he had never seen her fire a gun while she was in the car; that he had never seen her remove a gun from a red pocketbook; and, in fact, that he had not even seen a red pocketbook in the Pontiac. He also testified that he had lied when he reported that Foerster had shown him an ammunition clip. During Sundiata's trial and later in Assata's trial, he said he "assumed" that Assata had fired at him from the car because just before he heard a shot and after he had ordered her to put her hands in sight, she had made a gritting facial expression, bared her teeth, and emitted a growl. His remarks, I thought, seemed like some human beings' perception of how animals, particularly black panthers, prepare themselves for attack.

I made what I called a CARE package for Ray, Charlie, Sundiata, and Assata consisting of photocopied transcriptions of the Magnesinc and Baginski tapes, the station bible, and my analysis. For me there was one unassailable fact: the evidence we now had gave us a great opportunity to discredit all of Harper's testimony on cross-examination, whether he had acted from panic or cowardice and whether or not he had fired the first shot. We remained cautious, but we considered the Baginski tapes to be the most significant and helpful piece of material yet. For the first time we experienced a modicum of hope.

d in

or

66

Chapter 10

he trial was delayed from September 6 to October 9 while the administrative judge, Leon Gerofsky, decided our two motions. Our motion challenging the jury array charged that the county systematically prevented Blacks from being represented in the jury pool in the same proportion they were represented on voter registration lists (5 percent Black registered voters out of the 583,813 registered voters in the county).

In our second motion we maintained that the massive prejudicial pretrial publicity prevented a fair trial, and we supported our contentions with every newspaper article printed about Black Liberation Army activities since 1971. We would have added documentation of television and radio coverage, but we didn't have the money to pull together that information. Based on all of that, our motion requested a change of venue for the trial. We cited parallel circumstances that had existed in *Shepard v. Maxwell, Irvin v. Dowd,* and *Estes v. Texas,* in the latter of which the Supreme Court of the United States had said: "The court has insisted that no one be punished for a crime without a charge fairly made and fairly tried in a public tribunal free of prejudice, passion, excitement and tyrannical power. Along with these legal procedures is the requirement that the jury's verdict be based on evidence received in open court, not from outside sources." In *Irvin v. Dowd* the Supreme Court, setting forth the nature and extent of pretrial publicity that branded the defendant guilty of murder, had concluded that any conviction in a community so pervasively exposed to prejudicial pretrial publicity could be "but a hollow victory." And we ended our memorandum with a quote from a New York State Court of Appeals case that insightfully evaluated prospective jurors: "One cannot assume that the average juror is so endowed with a sense of detachment, so clear in his introspective perception of his own mental processes, that he may confidently exclude even the

unconscious influence of his preconception as to probable guilt
engendered by pervasive pre-trial publicity."

Gerofsky denied both motions, opining in relation to the first that jurors are chosen by computer from registered voter lists and suggesting that if there were fewer Blacks on the panel, the reason lay not in the very fair selection process but in the lethargy of the Black citizenry who did not bother to register. Having no further recourse (appeal from the ruling could not be made until after conviction), we reluctantly proceeded to trial.

On the day the trial began, October 9, 1973, police security, the most massive in the history of New Jersey, was virulent, jamming the streets surrounding the Middlesex County courthouse and saturating the courtroom. On the previous day Assata had been convoyed the seven and a half miles from the workhouse to the Middlesex County jail adjacent to the courthouse and was entombed in the basement, a large, windowless, vermin-infested room where she was on twenty-four-hour neon-lighted display and under heavy guard. She was the only woman who had ever been incarcerated in the fifty-six-year-old men's jail. Sundiata was also there, separated from the other prisoners somewhere above the first floor.

Preparations for the armed occupation of the city of New Brunswick had been under way for some time as members of the Sheriff's Department, the New Brunswick police department, and the police and unofficial plainclothes personnel from New York's Major Case Squad and the FBI joined forces. A reaction team of ten men from the state police and the city police department established a command post in City Hall from where they monitored activity in the entire city and were prepared to deal at a moment's notice with any bomb scares that might occur. They also prepared for an anticipated raid on police headquarters for securing arms. Guards were assigned to the judge and his family, members of the prosecutor's office, and each juror as he or she was selected. Closed-circuit television cameras and microphones were installed on each of the courthouse's five floors and in the courtroom where the trial was held. Only twenty spectators were allowed in the seventy-seat courtroom. Each was issued a pass and, after screening by a metal detector, was hand-searched.

Assata and Sundiata, handcuffed and in leg irons, flanked

by a small army of police, walked the short distance from the jail to the back door of the courthouse through a mob of reporters, a battery of flashlights, and curious onlookers straining to get a glimpse of the notorious pair. It was an atmosphere hardly saturated with the presumption of innocence and could not have helped but influence any juror with the defendants' guilt.

As soon as a trial begins, defense lawyers shift into another gear. All the probing maneuvers are over, and well-honed reflexive reactions to developing evidence emerge; you have to read fast, analyze fast, memorize testimony fast, and raise objections fast. The rules of evidence must spring to your mind automatically, enabling you to provide the legal basis for your objections as quickly as you make them. The beginning of the trial is the point when everything you have learned throughout the long pretrial phase has been integrated and solidified and when your years of experience as a trial lawyer blanket you with the security of familiarity. It is the time to check your appearance, cut your hair or manicure your nails, time to eliminate mannerisms that will attract the jury's attention to you rather than to the evidence being presented; you know that how you dress becomes as important as your legal presentations. Your concentration is keyed on each witness, probing for his or her weaknesses and jumping all over his or her hesitations. You give instructions to the defendant you represent: when to whisper to the lawyer and when to remain impassive in the face of the most damaging evidence. You are on center stage. It is what I call "show time."

My clothes were in sharp contrast to Assata's. She had asked her mother to buy ankle-length African dresses and *geleis* (African head wraps) to match, and they were so beautiful and colorful that each time she appeared in court every newspaper described what she wore as if the trial were an item on the fashion pages. I wore simple slack suits in navy blue, black, brown, gray, or tan. Sundiata's wife had brought him wonderful-looking African dashikis, and the two defendants were radiant in the drab surroundings of the heavily guarded courtroom.

Jury selection began on October 11. Jurors can be selected in different ways, depending on the rules of the jurisdiction. In New Jersey, as in federal courts, the judge conducts the voir dire, asking jurors questions that he or she has approved from a list prepared by the defense and the prosecution. (In New York State, the lawyers conduct the voir dire.) The defense and prosecution are each given a certain number of peremptory challenges—in our case ten each for Assata and Sundiata and ten for the prosecutor—whereby a prospective juror can be disqualified without a reason given. The judge has the sole discretion to remove a juror for cause (where there is clear evidence that the juror is not qualified to sit on the jury, either for expressed bias or other reasons), and there is no limit to the number of jurors who can be removed when this determination is made.

Judge John E. Bachman was a civil man, courteous and reasonable, implacable, and he always displayed a model judicial temperament, whether he ruled for or against a motion. For example, unlike other judges in later trials, he refused to cite Assata and Sundiata for contempt when they remained seated as he entered the courtroom—to the chagrin of the prosecutor, a squat man, ugly in face and in manner. When Assata objected to the tone of voice the judge used when questioning a juror, complaining that it suggested the answer and adding, "The same rules that apply to the lawyers should apply to the court," he quietly responded, "Your objection will be noted." He manifested a fairness that enabled him to reverse his own decisions. For example, when the trial began he ordered spectators banned from the courtroom during jury selection. After hearing our arguments protesting that he was creating "star chamber secret proceedings," he changed his position and stated on the record that the security precautions he had in mind were not as important as the perception of unfairness that closed hearings would suggest. And when we opposed the limited number of spectators allowed in the courtroom, he permitted all seats to be filled.

The first prospective juror to be questioned was a typical member of the jury panel. We had asked that, pursuant to the 1973 U.S. Supreme Court in *Ham v. South Carolina,* the judge inquire into racial attitudes. This juror, when asked about the racial composition of his neighborhood, said it was all white and unequivocally stated that he would not have a Black person living next door to him, describing a process where "Blacks make it a point to move into certain neighborhoods to break it up." By the third day only one of the sixteen jurors to be selected had been tentatively chosen by Bachman. When he learned that the jurors were discussing the case among themselves in the jury room and referring to newspaper articles, two things the judge had specifically instructed them not to do, he dismissed the entire panel. A new panel was installed and the voir dire staggered slowly forward. Then, on the fifth day, a prospective juror revealed that a friend of the dead trooper was on the panel discussing the case with the others; in addition, the prospective juror revealed the unanimous opinion of the entire panel that "if she's Black, she's guilty."

We immediately asked for a mistrial, which Bachman denied, but he dismissed that panel as tainted and called six hundred and fifty more. The following day, the first six jurors recited what was transpiring among this new group: they were openly reading the newspapers, discussing the case, and expressing their opinions that both Assata and Sundiata were guilty. The spectators were stunned into silence as they listened to each prospective juror's bald admissions and perceived the horror story unfolding in the back room where the jury panel sat waiting to be questioned. Bachman denied our second motion for a mistrial, stating that just because these panels were tainted he could not believe they were representative of the entire county. Before he called yet another set of jurors, however, he agreed to postpone the case to afford us time to prepare a new motion for a change of venue to present to the administrative judge.

On November 1, 1973, Judge Gerofsky granted our motion for a change of venue, moved the trial and the selection of jurors from Middlesex to Morris County, and set a new trial date of January 2, 1974, to allow the county time to make security arrangements. He now admitted that it was "almost impossible to obtain a jury here comprised of people willing to accept the responsibility of impartiality so that defendants will be protected from transitory passion and prejudice." While we applauded the removal of the case from Middlesex County, we were appalled at Gerofsky's choice. Morris County was one of the richest counties in the state, with the fewest Blacks and some of the most conservative voters in the country. Saddled with this reversal of fortune, we immediately swung our collective energies into substantiating the fact that we could not get a fair trial in Morris County, and we moved yet again for a change of venue to Essex County, which had a larger percentage of Black residents eligible for jury duty.

We raced relentlessly against the deadline, searching for unimpeachable authorities to support our motion. Charles Grey, one of the members of the National Black Assembly of New

Jersey, elected from Middlesex County, provided us with the demographics for each county in the state. We learned that of Middlesex's total population of 583,813, only 19,248 were Black, and the total number of registered voters, both Black and white, was 230,569. Morris County had the highest percentage of registered voters, 195,436 out of a population of 303,454. It also had the smallest number of Black residents, 6,954. Essex County had the largest population of any county in New Jersey, 929,986, as well as the largest number of Black residents, 270,736; its registered voters numbered 429,762. The politically sophisticated city of Newark was in Essex County; its voters had elected Imamu Amiri Baraka, Kaimu Mtetezi, and Hope Jackson as its assembly representatives.

Our contention was twofold. The first was the constitutional principle mandating that criminal defendants be tried by a jury of their peers. While certainly there isn't an identical experience shared by all Black people, nevertheless life is certainly more similar among Black people than it is between Blacks and the majority of Morris County whites. Second, despite the apparent objectivity of the grand and petit jury selection process, set forth in the official *Manual on the Selection of Grand and Petit Jurors, State of New Jersey* and heralded as fair by Gerofsky, the process was weighted against the possibility that Black jurors had an equal chance of being randomly selected for jury duty. We were fortunate to obtain the assistance of Professor Donald Payne, who had a Ph.D. from the University of Indiana and was teaching a graduate course in statistical data analysis at NYU. Using the demographic information we provided him and the jurors' manual, Payne prepared a report on the statistical probability of Black members being represented on the petit juries of Morris, Hudson, and Essex counties. Both Norman Lattimore, the Democratic county chairman of Morris County, and David Edwards, a member of the City Council of Morristown, Morris County, submitted affidavits attesting to the unpublished statistics of the number of registered Black voters in Morris County (from 2 to 3,000), which Payne used in his evaluation. We attached these affidavits to Payne's report and submitted both with our motion.

Payne's conclusions, supported by fourteen pages of statistical analysis, profiled in graphs and charts, was that the probability of Black jurors on any panel of sixteen (the number of trial jurors) was none in Morris County. He also described the inherently unfair and arbitrary procedures for juror selection as mitigating against an impartial selection system. For example, certain professional people who could request to be excused from jury duty were removed from the total voter registration list, thereby impeaching the system of random selection. Once a juror had served, he or she too was removed from the list. Additionally, Payne learned that jurors were not chosen from among all the registered voters, but only from those voters who returned questionnaires sent to them by the county commissioner. The assignment judge had the authority to remove from the list any person who did not return the questionnaire and replace that person with someone of his or her choice. Obviously, if the judge so chose, he or she had the power to bias the jury by this simple method. Payne concluded, "The power is particularly potent in the instance of minority representation. Since few representatives of minorities will appear on a jury selected at random, if these are stricken by the Assignment Judge, it is unlikely that a fellow representative will take his place."

We also attached to our motion a report of a survey to determine attitudes and biases in Morris County, conducted by the Center for Responsive Psychology, headed by Dr. Robert Buckhout, professor of psychology at Brooklyn College. The center surveyed more than five hundred registered voters during the first two weeks in November 1973 and concluded: "There is such a high degree of negative publicity of Ms. Chesimard and her background of arrests and charges, and so high a percentage of potential jurors already prejudiced, that there is no predictable probability that a fair jury could be selected in Morris County as the presumption of innocence has been so compromised among potential jurors that, failing to prove her innocence affirmatively, she would certainly be convicted." His survey showed that 76 percent of the voters questioned believed that both Assata and Sundiata were guilty.

As the entire defense team was racing to prepare this critical motion for submission before January 2, 1974, Judge Lee P. Gagliardi of the U.S. District Court for the Southern District of New York issued an order on November 28, 1973, demanding that Assata be returned to the state of New York to stand trial for the Bronx bank robbery of September 1, 1972. Trial was to begin immediately.

Chapter 11

No matter how widely publicized criminal accusations are, the only way a person can be prosecuted for a felony, such as a bank robbery, is by grand jury indictment. Once the indictment is filed, the defendant appears before the court and enters a plea of guilty or not guilty, a procedure called an arraignment. If the plea is not guilty, a date for trial is set, and the trial proceeds within a specified period of time, determined by the rules of each jurisdiction, unless it is postponed for a good reason. Between arrest and the time a petit (trial) jury arrives at its verdict, the defendant is presumed to be innocent, a presumption that can be overcome only by evidence that proves guilt beyond a reasonable doubt.

After Assata's arrest in New Jersey on May 2, 1973, indictments against her began to pile up. Arrests of alleged members of the BLA, official police department announcements promising future arrests, and police shoot-outs following stake-outs of alleged BLA members multiplied with accelerated frequency.

In the early morning hours of June 7, Andrew Jackson, whom the police had called a leader of the BLA over the past two years, was captured quietly in his New York City apartment along with his girlfriend, Denise Oliver, by FBI agents and New York City detectives. He was arrested on a federal warrant charging him with the August 23, 1971, Queens bank robbery. Named as co-defendants were Assata, Mark Holder, Ignae Ruth Gittens, and John Leo Thomas. Another federal warrant had been issued for his arrest for the April 17, 1971, murder of Samuel Lee Napier, West Coast circulation manager of the Black Panther Party's newspaper following a split with the East Coast Panthers. He was also wanted for his escape from the DeKalb County (Georgia) jail on December 12, 1971, after his arrest in a supermarket holdup and was wanted for questioning in the murders of police officers Gregory Foster, Rocco Laurie, Waverly Jones, and Joseph Piagentini. Additionally, he had been indicted in the January 2, 1973, murder of the Brooklyn drug dealer along with Assata, Melvin Kearney, and Twyman Myers and on July 20, 1973, was identified in a lineup as a participant in the ambush slaying of two Queens policemen, Michael O'Reilly and Roy Pollina, for which he was later indicted along with co-defendants Avon White, Jeanette Jefferson, Robert Hayes, and Assata.

Later on the day that Andrew Jackson was arrested, Fred Hilton was surrounded on a Brooklyn street and arrested as he was about to enter a building that had been staked out by police and the FBI on an informer's tip. A federal fugitive warrant had been issued for his arrest, along with the arrest of Assata and Avon White, for the September 1, 1972, Bronx bank robbery. According to *The New York Times*, Hilton was listed as one of eight wanted members of the BLA in a "recent intelligence advisory by the Police Department."

On June 9, the *Long Island Daily Press* devoted a four-page spread entitled "Dragnet for Black Lib Army Trio Tightens in Probe of Cop-Killings" to predicting the early arrests of members of the BLA, particularly Melvin Kearney, Twyman Myers, and Avon White. Photos of the wanted three, plus those of Jackson, Hilton, and Assata, were featured on one page.

On June 12, Assata was indicted for the September 1, 1972, Bronx bank robbery along with Fred Hilton and Avon White.

On July 20, Assata was arraigned for the August 23, 1971, Queens bank robbery. On the same day, Jackson, in addition to appearing for the lineup in the O'Reilly and Pollina murders, was also arraigned in Queens State Court for the murder of Napier.

In a press conference on August 24, the Brooklyn district attorney, Eugene Gold, announced that indictments had been returned against nine members of the BLA for additional crimes committed in Brooklyn, fulfilling the prediction of the *Long Island Daily Press*. The sensationalized reportage gave the names of the nine and released their pictures to accompany the story. Andrew Jackson, Melvin Kearney, and Twyman Myers were indicted along with Assata for the January 2, 1973, murder of a Brooklyn drug dealer. Fred Hilton was indicted for possession of weapons found when he was arrested on June 7. Victor Cumberbatch, already arrested for the murder of a New York City transit patrolman on June 5, 1973, Avon White, and Robert Hayes were indicted for a March 7, 1973, robbery of $350 from a

Key Food in Brooklyn. Ronald Myers was indicted along with Assata and Melvin Kearney for the December 28, 1972, kidnapping of a Brooklyn drug dealer. All were in police custody with the exception of Kearney, White, Hayes, Ronald Myers, and Twyman Myers. Kearney, White, and Hayes were arrested on September 12 by a large force of New York City police and FBI agents in a raid on a Bronx tenement the police believed was the headquarters of the BLA. Acting on a tip, they cordoned off the entire block and stationed themselves on the roof and in the basement of the building. Dozens of shots were fired as the police team crashed through the door of the suspected ground-floor apartment, and three policemen were injured.

Ronald Myers voluntarily surrendered to the police on August 25, the day following Gold's press conference during which he had identified Myers as being wanted.

On September 3, Herman Bell, the last of five alleged members of the BLA indicted in the 1971 murder of policemen Waverly Jones and Joseph Piagentini, was arrested after a stake-out in New Orleans, surrendering without a struggle when the car in which he was sitting along with his wife and two children was surrounded by a massive force of New Orleans police, FBI agents, and New York detectives. The others who had been indicted for the murders were Albert Washington, Anthony Bottom, and two brothers, Gabriel and Francisco Torres.

When Twyman Myers was killed by police on November 14 in an ambush shoot-out on a Bronx street after several days of a stake-out following a tip, Police Commissioner Cawley announced that the last of the leaders had been killed and that Myers's death had effectively "broken the back of the BLA." He was the seventh alleged member of the BLA to die in a police shoot-out.

I was representing Assata on all of the cases for which she had been indicted, appearing with her at arraignments and filing the usual pretrial motions, but the multiplicity of indictments disturbed me less than the growing number of alleged BLA members being arrested, and I was haunted by the prospect that one or all of them would plead guilty and falsely testify against her in exchange for a light sentence or other consideration. The September 1, 1972, Bronx bank robbery trial proved that my apprehensions were well founded.

There had been two indictments for this bank robbery. The

first, returned by the federal grand jury on November 21, 1972, charged Louis Chesimard (Assata's former husband), Paul Stewart, John Rivers, and Woody Green with having committed the robbery. The trial began on May 29, 1973, and ended in acquittal a week later. John Rivers had suspiciously pleaded guilty on the night of the robbery and testified for the government against Chesimard and Stewart during the trial. The second indictment was returned by the grand jury on June 12, 1973, and charged Assata, Fred Hilton, and Avon White with the crime.

Assata was arraigned following the second indictment on August 3, 1973, before Judge Lee Gagliardi of the U.S. District Court for the Southern District of New York. She pleaded not guilty and the trial was postponed until the termination of the New Jersey trial. During the pretrial conference held on September 26, I explained that the New Jersey trial had been delayed because of the many motions still being decided. Gagliardi extended the postponement of the Bronx bank robbery trial, and when a firm date of October 9 was set for the New Jersey trial, I wrote a letter so advising him. When the venue was changed to Morris County on November 1, it never occurred to me that the Bronx bank robbery trial or any other would intervene before the New Jersey trial date of January 2, 1974.

So when Gagliardi called me in for a pretrial conference on November 27, claiming surprise and annoyance because he had just learned of the postponement in New Jersey, and ordered the trial in his court to begin immediately, I was stunned. No one who had read the newspapers, and certainly no one in the legal profession, could have been ignorant about the postponement or the fact that it was caused by the change of venue. It was clear that Gagliardi was lying. And it was equally clear that he was trying to conceal his real reason for rushing to trial. Co-defendant Avon White had pleaded guilty before Gagliardi on November 24 and, although it was not reported by the media, had struck a deal with the U.S. attorney and Gagliardi whereby he had agreed to testify against Assata and Kamau (Fred Hilton). It was clear to me that White had been pressured into an early plea bargain to facilitate commencement of this trial before January 2, 1974, when the New Jersey trial was to begin, and before White recanted.

I explained to Gagliardi at the November 27 pretrial conference that from the time of Assata's arrest in May until the first week in August, I had not been able to prepare for even the New Jersey trial because I had not been permitted to confer with her privately and that even though we were not now technically on trial, I was actively engaged in the ongoing preparations and investigations to challenge the change of venue to Morris County. As I talked to this disagreeable, unreasonable, red-faced little man, a Nixon appointee to the federal bench and a right-wing conservative Republican resident of Westchester County, New York, a county strikingly similar in all its characteristics to Morris County, I realized that he had no intention of postponing the trial, despite the fact that he had just granted a postponement for U.S. Attorney General John Mitchell and former U.S. Secretary of Commerce Maurice Stans. They were on trial in the so-called Vesco case, charged with hampering a Securities and Exchange Commission investigation into Vesco's financial affairs in return for a large contribution by Vesco to the 1972 Nixon campaign. (Stans had also been Nixon's chief fundraiser in that election.) This was the only indictment they faced at the moment (although Mitchell was later indicted for involvement in the Watergate break-in and cover-up) and, with their battery of high-priced and well-connected lawyers, their claim that they needed more time to prepare for trial certainly was no more justifiable than Assata's very legitimate reasons.

Gagliardi rejected every argument I advanced. Trial was to proceed immediately, and that day he issued an order transporting Assata to New York State jurisdiction. I barely had time to sprint to the Middlesex County jail to tell her she would be moved the next day to stand trial in the Southern District Court. She listened to me speechless and expressionless. Her rage exploded the next day when she appeared before Gagliardi and he refused to grant an adjournment of even a few weeks. This was Wednesday, November 28, and he scheduled the trial for the following Monday, December 3.

I worked around the clock to research and prepare an appeal to the U.S. Court of Appeals from Gagliardi's decision, filing it on Friday, November 30. The hearing before the appellate court was heard on the next court date, Monday, December 3, the same date Gagliardi had scheduled the trial to begin.

During my research I had become aware of a major legal obstacle to a favorable decision: the Court of Appeals had no jurisdiction to postpone the trial, even if it did consider

Gagliardi's ruling to have been arbitrary. At best it could strongly urge him to reconsider, as it had done, successfully, in the Mitchell-Stans case. I argued in my petition that Assata's special circumstances required the court to make the same recommendation to Gagliardi.

In its opinion denying the petition, the Court of Appeals pointed out the differences in the two cases that, it claimed, precluded it from making the same recommendation. It stated, "A comparison of the two cases is instructive. The indictment in STANS was 46 pages, containing 16 counts, and was supplemented by a 60 page bill of particulars. The indictment in this case is three pages, containing three counts. Our dissenting colleague in Stans properly described that case as 'without precedent in the history of the country,' and the charges as 'somewhat novel.' The charges here, while serious, are not unusual."

The appellate court also pointed out that while Mitchell and Stans had made the request for adjournment jointly, Robert Bloom, Kamau's attorney, had repeatedly stated his client's readiness to stand trial, even if Kamau's trial were to be held separately from Assata's. In fact, as early as June and again in late September, while I was requesting a postponement in New York, Bloom had made a motion for severance and an immediate trial. A motion to sever a co-defendant—to have a separate trial for each—was one of two strategies used by some of the lawyers representing Assata's co-defendants. Separate trials for the other defendants would avoid the taint of negative publicity attached to Assata, which, at the time, seemed to guarantee conviction. The other reason was to slander an absent Assata with impunity for the benefit of other defendants.

In Bloom's first written motion for severance on July 6, he stated, "It is anticipated that the evidence against defendant Hilton will consist essentially of the testimony of an alleged co-conspirator, one John Rivers, a convicted felon. It is essential that in such circumstances every safeguard of the defendant's right to fair and unprejudiced trial be maintained. One very likely area of prejudice may arise if Defendant Hilton must proceed to trial with Defendant Joanne Chesimard. Many newspaper articles and magazine articles have appeared with regard to Joanne Chesimard and her alleged radical activities in the past year or more, and there has been extensive television and radio

reportage as well. As to Joanne Chesimard, it is respectfully
submitted that it would be difficult in the near future to afford a
truly fair trial to her, and, necessarily, to anyone co-indicted in
the same trial."

While Bloom's motion to sever Kamau from Assata's trial
raised questions in my mind about the feasibility of our presenting a common defense, I never suspected that he might be
dangerous to Assata. Then I read the earlier May trial transcript
that the assistant U.S. attorney, John H. Gross, gave me when
Assata was arraigned on August 3, 1973, material he was not
obligated to disclose to the defense.

Jesse Berman, Bloom's associate, represented Louis Chesimard. Louis was a college graduate with a respectable job who
had been honorably discharged from the air force. He was
clean-cut, was remarried with a child, and had no criminal
record. Relying on all of these qualities, which from a conventional perspective suggested a person of "good character," he
testified in his own defense, a rare occurrence in any criminal
trial, regardless of the defendant's background. The transcript
revealed that under Berman's carefully orchestrated direct examination, Chesimard testified that JoAnne Chesimard "was a
fugitive"; that during FBI questioning of him before he was
arrested, they had told him, "When we catch up with her we're
going to kill her"; that ever since Assata had been a fugitive she
had "always worn disguises"; and that she "always ran with BLA
members" and was "always armed." The implications of his
testimony were clear to the jury: Assata, a dangerous fugitive
who always carried a gun and was always disguised so that even
one who "knew her well could pass her in the street without
recognizing her," had forced him to obtain one of the vans
allegedly used in the robbery. He was an unknowing and unwilling participant. His entire testimony reinforced the violent
picture of Assata, so well portrayed by the media. But, of course,
his trial began on May 29, 1973, after Assata had been captured
in the shoot-out and her dangerous presence was safely behind
bars. Both he and Paul Stewart were acquitted. Gagliardi was the
trial judge.

I tried to repress my suspicions about Bloom. Was it fair to
attribute Berman's trial strategy to him? If, in fact, Chesimard's
testimony could be justified as "trial strategy," was Bloom's
severance motion an understandable move in the best interests

of his own client? I didn't know Bloom personally, but I did know that he had been one of the attorneys in the Panther 21 trial and was the lawyer for Dhoruba Bin Wahad (Richard Moore), Victor Cumberbatch, and Andrew Jackson. I tried to communicate my concerns about Bloom to Assata on more than one occasion, but the forced trial was so traumatic that she had neither the time nor the inclination to criticize her co-defendant's lawyer. In addition, in Assata's mind, Bloom was a "movement" lawyer and therefore to be trusted. In any event, I was stuck with him as co-counsel, regardless of my doubts, but I remained wary of him.

It was not until after the Bronx bank robbery trial that the full dimensions of Bloom's treachery were revealed to me, and my suspicions that Bloom was Assata's enemy were confirmed. On October 28, 1976, during a hearing before Judge Frank Vaccaro to set the rules for Andrew Jackson's pretrial lineup in the Brooklyn drug dealer murder, Bloom displayed a surprising willingness to rely on the credibility of Avon White, the informer who had pleaded guilty in the Bronx bank robbery case and who had testified against Kamau and Assata. Bloom advised the court that White had given him a handwritten statement to the effect that Melvin Kearney had confessed to committing the murder and to afterward removing the victim's identification cards from his body and giving them to "Joanne Chesimard and Woody Green." Green had been killed in a shoot-out with police before the indictment had been returned, and Kearney had died in 1975 while attempting to escape from the Brooklyn House of Detention. In his oral argument, Bloom not only insisted that Jackson was innocent but stated that he could prove the guilt of the real perpetrators, Assata, Kearney, and Green. Bloom told the court: "I want to prove that it was Chesimard and Green and Kearney that participated in the sharing of the identifications of the deceased. What I'm trying to do is this. It will be my effort to show the jury that certain people other than Mr. Jackson committed the crime." And it was revealed at the Queens bank robbery trial, in which Jackson was Assata's co-defendant, that Bloom employed an even more vicious strategy calculated to convict Assata.

What I did know at the time of the Bronx bank robbery trial, however, was that representation of those who were called members of the BLA was hot—a bonanza for young white lawyers like Bloom and Berman trying to hone their skills, establish a reputation, and gain the visibility guaranteed by extensive media coverage. To be assigned to criminal cases of indigent defendants, as most of the alleged BLA members were, these lawyers became part of the panels established in state and federal jurisdictions. While the payment they received did not compare with fees they might have garnered for representing other alleged major crime figures, they were paid something. In addition, they were entitled to services that would cost a privately retained lawyer (and his or her client) about a thousand dollars a day: free daily copies of trial transcripts and the services of investigators and other legal experts. My objection to these young white panel lawyers was specific. They formed a small, in-group cadre and shared an obsession with BLA cases; they were as suspect to me as was the fact that the same judges were repeatedly assigned from the "random selection wheel" to preside over BLA trials. Robert Bloom, Jesse Berman, and Judge Gagliardi exemplified my concerns.

On the afternoon following the Court of Appeals decision not to encourage Gagliardi to postpone our trial, Gagliardi called up the first 150 prospective jurors. And the battle was on. Assata refused to permit the judge to question them. As soon as he began a question, she interrupted him by standing up and demanding an adjournment, stating clearly to the jurors that she had not had time to prepare for the trial; each time Gagliardi had her removed from the courtroom by the marshals. At the end of the third day Gagliardi still had not been able to select a jury, and both Assata and Kamau had been taken from the courtroom on ten separate occasions. As Assata was forcibly evicted she accused Gagliardi of having made deals, of being bigoted, of having been bought and paid for, and of subjecting her to a lynching. She said he was "like a two-year-old baby, so unintelligent as to force a lawyer and client to go to trial when they were not prepared," charging that he was "bought and paid for by big business" and had "no concern for justice or Black people or for poor people or for any defendants except Mitchell and Stans." Finally, to avoid the brutality of the marshals, she would rise as they approached, saying in her usual quiet voice, "I will remove myself," and then stalk regally from the courtroom, trailed by Kamau and the marshals.

Gagliardi threatened to have the two defendants "gagged, bound, and shackled" if they continued their outbursts. They continued, and he asked Bloom and me which form of containment we preferred. Receiving no response, he made the decision himself and banned them from the courtroom on December 4. I refused to proceed in Assata's absence. I walked out of the courtroom, and that afternoon Gagliardi appointed another lawyer for Assata as alternative counsel, who was in place the next afternoon when I returned. Although he banned Assata and Kamau, on occasion he permitted them to return on their promise to "behave." When they were again quickly ejected, I again demanded Assata's presence and again left the counsel table, stating that I could not continue in her absence. Gagliardi shouted to the marshals, "Lock that door" as I approached the exit from the courtroom and cited me for contempt. That was on December 7.

The next day *The New York Times,* in its typical selective fashion, made no comment about the unfairness of the trial but instead headlined its editorial with the words "Order in Court" and said:

> The disruptive behavior of Joanne D. Chesimard and Fred Hilton during their trial on bank robbery charges once again raises the issue of the defense lawyer's responsibility for a client's conduct. Instead of urging Mrs. Chesimard to desist from her disgusting verbal attacks on United States District Judge Lee P. Gagliardi, Miss Evelyn Williams, the defendant's counsel, exacerbated the situation by trying to walk out of the courtroom in defiance of the judge's order to return to the defense table.
>
> Courtroom decorum is not a mere matter of social niceties. Without it, judicial procedures deteriorate, and society is eventually deprived of the benefits of a fair resolution of its grievances. Efforts to turn criminal trials into ideological circuses are as intolerable as the misuse of the courts for the purpose of persecuting political dissenters for alleged conspiracies. In either case, it remains the defense lawyer's professional and moral duty to help maintain court decorum rather than condone a client's disruptive protest, regardless of the latter's motives. . . .
>
> The point at issue remains nevertheless the same: It is essential that officers of the court, specifically including defense lawyers, comply with the judicial protocol that forms the cement of the rule of law itself.

With no other recourse available, both Assata and Kamau agreed that the only role the lawyers could take was to remain mute throughout the trial, to make no opening or closing statements, to cross-examine no witnesses, and to participate in no way in the trial, hoping to use Gagliardi's decision to obtain a reversal on appeal of the inevitable conviction. When they were not in the courtroom, Assata and Kamau were in the holding pen just behind the courtroom, where a loudspeaker had been installed. They emerged at selected times, as when Avon White and John Rivers testified, called them both "bought and paid for liars," and left. There were protests from the many spectators. On one occasion, when they chanted, "This trial is a racist frame-up, how can you have a trial without a defendant?" the spectators were ordered to leave the courtroom and several were arrested.

The government rested its case after one day of testimony, and, within hours after jury deliberations began, the jury returned, announcing they were hopelessly deadlocked and could not reach a verdict. They wanted to know why the defense lawyers claimed they were not prepared for trial as well as what had happened in New Jersey and why there had been no attorney participation in the present trial. Gagliardi told them that none of what had transpired was any of their concern and that they should limit their deliberations to the evidence. They asked permission to question Assata and Kamau, reflecting the state of their confusion, and their request was denied. Only Bloom felt that his client should abandon his Fifth Amendment rights against self-incrimination and voluntarily respond to questions from the jury.

On the third day of jury deliberation a mistrial was declared because the jury was deadlocked. We later learned that one Black juror had held out for acquittal because the refusal of defense counsel to participate gave validity to Assata and Kamau's charges that they were being denied a fair trial. We awaited the second trial, scheduled to begin immediately before another judge, with strange optimism because the prosecutor had presented all of his evidence, there had been no surprises, with the exception of Rivers's testimony from the May trial, and our chances of acquittal seemed at least possible. We knew that White and Rivers would command no more credibility before a different jury. In addition, the assistant U.S. attorney, Peter Truebner, who had also prosecuted the May trial, had told the jury in his opening statement that "the government has no fingerprints, no pictures of the defendants, no guns, no money or anything like that."

I knew that bank surveillance pictures had been taken but were not used during either the May trial or this one because they were so fuzzy that identification of anyone was impossible. And Truebner's admission to the jury that there were no photos simply meant that he would not introduce them into evidence because no one could be identified. But I also knew that the government will shape testimony to fit any conclusion it wants drawn, and I was not so sure that those photos would not suddenly emerge during the second trial, with White making an identification of Assata in the bank. Rivers had not been asked to even look at the photos in the May trial, and it was logical to assume consistency on the part of the prosecutor and to reason that he would not ask him suddenly to identify them now—because under no circumstances could Kamau be so fingered. In all previous testimony, Kamau was placed outside the bank waiting during the progress of the robbery in a getaway van. The only purpose of showing the photographs, which had been released to us with other potential evidence, would be to claim that one of the shadowy figures was Assata. So when Bloom, Kamau's attorney, announced that he was going to introduce them into evidence, I was outraged beyond my ability to describe.

I had been spoiled by my association with two great trial lawyers in New Jersey who always worked in tandem, always complemented each other's special talents, always were willing to concede that a decision unilaterally made was not advantageous to both defendants, and always, in times of honest disagreement, easily resolved conflicts. For example, when the New Jersey jury selection process began, Ray had decided, along with Judge Bachman, to seat only twenty spectators and consented to an "in camera" voir dire (held outside the public courtroom). After discussion with Sundiata, Charlie, Assata, and me, he understood the political necessity of an open courtroom and corrected his position with a brilliant argument before Bachman. And he was successful in reversing that decision. There were other instances, but the point is that we talked about strategy with each other in an open fashion and reached collective agreements.

Assata was adamant that the photos posed no threat to her but was unable to explain their advantage. When she insisted that I listen to what Bloom had to say, the burden of the months I had worked around the clock and the suddenly blatant demonstration of his treachery and Assata's refusal to see it as such crashed around me and unleashed my fury. Among other things, I told her that she could proceed for the balance of the trial with Bloom as her lawyer and that I was removing myself from the case. I felt that her failure to understand the significance of Bloom's stated intention to admit the photos into evidence was a clear rejection of my judgment and my ability as a lawyer. I could not prevent tears of anger as I made my motion to be relieved of the responsibility of representing her.

Arnold Bauman, the newly assigned judge, ordered the trial to begin on the day following the hung verdict, granted my motion to withdraw, and permitted Florynce Kennedy, the well-known Black feminist attorney, to be co-counsel with Assata, who cross-examined White and delivered her own summation. I thought this form of participation was an excellent maneuver, for it allowed Assata, a personable and convincing defendant, to reinforce her innocence directly to the jury without undergoing rigorous cross-examination. Few defendants can carry it off, but when they can there is no one better to explain to jurors, none of whom have ever been convicted of a crime, the evils of a judicial system embedded in an evil societal system. In the second trial there were no outbursts, no banishments from the courtroom, and total application to every legal detail. Prior to her arrest, Assata had never attended a trial and her limited knowledge of the practice of law came essentially from my heated comments to her during her adolescence when she lived with me. I would return home with daily complaints about the maze of inequality in which Black defendants were trapped, and she would listen in complete agreement, designating me the "last angry woman."

My fears about the photos had been right. Although Bloom did not introduce them into evidence, interestingly enough, Truebner did, and Avon White suddenly was able to identify one of the figures in the bank as Assata. The jury, questioned after their verdict of acquittal, said they had reviewed the surveillance photo over and over again. It had been the only piece of evidence they had to resolve in order to acquit because they had completely discredited Rivers's and White's testimony. The jury was finally persuaded that the figure in the photo was not Assata because White had described her as wearing overalls and the figure was wearing a jacket—a slim thread from which acquittal had dangled. The day after the verdict, on December 29, 1973, Assata was transferred to Morristown in Morris County to continue the New Jersey trial.

I have pondered the situation many times, and I have come up with a rationale for the position Assata took, which had nothing to do with disagreeing with my analysis or agreeing with Bloom. Instead, her need to maintain cohesiveness with Kamau, whether or not it meant her sacrifice in the process, was of paramount importance. It was a political decision she took but did not share with me, unfortunately—because I at least would have understood. Although, let me be perfectly clear, I would never have agreed with the decision whether or not it was politically correct.

In other political cases where I have been asked to represent one of multiple defendants, my first question is always Is Bloom one of the attorneys? If he is, count me out.

Chapter 12

While the acquittal in the Bronx bank robbery trial did not receive the same attention the trial had, it was nevertheless widely reported. The day following the acquittal, when Assata was immediately convoyed back to Morristown to stand trial for the turnpike shoot-out, radio and television news reported a new indictment in headlines such as "Joanne and Four Black Libs Indicted in the Shooting of Two Cops." Joan Carey, the Queens assistant district attorney, had announced the indictment against Assata, Andrew Jackson, Avon White, and two other "Army members still at large" for the attempted murder of two policemen, Roy Pollina and Michael O'Reilly, by shooting at them with submachine guns, sawed-off shotguns, and semiautomatic pistols on January 28, 1973, in St. Albans, Queens. This year-old charge, just translated into an indictment, was but another example of the conspiratorial efforts of law enforcement agents to extract indictments against Assata and to publicize them at crucial moments in her many legal battles. To them the Bronx bank robbery acquittal was an insult, and the existing untried indictments were not enough to satisfy their thirst for conviction. More insurance was needed and, even if she was not to be convicted on this most recent charge, the manipulated negative impact on the Morristown jury, still to be chosen, was well calculated to succeed.

The assault against alleged members of the BLA did not end with Assata. On the second day after the Bronx acquittal, Kamau was indicted and arraigned in Bronx Supreme Court for the attempted murder of two policemen, Joseph Lombardo and James Carey, on March 6, 1973, by firing fourteen shots at them during a high-speed chase. Kamau was indicted with "two unnamed other members of the BLA who escaped and who were still not identified." Also publicized in the newspapers alongside these articles was the beginning of the second trial in the New York Supreme Court of Dhoruba Bin Wahad, a member of the

Black Panther Party, for the attempted ambush murder of the two policemen driving in their patrol car on Riverside Drive in 1971, the first trial having ended in a hung jury on December 9, 1973. (Dhoruba was convicted in the second trial and sentenced to life imprisonment. After nineteen years of incarceration, including his time in prison before the trial, his conviction was reversed as a result of the heroic efforts of his attorneys, Elizabeth Fink and Robert J. Boyle, in January 1990. Documents they received through the Freedom of Information Act revealed the insidious and illegal withholding of favorable evidence during his trial, the intentional falsification of evidence, and the complicity of the government and the New York City Police Department in constructing his conviction to coincide with planned disruption against militant organizations and manufactured charges as specified in the FBI's COINTELPRO guidelines.)

The COINTELPRO offensive efficiently operated with the complicity of its primary media agents, the *Daily News* of New York and New Jersey. On January 7, 1974, the *Daily News* ran a feature story entitled "How the Cops Hunted the Last of the Black Libbers" and trotted out the well-reported November 14, 1974, ambush slaying by police of Twyman Myers, detailing how he had been fingered by a reported BLA member, Joe Lee Jones, and followed it up with a feature story on January 8 entitled "The Black Lib Army's Strategy in Blood." On January 10, 1974, the newspaper began a five-part series called "Black Lib's Diary," describing the alleged surprise existence of the diary of Denise Oliver, Andrew Jackson's girlfriend, who had been arrested with him on June 8, 1973, and reproducing handwritten pages from the diary. The excerpts described the despair of living underground and revealed that Jackson was "thinking of surrendering." The *News* prefaced the diary excerpts with the comment "The arrest of Joanne Chesimard, Sister Love to the Black Liberation Army, had a severe psychological impact on the militant band" and quoted from Oliver's alleged diary:

> Today it was Joanne who I never met   . but I feel as if I know her . . . even though it has been knowledge gained through the half-baked lies and propaganda of the news media. And today it was Zayd. I never thought he would wind up a corpse in New Jersey on the Turnpike. I suppose I assumed his existence would always be inevitable . . . but I was wrong. He dies and Joanne lives, ironic when you consider that Zayd had a great

will to live and Joanne, the anarchist, seemed to constantly tempt death. It was inevitable that Joanne would eventually be caught for her acts . . . but that is intellectual: and in the gut a certain misplaced pride glows—a sister, a get-down sister, right or wrong, a she not a he, has become a martyr.

Compounding the impact of this dredged-up and revitalized old news were stories of two trials of alleged BLA members that began on January 8: the New York Supreme Court trial of the BLA 5 (Herman Bell, Anthony Bottom, Albert "Nuh" Washington, and Francisco and Gabriel Torres) and the trial of Henry Brown, alleged BLA member, for the murders of policemen Foster and Laurie. Repeated in the news article about the latter was the death of Ronald Carter, killed in a gun battle with police in St. Louis in February 1972 and accused, along with Brown, of the police murders. Given prominence in the news stories were Brown's two escape attempts, the first from the Brooklyn House of Detention in April 1972 and the second from Kings County Hospital in October 1973.

If any residual anger remained from my confrontation with Assata during the Bronx bank robbery trial, it entirely dissipated in the face of this enveloping, artificially created negativity. The day after Assata's removal to Morristown, I met with her for an hour alone in a small room next to the courtroom and we talked without strangeness or bitterness. As always, we needed no protracted explanations or excuses. Slimmer and paler than when I had last seen her, she simply said, "Anty, I'm sorry, will you please be my lawyer?" and I said, "Of course I will." She was not triumphant about the acquittal, having already dismissed it, and, determinedly, was ready for this trial and the next one and the next one and the one after that.

As the jury selection process began, I was astonished by the dramatic changes that had occurred in both Judge Bachman and Ray Brown during the previous two months. The camaraderie and respect they had demonstrated for each other in the early days of the trial in Middlesex County—Bachman an experienced jurist and Ray an experienced practitioner who had appeared before him many times in his representation of major crime figures in New Jersey—had changed. Bachman was no longer impartial, no longer reasonable, no longer willing to apply U.S. Supreme Court decisions to the particularities of this case. Responding to citizens' anger over the increased cost of the trial to taxpayers because of the expensive security measures the county felt it had to install, to delays in the previous trial, to people's resentment over the bank robbery acquittal, to the cry for the conviction of these obviously guilty "animals" who did not deserve the civilized privilege of a trial, and to the public's need for quick and merciless "justice," Bachman reversed many positions he had previously taken.

Both Sundiata and Assata were Muslims. In the earlier part of the trial, no sessions had been held on Fridays, their day of worship, but Bachman rescinded this restriction and the trial continued six days a week in the rush to completion. During the first trial he had adjourned for the two or so days we needed to file motions for a change of venue from Middlesex County, but this time he refused when we filed the motion to move the trial from Morris County. Whereas before he had patiently listened to our arguments, now he made his decisions before we were finished and, once he had made them, stormed from the courtroom, leaving us talking to an empty bench. His face reddened easily and a stern, frowning countenance replaced the easy amiability I had been so familiar with.

And now, massed within Ray's consciousness was a rage at the inequities in the statutory standards for selecting jurors, which effectively excluded Blacks from either grand juries or petit juries, documented in the Buckhout and Payne surveys. In his vast experience, it was the one aspect of the criminal justice system he had never challenged, and it was as though he was determined to compensate for all those years when he had assumed its fairness. He engineered the attack against the process, insisted on presenting all the oral arguments himself, and pressed for a change of venue and appeal to the federal court when another motion for a change of venue was denied. Energized by the research that had been done, he skirted on the fringes of repeated contempt citations in his zeal. And that transformation, I'm sure, was permanent.

Each day of jury selection brought a new meaning to the words *tedium*, *frustration*, and *helplessness*. The voir dire droned on endlessly. Questions. Objections for obvious bias. Requests for additional questions. Motions denied. Another juror. The same questions. The same objections. The same denials for additional questions. The monotony was interrupted by new motions for a change of venue after the prosecutor used

his peremptory challenge to excuse one of the two Black jurors
on the panel and when Bachman refused to increase our peremptory challenges, which had been reduced from ten each for
Assata and Sundiata to five each when the trial had moved to
Morris County. When we discovered that several copies of New
York Police Commissioner Robert Daley's recently published
book *Target Blue*, from which excerpts had been published in
New York magazine, were prominently displayed in the jury
room, we moved for a dismissal of that panel and included the
incident in our motion for a change of venue to Essex County.
Bachman refused to dismiss the panel or to move the trial and,
contrary to his decision in the first trial, did not even excuse the
panel for taint but let go only the two jurors who admitted having
read the book. When discovered, each book had been turned to
a page in which Daley traced the movement of members of the
BLA across the country, describing the way in which Black
extremists managed to get from Harlem to Algiers with such
ease: "The leaders of this extremist wing were apparently Moore
(Dhoruba Bin Wahad), Andrew Jackson and JoAnne Chesimard.
They were the contacts in New York for wanted blacks from any
part of the country. JoAnne would make up phony identifications and from Harlem, fleeing Blacks would go to Canada, then
to Paris and finally Algiers."

In the streets surrounding the courthouse, the Ku Klux
Klan, banners prominently waving, circled the building, chant-
ing, "White power and death to the BLA." They clashed with
Assata's and Sundiata's supporters and provided an ominous
backdrop for the sham going on inside the courtroom. Then
suddenly, everything was interrupted by Assata's unexpected
illness, which would dramatically alter the direction of the
defense. Ray obtained the incomparable services of Dr. E.
Wyman Garrett, a board-certified obstetrician and gynecologist
from Newark who was licensed to practice in both New Jersey
and New York and whom Bachman permitted to examine Assata.
Dr. Garrett confirmed what she had whispered to us that she had
suspected: she was pregnant with Kamau's child.

As I listened to Sundiata's gentle teasing, I was absorbing
the impact of the news. I calculated the time remaining before
she gave birth and the barbaric conditions of her special incarceration, which there was no reason to believe would change.
The administration of prenatal care by despising prison doctors

was unthinkable, but I wondered if I would be successful in obtaining a private obstetrician. I wondered about the baby's survival in the airless, sunless dungeon of Middlesex County jail. Neither her mother nor I condemned Assata, and we quickly agreed to share the child's upbringing should she be convicted. We had long since adjusted to the fact that Assata was a product of the sixties, acting independently of the sexual restrictions that had so governed our lives and substituting a new morality. She was a fierce believer in women's rights, including the right to abortion, although she rejected that choice for herself. It was also understandable, in light of her solitary confinement for more than eight months without even conversational camaraderie, that the long days in the holding pen behind the Southern District courtroom with Kamau, a person she respected and trusted, would have provided the opportunity for comforting embraces to merge into intimacy.

After allowing Assata a short stay in Roosevelt Hospital, Bachman decided that he would not risk further delays in the trial for anticipated morning sickness or other discomforts that can accompany pregnancy, and he severed her trial from Sundiata's. Assata was returned to the basement of the Middlesex County jail to await the birth of her child in horrendous, inhumane conditions. The National Conference of Black Lawyers and Prisoners' Rights Organized Defense (PROD) filed a complaint in the U.S. District Court for New Jersey protesting the prison conditions and charging that Assata's constitutional rights as a pretrial detainee with no prior convictions were being violated:

> Plaintiff is kept in twenty-four hour solitary confinement, with no opportunity for fresh air, recreation, physical exercise, movies, T.V., social contacts and without minimum privacy in the exercise of her religious and personal needs.
> Plaintiff, in solitary confinement, is kept under twenty-four hour surveillance under electric lights by female matrons who keep a written log of her every movement.
> The basement cell in which plaintiff is confined alone for twenty-four hours a day has no natural light and poor ventilation. Utility pipes are exposed in the low ceiling and the floors are cement and damp. The cell is infested with ants and centipedes.

Additionally, Assata's diet was so nutritionally deficient

(even cheese, eggs, and vitamins were withheld) that it would not sustain an adult woman, much less a pregnant one. Dr. Marcella Katz, a nationally renowned nutritionist associated with the Institute of Human Nutrition at Columbia University, attached an affidavit to the complaint, setting forth her analysis of dietary deficiency and spelling out the danger to both Assata and her unborn child.

During the hearings on the complaint held in the federal court, Dr. Michael Oliver Smith, a New York psychiatrist, testified about the effects of sensory deprivation resulting from "the lack of natural light, lack of fresh air, lack of exercise, lack of recreational material, severe lack of human contact and lack of spiritual contacts," noting that "a great number of scientific studies completed in the past decade clearly have demonstrated that prolonged sensory deprivation regularly causes psychotic or schizophrenic breakdown." He concluded that if Assata had not been "such a strong and independent minded person, it is very likely that she would have had a psychotic breakdown well before this time." Dr. Smith was the only person except prison guards to see the inside of Assata's cell. He testified, "I have never seen a prison cell that was shrouded and hidden from the world in any way comparable to Ms. Chesimard's. . . . The effect of the lack of natural light, lack of fresh air, adverse temperature changes, water leaks and vermin is to create a consistently degrading and debilitating environment out of all proportion to conditions in other parts of the Middlesex County Jail or any other prison facility that I have observed."

The circumstances of Assata's confinement were a precursor to those in the Women's High Security Unit at the federal prison in Lexington, Kentucky, a special small-group isolation facility set up in October 1986 for political women and designed specifically to destroy Alejandrina Torres, Susan Rosenberg, and Silvia Baraldini, who were convicted of a variety of alleged subversive acts against the government. Amnesty International revealed in a 1988 report that led to a court-ordered closing of the unit, "This program [the High Security Unit] set up a hierarchy of objectives. The first of these is to reduce prisoners to the state of submission essential for their ideological conversion. That failing, the next objective is to reduce them to a state of psychological incompetence sufficient to neutralize them as efficient, self-directing antagonists. That failing, the only alternative is to destroy them, preferably by making them desperate enough to destroy themselves." The report concluded that these conditions were the same as the "dead wings" (isolation units) and "white cells" (cells painted in high-gloss white and illuminated around the clock with fluorescent lights) that existed in Germany's Stammheim high-security prison to accomplish the same goals. Stuart Grassian, in a report called "A Review and Delineation of a Clinical Syndrome," traced the development of psychological syndromes resulting from isolation that have been documented during the nineteenth and twentieth centuries in Europe and in Korea for U.S. prisoners of war. And, it must be added, the conditions of incarceration suffered by Sundiata after his conviction and by Sekou Odinga, Geronimo Pratt, Mutulu Shakur, and other political prisoners were no different.

The federal court dismissed the complaint and, while the appeal was pending, on May 10, 1974, New Jersey abruptly complied with one of the several warrants filed against Assata by the state of New York, and she was transferred to the Women's House of Detention on Rikers Island in Queens. But victory is measured not only by legal decisions. Assata was at last out of the dungeon and into the general population with other inmates. She was able to have visitors, fresh air, and nutrition that met the minimum requirements necessary to sustain her.

Following its well-established mode of operation, once she was in New York the government quickly held arraignments, pregnancy or no pregnancy. On May 11 Assata was arraigned before the Queens County Supreme Court for the January 23, 1973, attempted ambush murder of policemen Pollina and O'Reilly; on May 29 she was arraigned in Kings County Supreme Court for the drug dealer murder, and on May 30 she was arraigned in the same court for kidnapping a drug dealer.

Dr. Ernie Garrett wanted to continue as Assata's obstetrician, and the motion I filed in Queens Supreme Court to allow him to do so was granted. He had the tall, broad-shouldered, graceful body of a football pass receiver and was as jaunty in appearance as he was casual in manner. He wore the latest fashion in clothes and drove the newest model of custom-made Lincoln Continental sedan, but his large, soft, gentle-looking hands were the truest indicator of his personality. As soon as the court gave its permission, he visited Assata at Rikers Island frequently until the day she was moved to Elmhurst Hospital to give birth. He charged the family no fee, not even out-of-pocket expenses.

Technically, he was under the supervision of the Montefiore Hospital doctors, who were hired through city contract to provide medical services to the prison, and was required to accept their presence during each of his visits. Although he chafed at the insult to his credentials, his dedication to Assata and his need to visit her regularly, supervise her condition, and watch the progress of her pregnancy were more important. Despite the many times he made the long trip to Rikers from Newark only to be told that the doctor scheduled to be present with him was unable to be there, requiring him to make another appointment, his calm demeanor and quiet self-assurance never changed, to the chagrin of the hospital and prison administrators. As they persisted in these petty and unprofessional inconveniences in the face of his constant equanimity, they could not know that he recognized their attempted humiliation as but one of the many ways in which white professionals frequently try to denigrate the achievements of Black professionals and, therefore, they were unaware of the ease with which he deflected their intended impact on his performance.

Ernie's visits to Assata became more frequent as her delivery neared, and when he told prison officials that birth was imminent he was forced to pace impatiently until another Montefiore doctor arrived at the prison to confirm his diagnosis. Then he had to wait in the parking lot for the police convoy to arrive at the prison and follow the screeching caravan to Elmhurst Hospital in Queens. There, however, he was told by hospital officials that the court order permitting him to care for Assata during her pregnancy did not extend to delivering her child, and they would not afford him hospital privileges, although it was within their authority to do so.

I had visited Assata almost daily in those expectant days, always on the days Ernie had scheduled to see her because of the prison's constant tactics to prevent his medical examination and prescribed treatments. On the day of her labor and delivery Doris was visiting her as well. Doris's car was parked on the mainland side of the bridge connecting it to Rikers Island, while Ernie was parked in one of the island's reserved parking spaces set aside for prison officials. Doris and I rushed to the bus that took visitors from the island to the mainland and waited in the parking lot until the convoy passed, watching Ernie's pursuit with amusement. When we got to the hospital, at about 4:00 P.M., I was stunned to learn of the hospital's decision not to allow Ernie hospital privileges. It was too late to try to obtain another court order and Assata, her large Afro braided, sitting cross-legged on the hospital cot, arms planted protectively across her stomach, refused to permit any Elmhurst Hospital doctor to touch her and vowed that if Dr. Garrett could not deliver her baby, she would delivery the baby herself.

It was a stand-off of global proportions and one that was fraught with potentially tragic consequences. Ernie refused to leave the hospital and sat in the lounge consulting with me as I attempted to negotiate the stalemate. The Elmhurst Hospital doctors flitted in and out of Assata's room in increasing numbers as the night wore on and as birth became more imminent. Their attitude turned from contemptuous dismissal of the mere suggestion that they would allow a private doctor to deliver a prisoner's child to their stubborn insistence that their policy and decision were correct to their nervous realization that they might be forced to relent in the face of Assata's insistence that they not touch her. Finally they crumbled into unadulterated panic.

In the meantime, hundreds of Assata's friends and supporters had filled the streets in front of the hospital, loudly demanding that Dr. Garrett be allowed to deliver the baby, and the first-floor corridor was crowded with television cameras. It was only because of all of these factors combined that the hospital capitulated and permitted Ernie to deliver the baby. The officials and I, after discussion with both Ernie and Assata, fashioned an agreement among Assata, Ernie, and the hospital relieving the hospital of any responsibility that might result from the delivery performed by Ernie and permitting him to continue to treat Assata during her postpartum stay at the hospital. At about 4:00 A M on September 11, 1974, Ernie delivered a beautiful baby girl, Kakuya Amala Olugbala Shakur, whose birth I announced to the exultant crowd.

For the next two weeks Assata was permitted to remain at the hospital where she nursed Kakuya, the most pleasant memory she was to have for several months thereafter. On September 25, the hospital released Kakuya to Doris's custody and Assata was returned to prison on Rikers Island.

Chapter 13

On her return to Rikers Island, Assata resisted an internal body probe and was beaten and thrown into solitary confinement for two weeks until prison officials tricked her into consenting to the examination by lying that I had approved it. At the same time I was trying to obtain a court order enjoining the hospital from conducting this arbitrary examination. As brutal as it was, however, it was child's play compared with the court-engineered brutality that took place in December 1974. Sandwiched between them was a rare piece of good news.

On October 31, 1974, Judge Peter T. Farrell of the Queens Supreme Court granted my motion to dismiss the indictment for the January 28, 1973, ambush murders of policemen Pollina and O'Reilly. I had filed what is called an omnibus motion in response to the indictment—a catchall challenge composed of various forms of relief, including the dismissal of the indictment because it was based on insufficient and illegal evidence that had been presented to the grand jury. This part of the motion had so seldom been granted in the history of criminal law that I had no expectation of success. And certainly not given the hysteria of the times, which demanded that Assata be arrested, indicted, and convicted of almost anything. As with all the other indictments against her, this one had been presented to the grand jury after her capture. When it was dismissed, I knew the evidence had to have been so paper-thin that it would not support even the newspaper fabrication on which it was based and must have been so transparently illegal that the judge could withstand the criticism that would be hurled against him for his decision.

The celebration terminated on December 11, 1974, when Judge Jacob Mishler of the federal court in Brooklyn, assigned to try the Queens bank robbery case, issued an order for Assata "to submit to the photographing of her person by Agents of the Federal Bureau of Investigation for the purpose of comparison of such photographs during the armed robbery of the Bankers Trust

Company" (the Queens bank). Mishler had issued an earlier order for her appearance for such photographs, with which she had refused to comply. Because of her own illness following childbirth, the traumatic separation from Kakuya, and the brutal nature of her treatment by the corrections officials when she returned to Rikers Island, she had not been physically able to appear anywhere for any purpose. Outraged by Assata's refusal to voluntarily appear before him, Mishler ordered that "the defendant, having refused to voluntarily leave her place of incarceration at the New York Correctional Institution for Women," would be "accompanied by United States Marshals for her appearance" on December 31, 1974. He further ordered that "the United States Marshals transport the defendant Joanne Chesimard from her said place of incarceration to the United States Courthouse . . . in Brooklyn . . . employing such force as is reasonably necessary to accomplish her transportation and appearance for said photographing."

We anticipated the worst, and it happened. Assata, still weak, did not resist transportation by the marshals to Brooklyn. In the meantime, I had prepared a motion before the Court of Appeals for the Second Circuit to prevent the photographing, pending a decision on the legality of Mishler's order. I filed it in the assistant U.S. attorney's office in the Brooklyn courthouse late in the afternoon of December 30, but because of the many affidavits I needed to support the motion, I was unable to file it that day in the appellate court, which was located in Foley Square in lower Manhattan, because I simply did not have the time. The next day I asked Mishler for a two-hour adjournment so that I could cross into Manhattan to file the motion, and he refused.

I entered the strangely empty, isolated courtroom where the photographing had been scheduled to take place at 9:30 A M on December 31. The silence was reminiscent of a back alley at midnight, the threat of an assault lurking in a corner, unseen, waiting for the right moment to attack. Open, serene, innocent, unthreatening, the room nevertheless could not conceal the aura of the Nazi concentration camp "shower rooms" that invited the unsuspecting Jews of Europe to their death in the gas chambers. But this time the commander of the camp was a Jew.

Assata was brought in with her usual police escort. The court reporter entered and adjusted her stenotype machine. Five marshals followed her, together with two FBI photographers, their cameras at the ready. When Mishler strode into the room and sat at the bench, he ordered the photographing to proceed. Before it commenced, I advised him that, regardless of any other considerations, Assata had already been photographed when she was arraigned in 1973 and that this session was unnecessary. Robert Clarey, the assistant U.S. attorney, explained that the mug shots, although taken from several angles—front and both right and left side profiles—did not reflect the exact angle of the bank surveillance photos and were therefore worthless for comparison.

Mishler brushed aside my reminder with the following statement: "Let's get this over with. I directed that the photographing be done and it was for the purpose of determining that the defendant was in fact of the same height, build, general outline as the one who held up the bank. Now, if your expert feels that the height of the hair or the coiffure should be about the same to take that into consideration, fine. I am not going to make any further directions. I have never seen so accurate a photograph of a face" (referring to the similarity he perceived between the bank surveillance photos and Assata).

That statement alone was sufficient to support a motion for his removal as the trial judge. But he continued to manifest his bias. Clarey said he needed the photos "because her large afro concealed her face, and, on trial, I anticipate a great deal of difficulty to force Miss Chesimard to wear glasses and comb her hair back in a courtroom."

Five United States marshals climbed all over Assata, forcing her down on the floor of the courtroom. Two held her body, two held her head, and one, his arm around her throat, attempted to push her chin upwards for the photographer who was poised for the correct angle standing on top of a table. Mishler said, "Let the record show Mrs. Chesimard is attempting to distort her features." And Assata, her throat being throttled, screamed, "Let the record show that I am refusing to take pictures which are unconstitutional. Let the record show I am refusing to be framed."

As the assault continued, Mishler, a short, chinless, gray-haired man, leaned over the elevated courtroom platform on which he had been sitting, looked down to the melee on the floor, and said to the marshals, "You take any force . . . take any force that is necessary. . . . The orders of this court will be obeyed by Miss Chesimard or anybody else, and she has no special rights here. She is not going to get away with it just because she is obstreperous and disruptive." When I made repeated objections, charging the marshals with unconscionable brutality, Mishler said, "That's the only way they can get a photograph. I direct that they do it." When I pointed out that Assata had a bullet in her chest and a paralyzed arm, in addition to still recovering from childbirth, he stated, "She certainly seems to have enough strength to resist five marshals."

When I continued to describe, for the record, each attack and the nature of the force being used against her, putting objection after objection on the record, Mishler repeated to the marshals, "Use all the force that is necessary." When I pointed out that a defendant is not obligated to prove her innocence, Mishler replied, "Meaningless shibboleths have no place here. She refuses to show what her face looks like. I can anticipate what the trial is going to be like. Photographer, take a photograph showing her head down, refusing to put her head up. That is the kind of photograph I want." When I asked where the court reporters were, invisible behind the flying bodies, Mishler said, "We have two of them. We don't want to miss anything here. I can see a Civil Rights 1983 action on this" (referring to an action brought in federal court for damages when constitutional rights are violated).

The judge discontinued the attempt to photograph after Clarey said, "Your Honor, the photographing at this point is meaningless because we are not getting the angles we need for comparison." At that point Mishler asked, "Now, have you got any bruises on you, Ms. Chesimard?" And Assata stormed back, "Inside and outside. I have so many bruises this court cannot even begin to understand. What do you mean, do I have bruises?" Mishler responded, "I find this defendant is obviously in contempt of court," and directed Assata to appear at her trial with the same hairdo depicted in the surveillance photograph.

I have been asked repeatedly how I could remain calm while watching such punishment being inflicted on my niece, and I've replied that if Mishler was to be removed as trial judge, his constitutional violations had to be put on the record, regardless of the pain I felt. Assata finally was led from the courtroom to a downstairs cell. I raced to her and demanded that a nurse, the only available medical person, be brought immediately to examine her. We were not aunt and niece. Not mother and daughter. But two women in an alien world, sharing an anguish neither could extinguish for the other. Me doing my legal thing and Assata doing her necessary thing. The only weapons we had.

My motion for Mishler's removal from the trial was granted, and when the case was tried on January 5, 1976, Judge Jack Weinstein was assigned. When the series of photographs was offered into evidence by the assistant U.S. attorney during the trial, Weinstein excluded them, stating, "I would be inclined to exclude that. I will allow you to introduce proof that she refused to be photographed, but I believe this comes close to shocking the conscience of the Court. If that exhibit was obtained in this forcible way, I won't allow it. It's the equivalent of forcibly pumping somebody's stomach."

Chapter 14

Gagliardi had held me in contempt for simply trying to leave the courtroom during the Bronx robbery trial. I had not used profanity or verbal abuse, nor had I called him a racist pig or otherwise accurately described him. I was cited for contempt on December 5, 1973, and sentenced on February 4, 1974, to a ten-day prison term in a maximum prison facility, a sentence that Gagliardi refused to reconsider absent my apology, which I refused to give. William Kunstler appeared with me at the sentencing, along with Conrad Lynn. Leroy Clark, a professor at New York University, O. T. Wells of the National Bar Association, Haywood Burns of the National Conference of Black Lawyers, and James Larson and Arthur Kinoy of the Center for Constitutional Rights prepared the appeal to the U.S. Court of Appeals for the Second Circuit, which affirmed Gagliardi's decision. On January 13, 1975, the U.S. Supreme Court denied certiorari (it refused to review the lower court decision). Later that day Barrett Prettyman, the Washington lawyer who had filed the appeal before the Supreme Court, called to tell me its decision and the next day I surrendered to the United States marshal, whose office was located behind the District Court on Foley Square in lower Manhattan.

The marshal's office was unaware of the Supreme Court's decision, and there was rank confusion when I arrived since a warrant of arrest had not yet been lodged. But that was one of the reasons I voluntarily appeared—to avoid a midnight raid by the Joint Terrorist Task Force or apprehension in some other situation entirely beyond my control. And it was the best possible time for me during a lull in Assata's trials.

January 14 was a bitter cold day. The upper New York State countryside was covered with snow as the marshals drove me the considerable distance to the Maximum Security Unit of Westchester County jail in Valhalla, New York, my hands tightly cuffed behind my back, and it was late in the day, almost dark,

136

when I arrived. I had interviewed many prisoners incarcerated throughout the state of New York and quite a few outside, including some in federal correctional facilities. But visiting prison is one thing; being in prison is another. There are, of course, the army-like rules and regulations given to you after everything in your possession is removed and inventoried and after the strip search, including a rubber-gloved anal probe. The directives included the following commands: "All inmates will arise at 6:30 A.M., lock-in at 10 P.M. Lights out and radio off at 11 P.M. You must be clean and neat in appearance at all times. Showers must be taken at least every other night, although you may shower nightly if you wish. You are NOT to enter another inmate's room at any time. At the discretion of the Corrections staff, your cell may be changed at any time. Also, your person or cell may be searched at any time." Etcetera.

My cell was exactly seven by six feet. It contained a narrow cot, a small table, and a bathroom through a doorless opening. The communal shower was down the hall, but there was no cold water and the hot water was scalding. I soaped first and then rinsed quickly, exposing myself for only a few minutes. But there were many avoidances I had to learn from the other inmates. When my face and body broke out in a sick-looking rash, they told me it was from the sheets and the soap, both of which contained more lye than cleansing agents. While I could buy other soap at the commissary, the only way I could escape the sheet contamination was to put the blanket on top of the sheets and sleep on that, leaving myself uncovered except for the very short blue hospital-like gown that had been issued along with a blue uniform. Every hour during the night the guards penetrated each cell with a piercing flashlight, and I learned to sleep with my head facing away from the cell door and on my stomach to avoid being awakened by it.

Before I surrendered I had decided to engage in a hunger strike as a political protest. At first I was allowed to sit in the cafeteria with the other inmates while they ate food that justified their comment "You may enter jail slim, but, forget it, you will come out fat." It was grease, grease, and more grease, and had I not made the choice beforehand, the food would have forced me into a hunger strike. After two days, however, the prison officials decided that my noneating presence in the cafeteria was potentially inciting and locked me in the library during mealtimes.

When there was no one available to escort me to the library, I was locked in my cell. After the fourth day, the prison doctor suggested that I eat if I knew what was good for me, and that night I had nightmares about force feeding and woke up screaming. But I stuck it out through the ten days and even collected a few bets from the corrections officers who had wagered I could never do it. I was a daily item of discussion and was carefully watched to detect the ingestion of any food. Once, when I purchased several candy bars and cookies from the commissary, the guards said, "Oh, that's how she does it." The inmates quickly came to my defense and told them, "The food's not for her. She gives it to us."

I cannot now independently recall the days I spent there, but I did write daily notes, to the consternation of the guards, who felt that I might be a threat to the institution when I was released. After the inmates told me of their concern, I kept my notes with me at all times. As I look at them now, I see that, despite my bravado, I was frequently nauseous from lack of food during the first four days, but I have no notation of vomiting. I was also depressed and headachy, in a bad mood, and hardly the courageous person I thought I would be. One of my notations is underlined: *"I want out of here! I want to go home!"* But from the first day, I wanted to get to know the sisters, and for the first time in my life I used that term easily, without thinking. The fifteen of us who shared the wing were Black, as were most of the women in the whole facility. They were felony repeaters and constantly complained to each other about the raw deals they had received from the courts and their lawyers, the unjustified convictions, and the frame-ups. Once they stopped viewing me with suspicion, as a ten-day outsider, they used my legal knowledge to write letters to their probation and parole officers and to their lawyers.

The jail was modern in design, both inside and outside, concealing the corrosive neglect of certain signs of a bygone time when rehabilitation was more than a concept. There was an enormous gym in which broken equipment rotted against the walls. The machine in the sewing room was inoperable, and the typewriter had no ribbon. I spoke to the corrections officials about the missed opportunity the equipment represented and wrote letters to the State Department of Corrections calling attention to their state of disrepair, which was signed by all of the sisters in my wing. The other women began to feel they had some control over their lives and responded to my demands that reasonable responses should be made only to reasonable requests. I had no objection to scrubbing my cell or mopping the area of the jail in which we were housed, but when our tasks included cleaning the rooms and the toilets of the corrections staff, I refused. Fortunately, after threatening disciplinary action, the guards reconsidered and, at least during the time I was there, cleaned their own quarters. These were small, inconsequential things, but to be able to determine even a minuscule element of one's existence is an intricate, inseparable ingredient of human dignity. Stripped of even that, the animal residing in all of us will emerge.

During breakfast, lunch, and dinner, when I was in the library, I reread *Soul on Ice* and Angela Davis's books until the guards realized the books were there and removed them. At first the sisters would come in to ask me legal questions. Then they were banned from the library and replaced by the guards, who sought my opinion about their own legal problems. So I struck a bargain with them and thereafter, to my amazement, half my time was shared with them and half with the inmates. When the guards learned I was JoAnne Chesimard's lawyer, their search for free legal advice did not abate. When the sisters asked me if I was Assata's lawyer, they asked from the side, slipping the question in between deals in a card game, pretending no real interest, but, just as an item of possibility, was I? We had a good relationship and that information neither lessened nor enhanced it. They had read the newspapers but didn't really understand what Assata was all about except that she was a "bad sister" and "right on."

Most of the afternoons, between lunch and dinner, we played cards—spades and hearts. I'm a great poker player and had spent many three-day weekends in poker games with friends. So I learned the other games quickly, and the highlight of my incarceration happened when Hazel, the most reluctant to accept me, noisily claimed me for her "steady partner," interrupting my reading or writing in my cell by yelling, "Come on out. The game is starting." They made large jars of Kool-Aid to drink during the games, especially for me, so that I would have some nourishment. I became their project and they protected me, frequently offering to push my mop because they felt I might be getting too weak. I didn't feel weak at all—as a matter of fact until the day I was released and for about four days afterward, I no longer felt any hunger. I drank gallons of water and would have taken vitamins, a daily prejail habit, were it not for the fact that I didn't trust the officials. They might have given me anything and called it a vitamin.

One of the most annoying aspects of prison life is the nomenclature used by the corrections people. "Ladies, time for medication" was a euphemism for the tranquilizers given out three times a day, when the sisters lined up in eager anticipation before the pill-laden carts. It was always "ladies." "Ladies, lights out." "Ladies, time to get up." "Ladies, commissary, mail, food time." "Now, ladies, behave yourselves." The mother wore a uniform and had total power. The children pouted but silently complied. Only one letter a week could be mailed, and despite Supreme Court decisions to the contrary, each one was read by the guards. Visits were restricted to family members or lawyers, so while Doris, Bevvie, and my brother-in-law visited, my best friend, Doe Burke, couldn't. Flo Kennedy was an unauthorized surprise and was disappointed that I was too weak to attend the dinner party she had planned for me at a Harlem restaurant upon my release.

While Westchester County jail represented imprisonment under the least brutal conditions afforded the minority poor, perhaps in the entire country, it did not equal the facilities for convicted white-collar criminals or governmentally approved robbers and burglars, like the Watergate gang, with their tennis courts, golf courses, and swimming pools. But given the repressive nature of confinement itself, at least it was as humane a separation from society as was permitted to those unprivileged among us. Imprisonment is more than isolation from the world. It is confinement in an artificially engineered society with forced associations and supervision of a kind not experienced since childhood. Decisions are wrested from you. When to sleep. When and what to eat. What to read. One radio station fixed in place for you, its dial positioned too high to be changed. Forced submission to arbitrary authority pervades the smallest detail of your daily movements. The staff is alert to the slightest deviation and is quick to force submission with threats of solitary confinement or the withholding of mail or medication. Only internal flights from prison walls are possible.

Dealing with the abrupt separation from your life, adjusting to prison rules and regulations, and resisting a natural instinct to defy senseless, meaningless commands are the most difficult feats to successfully accomplish. When you enter an environment that renders you helpless, not only do you relinquish control of yourself, but your dignity is removed with the removal of your clothing, replaced by prison uniformity, and closeted as your clothing is, elsewhere. The hunger strike enabled me to maintain control over what I put into my body and to withstand any possible erosion of my will to resist the daily demands for total submission. But I was there for only ten days. As I marked each day off on the calendar I had made, I knew that had my sentence been longer I would have had to find another device for my own survival.

The sisters gave me a party the day before I left. They had purchased Kool-Aid and cookies from the commissary and decorated the card table with handmade good-bye cards. I still have Hazel's gift, an attractively bound pink-covered telephone book that Avon handed out to its salespeople. Inside the cover she had written:

> To Evelyn Williams. From a friend. Evelyn, it was a pleasure to have you as a short friend. I hope we will see each other again but not in a place like this. Good luck in your work.
>
> Your pal,
> Hazel.

P.S. You are a good cards player.

The contempt citation was a criminal misdemeanor, but Gagliardi could have cited me for civil contempt, which would not have been a crime. And, had the circumstances in any way justified it, he could have charged me with contempt as a felony, which, regardless of the length of the sentence, would have resulted in automatic disbarment. Instead he let the Appellate Division of the Supreme Court of the State of New York, First Judicial Department, tie up the loose ends for him.

On May 13, 1975, I was served with a petition signed by the Association of the Bar of the City of New York. The bar association had been created by an act of the legislature of New York in 1971 to "elevate the standard of integrity, honor and courtesy in the legal profession" and is the only one of all the bar associations in the city anointed with the responsibility to initiate disbarment proceedings. It is also a bastion for corporate lawyers and large law firms and, since its inception, has discouraged minority membership. The petition stated that "on or about March 5th, 1975, the Executive Committee of the Association of the Bar duly approved the request made by the Committee on Grievances of the Association for authorization to prosecute the respondent, *without hearings*, before the said Committee on Grievances." John Bonomi was chief counsel to the Committee on Grievances of the association.

The petition recited the part of the transcript of the Bronx robbery trial that reflected my allegedly offensive conduct, as well as the Court of Appeals' decision affirming Gagliardi's order. Among other things, it reiterated the Court of Appeals' opinion, which held that Gagliardi had "offered Ms. Williams the opportunity to purge herself of her contempt, and she had declined. The court asked Ms. Williams if she had anything to say in defense of her contumacious conduct, and she stated that she did not consider her conduct contumacious." The bar association petition was fifty-two pages long. I prepared a response and waited for action to be taken against me. I had no way of knowing what to expect, since a hearing in which I could have introduced other evidence had been denied. But disbarment was the action implicitly being sought by the bar association, and I was prepared to appeal if that decision was made. In the meantime, I continued my preparation for Assata's cases that were still awaiting trial. But I was fortunate. The presiding justice of the Appellate Division refused to act on the petition and dismissed it out of hand. His reason was that I was being selectively and prejudicially prosecuted and he would not permit it. I might add that Justice Harold Stevens, now dead, was also Black. I am now associated with Stevens, Hinds and White, the Harlem law firm founded by his brother, Hope Stevens, long a prominent community activist before his death.

Six days after I received notice of the bar association's disciplinary action, on May 19, 1975, I was almost murdered. The day, Malcolm X's birthday, had started out pleasantly. I had lunch with a young, recently married couple, both of whom had graduated from New York University and had been active in the Martin Luther King Center and were part of the defense committee for Sundiata and Assata. They were expecting their first child, and the conversation centered on their preparations, their jobs, and their plans to leave the city to better raise their child. I was relaxed, pleased to see the young, happy-with-life faces charting their lives with the confidence and fearlessness vested in the young. Apart from a few such pleasant interludes, I was always preparing for Assata's remaining cases.

I still did not know the order in which the cases would be tried, although I had expended every effort to find out. But in two cases, the Queens bank robbery case to be held in the Eastern District federal court and the drug dealer murder case to be held in the Kings County Supreme Court, one of Assata's co-defendants was Andrew Jackson. And Robert Bloom was his lawyer in both. While I believed Assata's trial should be severed from Jackson's in each case, she rejected that plan and continued in her firm position that unity among the co-defendants must be maintained. But there had been no joint conferences between Assata and Jackson, although my motion for such a conference had been allowed. I felt that only a convenient time for the meeting had to be arranged.

Despite my reluctance, I left several messages at Bloom's office asking him to call me to set a time. When he didn't return my calls, I wrote to him, but he still did not reply. What I didn't know was that there was a very logical reason for Bloom's refusal to discuss joint trial strategy. His strategy had already been put in place. Unknown to everyone except the U.S. attorney, the judge for the federal court in the Eastern District, and Bloom, Jackson had already pleaded guilty to the indictment and, in a sealed statement made at the time of his plea, had identified Assata as one of the bank robbers and promised to testify against her at the trial in exchange for the government's promise of leniency.

While the former students and I were dawdling over coffee at lunch that day, Martha Pitts, also a former member of the Martin Luther King Center at New York University and a member of Assata's Cell, a defense committee formed to protest her jail conditions, came into the restaurant. I had not expected to see her but was agreeably surprised. Martha was a registered nurse, and her medical knowledge had been invaluable in helping me understand the shorthand nomenclature of hospital records and coroners' reports.

I mentioned the difficulty I were having trying to reach

Bloom and said I needed to know when he would be available for a joint conference. I knew he was in the Bronx Supreme Court on trial with Victor Cumberbatch, but I had been reluctant to make the trip there or to have to talk to him. When Martha offered to go there with me, right then, I welcomed her suggestion and we left the restaurant and took the train to the Bronx.

We walked into the courtroom in which the trial was being held before Judge Ivan Warner, and the court officer immediately waved us out. We left, but since courtrooms are always open forums, I wanted to know why we were prevented from entering, even as spectator members of the public. The only time courtrooms are closed is during the judge's charge to the jury before the case is given to them for their deliberations. And even then, all those who are seated before the charge begins are allowed to remain. On such occasions, the door to the courtroom is locked and a sign posted saying, "Jury is being charged."

I opened the door and motioned for the court officer, a tall, heavy Black man, whose name I later learned was Augustus Argrett, to come into the corridor. He did so, explaining that no one was permitted into the courtroom because the jury was being selected. I asked, really knowing differently, whether it was a proceeding whereby the public was excluded. He said it wasn't but explained that the judge did not want spectators sitting alongside potential jurors. I had noticed when I had entered the large courtroom that there were only a few people there, and I remember comparing the sparse attendance with that at Assata's trials, where supporters not only filled the courtroom but lined the halls waiting for a vacated seat.

I mentioned that there were plenty of spaces in which we could sit and be far removed from any of the potential jurors, leaning against the wall next to the courtroom as I talked, conversational, really quite happy that circumstances beyond my control prevented me from contact, at least on that day, with Bloom. I told him that I was a lawyer and asked him if he would give Bloom a note from me, explaining that I had to arrange a joint conference with him and my client on another case, JoAnne Chesimard.

He looked at my note, written on the back of one of my cards and, without warning, lunged at me. Both his hands tightened around my neck, and he wrestled me backward by the throat to the end of the corridor. The fury of his attack was like a tornado. Sudden and deadly. All I could do was scream. My off-guard, off-balanced movement backward permitted no other response. But my screams were sufficiently compelling to alert every courtroom on the floor, from which court officers poured. Collectively, they pulled him away from me. Once we were separated, to my amazement he again approached me, forced my arms behind my back, handcuffed me, and said, "You're under arrest."

The court officers surrounding me talked to him, trying to dissuade him. But he was adamant, pushing them away with the same force he had used on me, sending one smashing against the wall. He was completely out of control and dangerous to everyone. And the court officers, unsuccessful in their appeals to him and fearful of his massive, unleashed rage, stepped away. I could use many adjectives to describe him and his actions, but none would be adequate.

By the time I was brought from the holding pen in the courthouse to two other police stations, terminating at the 42nd Precinct, chained and shackled to other prisoners, it was about 6:00 P.M. My neck was swollen to three times its normal size and I could not speak. There was a loud ringing in my ears, which persisted over the next several days and which my doctor told me was caused by the pressure exerted on my neck. Both my wrists were sprained, and black and blue colorations surrounded the large lumps on both my arms. My chest was scratched and the jacket to the gray suit I was wearing was ripped, the handle of my pocketbook was torn off, and my briefcase was missing. Fortunately, because I had not planned to do any legal work that day, it contained nothing of significance.

At no time was I told why I was being arrested or the nature of the charges against me. I was refused a telephone call as well as medical attention, which I repeatedly requested. Mug shots and fingerprints were taken at both precincts. My right hand was so swollen and stiff that the police officer at the 42nd acknowledged, as he tried to move my ink-stained fingers across the fingerprint sheet, that the injury was apparent to him. But the complete horror of the drama was still to be unreeled.

I was strip-searched at both precincts, but the search conducted at the 42nd Precinct by Police Officer Canby, a white woman, was the most vicious and most humiliating I had experienced. It was held in the filthiest bathroom I had ever seen in my life, the floor covered with excrement, alive with a nauseating odor. When Canby completed the search, she returned my clothes to me, but before she gave me the slacks to the pants suit I was wearing, she held them up to my face, then dropped them and stepped on them, mashing them into the floor. I looked at her for a long time, knowing I would never forget that face.

Afterward, before I was put into the cell in which I spent the night, every scrap of paper in my wallet and pocketbook was removed and examined by Canby. Her reason was that my several credit cards and other identifications might be stolen. The cell contained an uncovered iron bench and a toilet that could not be flushed from the inside but only by the guards from the outside, and there was no toilet paper. To get some, it was necessary to ask the guards and they refused either to give me toilet paper or to flush the toilet in my cell. No food or water was offered, and no pillows, sheets, or blanket were given to me. At 11:30 PM I was told that I would not be arraigned until the morning and to enjoy my stay.

I spent the night sitting on the edge of the bench in my underwear, the stained slacks distanced as far away from me as I could place them. I was disoriented because, along with the belt to my jacket and shoelaces, they had taken my glasses and I could see little in the gray dimness, not even the filth on the walls and floor of the cell. I gently felt my cricoid cartilage and remembered how easily death is caused by its fracture. Martha Pitts, also arrested with me but not in any way touched by Argrett, was in the cell across from me. She tried to converse, but I couldn't answer. And, anyway, my pain and fury were too great to have communicated even with God.

I smoked cigarette after cigarette, which, strangely enough, had not been taken. By 8:00 A.M, when all the cell doors opened just prior to bringing the prisoners to arraignment court, the entire area was filled with the smothering stench of excrement and unwashed bodies. There were about nine women in addition to Martha and me who had been there for the night. One white woman was courteously given medical attention for a severe headache. My requests had been ignored. There was no water to wash my face or rinse out my mouth. There was no mirror to adjust my hair or in any way smooth out my appearance to be somewhat presentable before the court. Disheveled, my clothes smelling from the residue of the bathroom floor, ragged, exhausted, and in pain, I was taken to the courthouse again in a police van and again shackled to the other prisoners.

It was only in the courtroom that I learned of the charge against me. It was a felony complaint, assault in the second degree, under the following circumstances: "Deponent [Argrett] states that at the above time and location, the defendants together and acting in concert did accost a juror and did scream and attempt to forcibly enter the courtroom and when refused admittance, the defendants did intentionally cause deponent physical injury by struggling with him and kicking him in the shins. Deponent further states necessary force was used to effectuate the defendants' arrest."

I was, of course, surprised that Martha had been arrested along with me. But that the complaint against us was identical defied credulity. I remembered seeing her, as I was being throttled down the hall, leaning against the wall of the corridor in what appeared to me to be a rather casual posture, considering the circumstances. In any event, I represented both her and myself and was barely able to talk to either the assistant district attorney or the judge, both of whom looked at the felony complaint and barely concealed their disbelief. On application of the district attorney, the complaints were dismissed, immediately and without a hearing. I had called Doe that morning and she picked me up from the courthouse and drove me home, where I scrubbed and went to my doctor, who referred me to a throat specialist. I stayed home for week, healing, and did not need a medical evaluation to know that I was indeed lucky to have survived.

Chapter 15

A presiding judge establishes the emotional climate that shapes a trial and influences the attitude of jurors, the conduct of defense and prosecution lawyers, as well as the behavior of defendants. Judge William Thompson was the trial judge in the Brooklyn Supreme Court on September 6, 1975, when the drug dealer kidnapping case began. He was an energetic Black man in his early fifties who power-walked around the courtroom whenever his presence on the bench was not required, his long black robe flying behind him in the wind of his energy. He barked orders to the court attendants and ruled the courtroom with both humor and authority. Throughout the long, four-and-a-half-month trial, his unflagging, upbeat personality charged the atmosphere, filling it with his crisp decisions delivered in the well-defined enunciation of a native New Yorker, and, despite any preconceptions he might have had, he was always evenhanded and legally substantive, whether he ruled for or against the defense. Judge Thompson is now a justice of the Appellate Division of the Supreme Court of the State of New York.

Assata, Melvin Kearney, and Ronald Myers were charged with kidnapping a drug dealer from a bar in the Bedford-Stuyvesant section of Brooklyn, drugging him, and demanding ransom for his release. Ronald Myers was a tall, thin, graceful, somber, employed nineteen-year-old who was as innocent of political activity as he was of the charges. When the indictment was announced in the media, he obligingly surrendered, never doubting that the mistake would be corrected and he would be released. To his disbelief, he was sent to jail for two years before his medium-income family was able to post the enormous bail that had been set. His lawyer, James Carroll, was outraged, and while our relationship was cordial, he clearly preferred to distance himself from Assata and me. I understood the strain under which he was functioning and sympathized with his position. He was a novice lawyer, a friend of Ronald's family, and it was the first time he had been involved in a case of this negative political dimension representing a client whom he believed to be completely innocent. I shared the results of my investigation with him and did not intrude on his well-justified anger. Melvin Kearney, a muscular young Black Panther, full of laughing disregard for the "system," died while attempting to escape from the Brooklyn House of Detention a few days before the trial began, when the rope he used to lower himself from the eighth floor broke. The news was traumatic, staining the beginning proceedings with its tragedy and forcing hurried adjustments in strategy.

In New York state courts, lawyers conduct their voir dire of prospective jurors, and this lengthy trial was equally divided between jury selection and the trial itself. There are several obvious advantages of lawyers conducting the voir dire. A lawyer can flush out suppressed attitudes and biases by instant follow-up questions rather than waiting for the judge to ask them after he or she completes the first interrogatories. The tone of a lawyer is completely different from that of a judge, particularly a prosecution-oriented one who will try to rehabilitate a juror's bias or already established opinion. Additionally, a trial lawyer is able to respond to a juror's mood swings, reactions to the defendant, expressions, nervousness, or efforts to control animosity, which the intervening role of the judge dilutes. So I was pleased, at last, to be able to directly speak to jurors, to ask them questions that reflected our defense strategy and also exposed the weakness of the prosecutor's case, thereby preparing the chosen jurors for the evidence to follow.

My investigation revealed several surprises: the bar in which the kidnapping allegedly occurred was not owned by the main witness for the prosecution, was operating illegally, and was managed by her boyfriend, the self-described kidnapped drug dealer, who had a long criminal record. His Bureau of Criminal Investigation sheet reported convictions but no sentences, a red flag to the possibility that he had cooperated with the police or the FBI. In light of the just released Church Committee COINTELPRO report, I suspected that he was either a paid informant or an actual agent for the FBI and, to introduce this element into the consciousness of the jurors, I asked each of them whether they could give the same degree of credibility to him as to any other witness were it revealed that he was an FBI informant. It was the prosecutor's heated objection to this question, stating that there was nothing to indicate an FBI relationship with any of the prosecution's witnesses, that alerted the jurors to the significance of such a link. The objection was overruled, and by the end of the voir dire the jurors chosen, each of whom had been seated in either the courtroom or in the jury box during the voir dire of other prospective jurors, had heard this question over and over again and were well aware that this malevolent possibility could arise during the trial. When it did, the prosecutor was trapped by his protests and appeared to have been intentionally concealing information that he was legally obligated to reveal to the defense once the witness was put on the stand. Except in the case of an affirmative defense, such as insanity, alibi, or self-defense (when the defendant has the burden of proof and is compelled to take the stand), the defense must shred the prosecution's case to prevent him from establishing guilt beyond a reasonable doubt through either cross-examination or introduction of evidence to rebut the prosecution witnesses.

Our motion for Assata to act as co-counsel was granted, and, elegant in a long, colorful African dress, she delivered the opening statement, outlining the philosophy of the BLA and its response to the injustices dealt to Black Americans and asking the jury to judge her solely on the issue of guilt or innocence of this particular crime and not by her admitted association with the BLA. The testimony of the bar owner that she was licensed by the State Liquor Authority and the Alcoholic Beverages Commission to operate the bar was discredited by subpoenaed records and witnesses from both agencies, which revealed that she had never been issued a liquor license, and by the real owner of the bar, who testified that he did not know her and denied giving her permission to operate the bar, which he said he had closed.

Subpoenaed Kings County Hospital records of the drug dealer, who testified that he had struggled out of hand and leg cuffs and made his way to the emergency ward to have his stomach pumped, proved not only that his body contained no drugs except a trace of cocaine but also that when he entered the hospital he did not report he had been kidnapped. And under Carroll's cross-examination, the drug dealer admitted that he was in fact a paid FBI informant, but he invoked his Fifth

Amendment right and refused to testify further. And when his identification of Assata as being present in the bar became less than certain, the prosecutor called a cross-eyed witness with obviously defective vision to testify that he had seen Assata in the bar on numerous occasions, including the night of the kidnapping; to buttress his identification, he said that she had spent several weekends at his house. I could not resist asking him a ridiculously dramatic but dangerous question most frequently interjected into B movie criminal trials: "What is the color of her eyes?" I ended my cross-examination when he said he didn't know.

Desperate by now, the prosecutor moved to admit into evidence all of the weapons recovered on the New Jersey Turnpike that had been introduced at Sundiata's trial as well as other papers and documents found in the Pontiac that had not been introduced into evidence. A handwritten note demanding $25,000 ransom, signed "Black Liberation Army," had allegedly been left at the bar, and I had fully expected a pretrial motion for samples of Assata's and Ronald's handwriting to be taken. None had been made, and I supposed that the prosecution intended to make a comparison of the writing on the note with some handwritten materials that had been found in the trunk of the Pontiac. These items were clearly inadmissible at this juncture of the trial without proven connections to either Assata or Ronald, and both motions were denied. I made the briefest summation of my career and the jury took just eight hours to return a verdict of not guilty.

The trial ended on December 16, 1975, and Assata was ordered to proceed to trial in the Queens bank robbery case on January 6, 1976, before the U.S. District Court for the Eastern District. This was the case in which Judge Mishler had been removed after ordering the vicious photographing session of Assata by U.S. marshals. By now, not only my own resources but those of Doris and Doe, who had amply supplemented my efforts, had dwindled, and I had been forced to accept a few cases simply to pay my bills. One trial had been postponed for the umpteenth time, and once Assata's Brooklyn trial ended, I was directed to begin my other trial immediately. When Jack Weinstein, the judge who had replaced Mishler, refused to grant an adjournment of the Queens bank robbery case, it was necessary for Assata to find another lawyer.

Stanley Cohen was recommended by one of the defense committees who had visited Assata while she was on Rikers Island, and Afeni Shakur, a defense committee member and a professional paralegal, was given permission to sit at counsel table as Cohen's legal assistant. Unlike Mishler, Weinstein was a thoughtful judge who voiced no anticipation that Assata would disrupt the court as Mishler had predicted and was impervious to her political associations. He expressed judicial concern about the violation of her constitutional rights when the photos that had been taken at Mishler's orders were shown to him, and he conducted the trial with the dignity and legally balanced acumen that anyone charged with a crime in this society has the constitutional right to expect. He repeated his impartiality, stating, "My sole interest is to see that the case is fairly tried."

The evidence linking Assata to the crime was the bank surveillance photographs, the identifications made by the bank tellers at the time of the robbery, and Andrew Jackson's statement that Assata was a participant, made at the time he pleaded guilty to the indictment in exchange for a favorable sentence. Stanley Cohen's first motion was to ask for a subpoena for Jackson to testify at the trial, advising Weinstein that he had spoken to Jackson a few days before the trial began and that Jackson had recanted his statement, alleging that he had been coerced into making it by the assistant U.S. attorney, who had refused to accept his plea unless he implicated Assata. But Stanley's master stroke was to also subpoena Robert Bloom, Jackson's attorney, who was present along with the assistant U.S. attorney at the time Jackson pleaded, to testify about the conditions under which the plea had been given. Once entered into the record, the plea bargain had been sealed, hidden from the defense, and would not have been disclosed until after Jackson's trial testimony. Stanley further advised Weinstein that Jackson would also testify that Assata was innocent of having taken part in the bank robbery. Stunned that the sealed conditions of the plea had been discovered and faced with Stanley's threat to publicly expose his complicity in framing Assata, Bloom quickly admitted to Weinstein that Jackson had been forced into making the plea but asked that he be permitted to stipulate that fact on the record rather than testify about it in open court before the jury, claiming that he planned to go on vacation to Mexico and California the next day. Weinstein nevertheless ordered him to remain in the state and to be available to the defense as its witness. Bloom's testimony was not required, however, because Jackson refused to take the stand against Assata and his statement became a nonissue.

The prosecution's repeated efforts to introduce the "Mishler photos" were rejected by Weinstein, who said, "I have told you, you may not use that photograph while it shows all those hands and people holding the defendant down." The prosecutor's alleged purpose in displaying the photos to the jury was to prove that Assata had resisted the comparison poses; her avoidance, he would allege, inferred guilt. Assata countered in her opening statement to the jury that she had refused to be forcibly posed or to have her appearance artificially altered to resemble a bank robber and that she was innocent of the charges.

The bank employees present during the robbery who had identified Assata as a participant to the FBI admitted that the only photo they had been shown was a mug shot with the words "New York Police" printed across her chest and the Bureau of Criminal Investigation serial numbers, an illegally suggestive procedure designed to classify her as a criminal. It was a most potent device when none of the other photos were so defiled. Other tellers could not identify Assata, and the prosecution's main witness, the head teller who had been specially trained to identify bank robbers, after stating he was positive that Assata was the bank robber, admitted, under Stanley's caustic, penetrating, and persistent cross-examination, that she "resembled" the bank robber. The trial transcript records the following questions and answers.

Stanley: Have you ever been told that you resemble someone on TV?

Teller: Yes.

Stanley: Whom have you been told you resemble?

Teller: Robert Stack.

Stanley: Are you Robert Stack?

Teller: No.

Devastated, the teller finally answered "yes" to Stanley's question "So, in all fairness, you would have to say the possibility exists that you might be mistaken?" At which point Stanley said, "Thank you. I have no further questions."

Assata was acquitted on January 16, 1976, after the prosecution's FBI photographic expert admitted that, even after using the most recently developed computer comparison equipment, he could not prove that the person in the surveillance photo was Assata. And on that same day, Assata was returned to the state of New Jersey to stand trial for the third time in the turnpike case.

Chapter 16

When prosecutors in New Jersey and New York agreed to force Assata to stand trial on all of the indictments outstanding against her in New York before she was returned to New Jersey, they envisioned her return as a convicted felon, not a winner in every case she faced. And now New Jersey was restored as the most viable forum for conviction.

Assata was again interned in the Middlesex County jail basement, and again the National Conference of Black Lawyers filed a federal court action to have her removed. The banning of all visitors except attorneys and the weekly half-hour visit for her family, which now included Kakuya, was reinstated, and I visited her at least three times a week, bringing her the math books she requested to keep her mind alert. She always smiled when she saw me, but sometimes the effort she made was too painful for me to watch. Immaculately clean, from her fingernails to her well-groomed hair, she walked up the stairs from the basement holding her head high, her back straight, giving no appearance of submission.

We small-talked about the family, about the baby, about the federal action brought to release her from solitary confinement, about nothing in particular, and we played tic-tac-toe and did crossword puzzles together. I became increasingly concerned about her obvious despair that she would not be acquitted in this trial, which grew as significantly as her color paled from a robust brown to yellow. I didn't share my feelings with her mother or with anyone else, for that matter. It was her private war and I just did all I could to provide a little relief, continuing to work on the legal actions to release her. She wrote a poem for me on my birthday which I think accurately describes our visits:

WORDS TO ANTY
During these crazy times
when madness holds us in its grip
and teases us with freedom,

During these sorry times,
when tears are not shed
because we need them
to keep on getting up.

During this time,
when words are not worth too much,
we talk in whispers
though secrets long have fled.
And spend our words
on tender bickering.
Then, impatiently go on
to conversations we have had before

During this time, when words
are flimsy hopes,
or empty lies
surrounding empty deeds,
but, in a tragic way, now,
our words are all we have.

So let me tell you now.
i love you.

Happy Birthday.
Keep on getting up.

That was the extent of her hope as the trial approached. Theodore Appleby had replaced John Bachman as the trial judge, and his pit bull determination to succeed where other jurisdictions had failed was reminiscent of Gagliardi and Mishler and as hypocritical as the patriotic slogans used by the gang of white students in 1976 who, opposed to busing, stabbed Black people on the streets of Boston with the staffs of American flags. But Appleby and Edward Barone, the newly assigned prosecutor, were more than adequately aided by the disarray of the defense lawyers. On February 14, 1976, during pretrial preparations, Raymond Brown's unanticipated motion to be relieved as New Jersey counsel had been granted. I tried to absorb the panic his absence created by remembering that Bachman had forced him to appear every day in Sundiata's trial, along with Sundiata's own lawyer, Charlie McKinney. And now, to add the months of preparation and trial appearances to the monetary sacrifice he had already made was an unreasonable expectation.

Stuart Ball, a rich, young white labor lawyer, replaced Brown as New Jersey counsel and moved to admit to the case Stanley Cohen, Assata's lawyer in the Queens bank robbery case, whom he knew. Ball's first motion was to ask the court to overturn the 1973 order changing the venue from Middlesex County to Morris County. I so vehemently voiced my objection to this unilateral action that he requested that he be relieved from the case after the court gladly granted the motion. His motion to withdraw was denied, and Lawrence Stern, another young white lawyer from New York who had limited experience with some of the BLA cases, joined the defense team along with Lewis Meyers, a member of NCBL from Mississippi who had participated in the federal civil suit to transfer Assata from the Middlesex County jail. Motions were made and motions were denied. Among the denials, the most prejudicial, as they affected our right to a fair trial, were the one asking for a free daily copy of the trial transcripts, which were automatically granted to all indigent defendants and for which Assata was eligible, and the motion that court not be held on Fridays to respect Muslim religious practice, also automatically granted in most jurisdictions. Both those motions had been ordered in the earlier part of the trial.

Then Stanley Cohen mysteriously died in August 1976. The circumstances of his death and its cause have not been determined to this day. Upon his death, the New York City Police Department removed all legal materials relating to Assata's case from both his home and his office. I had to file several demands for their return from the property clerk's office, where they had been impounded, and finally had to obtain a court order before they were released to me. Even so, what I received was of no value. The question about what material was withheld or destroyed still remains unanswered.

After Stanley's death, Assata insisted on adding another lawyer, buying into the others' argument that the days when major criminal trials were conducted by only one or two lawyers were over. Therefore, I asked Bill Kunstler to join us. His first act, while the appeal seeking Assata's transfer from confinement at Middlesex County jail was still pending, was to talk to Sheriff DeMarino and then hold a press conference to express his pleasure and satisfaction with the jail because "it is so conveniently located near the courthouse." It was but another manifestation of the absence of coordination among the members of the defense team and of a strange unwillingness of everyone involved to accept the fact that this trial had a history. Except for Bill and me, there were no experienced criminal trial lawyers on the "team," and the clashes between the others and me were serious.

For the second time in my legal career I became aware of the disdain with which men perceive women in competitive arenas, the first having been at NYU, where I was only one of a few female law professors. It was not that I was unaware of sexism, but I had always been more aware of racism, and my ability to cope with that was second nature. I was also a little unprepared because, since childhood, my best friends and closest associates had been male. I must admit I was not tactful in my comments to the other lawyers, but tact is not my strongest characteristic under any circumstances. Among the many decisions they made that I disagreed with was their plan for Assata to take the stand to relate the events of that night on the turnpike, even though I understood it was a calculated risk that relied heavily on her proven ability to be persuasive before a jury. The problem as I saw it, however, was that, first, Assata had never been subjected to cross-examination and, second, she had been living for more than a year in solitary confinement. I knew the trauma she had suffered, and I wondered if she could circumnavigate the prosecution's traps, despite her steel will to do so. But the other defense lawyers seemed to be oblivious to any effects this devastating experience might have. They met with Assata every day and criticized me for not participating in the conferences, even though I explained that when I left New Jersey I had to travel to the Bronx to spend the night with Doris, who had just undergone a serious gallbladder operation, and to care for Kakuya. They sought Assata's legal opinion in developing a trial strategy, entirely discounting the one that had been developed by Ray, Charlie, and me in 1973. It was as if this was the first time the case was being tried, and Sundiata, sentenced to life imprisonment plus thirty years, had been convicted of a different crime. (Sundiata was first sentenced to the newly created Management Control Unit at Trenton State Prison and then was transferred, under the Interstate Compact Act, to the highest-security federal prison in the United States at Marion, Illinois, for eight years, longer than any other prisoner. There he was exposed to tuberculosis before being transferred in July 1987 to Leavenworth, Kansas, where he remains.) While Assata was a political tactician par excellence and was certainly helpful in that regard, she was hardly a legal tactician. I saw the strain as she rose to each occasion, wielding an almost hypnotic influence over the lawyers and, at the same time, needing answers herself. She became weary of them, weary of the trial, and weary of all the futile efforts. Weary, but driven to go on.

The team had distributed trial assignments to each member and had decided that I would not make the opening statement, cross-examine Trooper Harper, conduct Assata's direct examination, or sum up. I watched their infighting for center stage with amazement and contempt, mixed with horrified apprehension when I learned that the lawyer who would directly examine Assata had never before performed this delicate, intricate form of questioning, which required quite different skills from those needed for cross-examination of a prosecutor's witness. Worse, he didn't even seem to understand the difference. Despite my opposition to Assata's taking the stand at all, I knew at least that if I examined her there would be high drama, if for no other reason than our contrasting personalities and well-publicized family relationship. And, of course, I had been preparing my cross-examination of Harper for four years and was sick at the lost opportunity. Not that anything any of us did or did not do would have affected the outcome of the trial.

But there was a significant and critical difference between my strategy and that of the rest of the team: I wanted to attack every vulnerable witness mercilessly, to exploit every contradiction, expose every lie he or she had told in every previous document or sworn testimony, including that given in Sundiata's trial, and to place every objection on the record in preparation for the appeal of the verdict, which I had no doubt would be guilty. The "team," on the other hand, believed they could win despite the bias and hostility of the jurors, the judge, and the county. They approached the trial as if they could assuage this Middlesex County jury, which Appleby had ordered sequestered for the duration of the trial, by shortening the length of the trial and, therefore, the length of their confinement by shortening the cross-examination of the prosecution's witnesses. They believed that they would thus extract impartiality from the deeply entrenched prejudices of the jury and the court.

Appleby's vindictiveness would not be appeased. When Bill Kunstler appeared before a group of Rutgers University students on October 21, 1976, and spoke about the need for all students, as well as all citizens, to be alert to injustices prevalent in the legal system, to participate in Assata's trial by their courtroom attendance, and to protest Assata's "violent jail conditions," Appleby issued an order for Bill to show cause why he should not be removed from the case, citing violation of the New Jersey canon of ethics and his own gag order. During the two-week hearing held in December 1976, just a few weeks before the trial was to begin, Appleby abruptly abandoned his order. Bill had testified, "I consider I have done absolutely nothing wrong. I did say I was going to refrain from public utterance that could interfere with the administration of justice and I adhere to that," adding, "I will say absolutely nothing about this case under any circumstances. Her Sixth Amendment rights to counsel are more important than my First Amendment rights to free speech." Appleby said that he believed in Assata's right to counsel of her choice and that the necessity to avoid further delay outweighed Kunstler's "questionable behavior," adding, "He may be guilty of the acts, but a fair trial has not been prejudiced." Bill had been represented at the show-cause hearing by Morton Stavis, a Newark, New Jersey, civil rights lawyer associated with the Center for Constitutional Rights, but the entire defense team had been engulfed in the proceedings and had been effectively sidetracked.

Undaunted, Bill filed a motion for Appleby's removal in January 1977 when he learned that Lawrence Blasi, a member of the prosecutor's investigation staff, had attended an event sponsored by Cheryl Clarke, a poet and member of the JoAnne Chesimard Defense Fund. The event, called "An Evening of Poetry," was held at the Washington Square United Methodist Church on January 4, 1977. Harry Belafonte was the host, New York Supreme Court Judge Bruce Wright was the keynote speaker, and poets Audre Lorde, June Jordan, and Susan Sherman read their poetry, while I read Assata's. Blasi had appeared as a witness against Bill at the hearing aimed at his removal from the case and was the only one who had lied about Bill's Rutgers

University speech, which formed the basis for Appleby's charge of ethics violations. He had testified that Bill had discussed Assata's innocence, which not only was untrue but was refuted by the testimony of two reporters who were present and had taken verbatim notes. So when Appleby directed Blasi to appear at the poetry reading, Bill was apoplectic and charged the judge with acting in conspiracy with the prosecutor, stating, "The communications between the judge and prosecutorial authorities are violative of the spirit of fair play in American courtrooms." In his oral argument for Appleby's removal, Bill told him, "There is nothing more sacred than the defendant's right to an impartial judge. I think you will say you are impartial, but if you believe you are not, you ought to step down and not continue a charade where you have hostile attitudes toward the defendant and her counsel." Appleby retorted that the best evidence of his impartiality was the fact that Bill still remained in the trial, and he refused to disqualify himself.

Appleby's relentless persecution of the defense team and the National Jury Project, whom he accused of tampering with prospective jurors as they conducted their survey of attitudes in the county, extended beyond the courtroom. During jury selection, Lennox Hinds, not a member of the defense team, held a press conference on January 20, 1977, protesting Appleby's decisions and the atmosphere of partiality, unfairness, and bias he projected. Lennox accurately described the trial as a "travesty," adding that Appleby "does not have the judicial temperament or racial sensitivity to sit as an impartial judge," that "it was only after the trial began that we began to have fears that what we are seeing is a legalized lynching," and that Appleby was asking prospective jurors self-serving questions that were leading to the "creation of a hangman's court." And he stated, "It will be a kangaroo court unless the judge recuses [removes] himself," and a "kangaroo court means a guilty verdict."

Appleby's thunderous reaction to Lennox's statements was not officially launched until the end of the trial, when he prodded the Middlesex County Ethics Committee to initiate disciplinary actions against Lennox, claiming he had violated the canon of ethics and Appleby's gag order. However, since Lennox was not one of the trial lawyers, he was not bound by the gag rule. It was only because the Garden State Bar Association, the New Jersey Association of Black Women Lawyers, and the NCBL brought federal action to stop the disbarment proceedings that Hinds was finally vindicated and his license to practice law preserved.

During jury selection, while the defense had five remaining peremptory challenges and there were still five jurors to be chosen, I took a day off to nurse the cold, sore throat, and fever I had suffered all week. I so advised the others the day before, adding that given the fact that more jurors would be excused for cause and by our exercise of our remaining peremptory challenges, jury selection would continue for at least two more days before the final panel would be chosen. At one o'clock I received a telephone call from a member of the defense committee advising me that the jury had been selected that morning, that the jury box had been filled, and that opening statements would begin that afternoon. I raced to the courtroom, knowing I was too late to change anything. The explanation of the other lawyers was that the results of the field survey conducted by the National Jury Project had ascertained that all of the remaining jurors held the same degree of prejudice, so it didn't matter which ones were chosen. I not so patiently reminded them that a critical argument for reversal of a conviction on appeal had been destroyed. When the defense challenges a juror for cause (for example, for bias) and the court refuses to exclude the juror, the defense must use a peremptory challenge. The typical defense strategy is to use all of the peremptory challenges and then move for additional ones. If that motion is denied and if, on appeal, it is clearly shown in the record that biased jurors were seated, there are possible grounds for reversal of the ultimate verdict. But if the defense puts its satisfaction with the jury on the record, as it is required to do before the entire panel is sworn in, and has not used all of its peremptory challenges or has failed to move for additional ones, the argument cannot be made on appeal that the defendant was precluded from selecting a fair and impartial jury. But that was only one of the many irreversible mistakes the team had made, and Assata went to trial with a jury consisting of five unchallenged jurors who were either relatives or close personal friends of state troopers or of state law enforcement officers.

After Barone made his opening statement to the jury and Lewis Meyers opened for the defense, the prosecution put Captain James Challendar on the stand as its first witness. He had been in charge of operating the Magnesinc tapes on the night of the shoot-out, and I had successfully convinced the team that

I was best qualified to cross-examine any witness who had been involved in any way with the turnpike conversations recorded on the Magnesinc tape as well as the Baginski tapes and the station bible, even though the crucifixion I had planned for Harper was not to be.

I began my cross-examination of Challendar with an innocent, inquiring tone, establishing the authenticity of the tape and his identification of each voice recorded on it. I then asked him about the procedures used by troopers on the turnpike when they made stops and under what circumstances more than one trooper was ordered to assist in making a stop for a minor traffic violation. I gradually directed his attention to the tape, which contained Palentchar's voice. Just after he admitted that Palentchar's response of "Meet you at the pass, partner" was "unusual," "unfortunate," and one he "would not have made," and just as he had reached the stuttering stage in his effort to avoid the clear implication of those words—that a gunfight had been anticipated—the other defense lawyers slipped notes under my hand. I glanced at them and read, "You've crossed enough." "You're antagonizing the jury." "This isn't Brooklyn." "Shut up and sit down." It was at that point, as I struggled to resume my cross-examination with some degree of composure, that I made the decision to withdraw from the case. Better to do so now, at the beginning of the trial, and use my absence from their weighty mistakes to free myself to point them out on appeal. This time Assata understood, and I read about the unfolding travesty in the newspapers.

On March 25, 1977, Assata was convicted and sentenced to life imprisonment, but Appleby's hunger for retribution had not yet been satisfied, and on April 25 he added thirty-three years to her sentence for contempt of court because she refused to rise when he entered the courtroom. He plunged to the depth of his hatred by directing that she be removed from the Clinton Correctional Institution for Women, to which she had been sentenced after the jury verdict, and ordered her placed in solitary confinement in the Yardville State Prison, an all-male institution in which a female prisoner had never been incarcerated. I filed an appeal from the conviction and, once again, NCBL, PROD, and I filed an action in federal court protesting the Yardville sentence. The District Court dismissed the suit, and while the appeal was pending New Jersey once again transported

Assata back to the state of New York to stand trial for the two remaining indictments against her: the Hilton Hotel case and the murder of the Brooklyn drug dealer. Motions to dismiss these ancient cases, because the failure to bring them to trial sooner had denied her the statutory right to a speedy trial, were granted, the last occurring on March 24, 1978.

In the interim, the federal appellate court in New Jersey reversed the U.S. District Court, ruling that "any confinement of plaintiff at Yardville Correctional Facility could only be for a very temporary period, a matter of days, without jeopardizing plaintiff's constitutional rights." But by then New Jersey had consolidated its plan to transfer Assata directly from New York to the federal prison for women in Alderson, West Virginia, by implementing the Interstate Corrections Compact Act of 1973, as soon as the New York cases terminated. With the able assistance of Jonathan Lubell, I filed an action in the U.S. District Court for the Southern District of New York asking for an injunction preventing her removal to the state of West Virginia on the grounds that the great distance between it and the residence of her appeal lawyer, the New Jersey public defender's office (who thereafter appointed me its representative to prosecute her appeal), stripped her of the fundamental right of effective counsel and access to the courts and thereby deprived her of her right to assist in the preparation of her appeal.

William E. Norris, the deputy public defender responsible for the operation and functioning of the appellate section of the public defender's office, joined in my motion.

The motion was also supported with an affidavit by Dr. Mutulu Shakur, director of the National Task Force on COINTELPRO Litigation and Research.

The New York federal court refused to grant the injunction and Assata was transferred to Yardville for the transfer hearings, held on April 3 and 4, 1978. The Interstate Corrections Compact rules did not allow an inmate to be represented by a lawyer at the hearings, and Assata reluctantly acted as her own lawyer, conferring with me frequently as I sat just outside the closed doors of the hearing room. The decision of the New Jersey Corrections Department to transfer her to the federal correctional facility at Alderson, West Virginia, was appealed and affirmed. Shortly thereafter she was convoyed to the maximum-security unit at Alderson and was housed with Nazi Aryan Organization members who threatened her life on a daily basis—until one meaning-ful confrontation when she permanently dissuaded them from further efforts, advising them that "if someone's mother was going to cry, it wasn't going to be mine."

When Assata told me that the federal prison officials were planning to remove her to an even more remote federal prison in the Virgin Islands rather than to place her in general population once the maximum-security unit had been declared unconstitu-tional, I filed an injunction suit in the West Virginia federal court. Whether this action forced the United States Bureau of Prisons and the New Jersey corrections officials to reconsider another transfer, I have no way of knowing. But within days, on February 20, 1979, Assata was returned to New Jersey and placed in the maximum-security unit at Clinton Correctional Institution for Women.

In the meantime, I was feverishly trying to perfect her appeal. Every roadblock, every delay, every excuse was given by the prosecutor to withhold the trial transcripts and to prevent me from inspecting evidence he had admitted during the trial and still had in his possession. The clerk's office, where all motions are filed and docket sheets of the course of the trial are maintained, had misplaced most of the materials relating to the trial, so I was forced to attempt to obtain copies of motions and related orders from the defense team, none of whom could locate them. At the end of a trial all exhibits that have been admitted into evidence by either side are returned to them. Missing was the critically important four pages of the station bible, a defense exhibit, and while someone on the defense team should have had a copy, which I could have used to make my appellate point, the original entries were part of the permanent log maintained by the state police. The police refused to permit me to see the log, let alone photocopy the relevant pages, and the prosecutor's office claimed ignorance of their existence. After all of my many persistent efforts failed, I appealed to the Office of the Public Defender, documenting my attempts to obtain the transcripts and items of evidence. That office responded with a motion before the Superior Court of New Jersey, Appellate Division, asking the court to order that the transcripts be produced. Mark D. Sperber, assistant deputy public defender in the appellate section of the office (headed by Stanley Van Ness, who had worked closely with me during this period and without whose support and invaluable assistance I would have gone berserk), itemized in his affidavit each trial transcript that had been withheld. Additionally, I did receive four transcripts with critical pages missing. Mark's motion pointed out that without the use of these pages Assata's rights to due process were being violated. Mark also said that Louis Finkel, the supervisor of court reporters in Middlesex County, had told him that he doubted whether anything further could be done to recover the missing material.

The appeal was in this incomplete, compromised, and sabotaged state on November 2, 1979, a day celebrated in the Black community as Black Solidarity Day, when the 3:30 P.M. news flash crackled over the radio and interrupted TV programs: Assata had escaped from the Clinton Correctional Institution for Women and a nationwide hunt for her was under way.

Part III

Chapter 17

My first reaction of disbelief mingled with a sustained hot flash of exultation when I heard the news. How was it possible for anyone to escape from South Hall, the maximum-security unit of Clinton Correctional Institution for Women, isolated from the other buildings in the five-hundred-acre complex and surrounded by a fifteen-foot chain link fence topped with two feet of barbed wire? I reconstructed my many visits there and visualized the locked gates separating the grounds from the long, winding road in from the highway; the checkpoint registration shed where identifications were compared with lists of approved visitors and where one's person and possessions were searched; the armed guards who drove the prison van from the checkpoint to South Hall; the first electronically operated door the accompanying guard directed be opened; the first room entered, separated from the visiting room by another electronically operated door; the visitors' room where, behind a large, completely enclosed bulletproof bubble, the guard who operated all of the electrical equipment was stationed; the steel door located behind the guard facing the entrance to the area from which the inmates entered the room. I repeated to myself, How was it possible? And I could find no more answers than the New Jersey corrections officials could.

I didn't leave my house for the next week except to go to the store for the daily papers, which gave only sketchy accounts of what, I was amused to read, they called Assata's "liberation." The November 4 *New York Times* reported the official version of the escape as provided by James V. Stabile, a spokesperson for the Department of Corrections:

> One man arrived first and checked through the registration building. He was not searched; he carried two handguns, apparently .45 caliber. He was driven in the van to South Hall by a guard, who then escorted him through the chain-link fence and the main door. Then he was ushered through

another locked metal door that opens into the visiting room. That door is operated electronically by a guard in a glass booth.

Shortly afterwards, the two other men arrived at the main gate, cleared the registration building, again without being searched, and were driven to South Hall by the same guard who had escorted the first visitor. He took the two men through the fence's locked gate.

Upon reaching the metal door, one of the two men drew a pistol and seized the man who was escorting them. Simultaneously, the man who had been talking with Miss Chesimard came up to the glass booth, drew two pistols and pointed them at the woman on guard there.

She complied with an order to open the metal door. Miss Chesimard and the three men took the two guards as hostages. Miss Chesimard, a Muslim who also goes by the name of Assata Shakur, and the three men transferred to two cars after driving the commandeered van across a hilly field. The field separates the grounds of the prison and a nearby state school for the mentally retarded. The getaway cars had been in the school parking lot.

The Newark, New Jersey, *Star-Ledger* gave a slightly different version of Stabile's remarks. The paper reported that when the two men entered the prison with the male guard driving the van, "Chesimard and her first visitor had their guns trained on a female guard in a bullet proof control booth. Although the guard was supposed to have remained in the booth, which operates the unit's doors, she came out when ordered to. Chesimard and the others handcuffed the guards and herded them into the jail van for a ride to a parking lot at an adjacent school. There they piled into two cars, a blue Lincoln and a blue compact car, either a Comet or a Maverick. Chesimard got into the smaller car which bore New Jersey license plates. The guards were left in the van unharmed."

On November 3, the FBI issued a warrant for Assata on charges of illegal flight after it was assumed she had left the state of New Jersey, eluding helicopters, roadblocks leading to bridges and tunnels, airports, bus terminals, and other nonvehicular routes of travel. A white woman in her early twenties was believed to have been the driver of one of the cars, and sketches of her and the three Black men based on the descriptions provided by the guards were published, along with the names the men had used: Dingus Obedele, Kweli Olugbala, and Jerri Patterson. Officials admitted that "the names were most likely fictitious" and that the addresses they had on file for them proved to be vacant lots or nonexistent, adding that they were nevertheless positive the men were members of the Black Liberation Army. Criticism of the "inadequate security" at the prison mounted, investigations were demanded, and state prison officials considered reorganizing security to include tank traps of the Normandy beachhead type. The *Star-Ledger*'s editorial proclaimed, "Joanne Chesimard's escape from the Clinton Reformatory is more than an embarrassment. It's a disgrace." Corrections Commissioner William Fauver glumly remarked, "I'm not sure we're going to make any changes. I'm not sure any changes could stop something like that escape." According to the *Courier-News,* a central New Jersey paper, police said, "No shots were fired and no one was injured in the escape," which "went so smoothly and quietly that other corrections officers inside the maximum security building said they were not aware of any problem until the alarm was sounded," and state police and prison authorities called the escape "well-planned and arranged . . . with obvious knowledge of the area." Clinton Pagano, state police superintendent, predicted, "We will recapture Joanne Chesimard and return her to the place of 'rescue,' whatever effort that takes. You can take that to the bank."

I searched my memory for a scintilla of indication that Assata had been planning to escape. I suppose I was given a clue to her ultimate intentions during the week in the spring of 1979 when she was returned from Alderson to Yardville to aid in the preparation of her appeal. I remembered what she said when she put on a necklace I had given both her and Kakuya with a subway token as a pendant: "You can never tell. I just might need this one day."

And again, I might have sensed a hint on my last visit to her at Clinton two weeks before November 2. Usually I notified the prison of the date of my visit and called the local cab company to wait for me at the station, since there was no bus to the prison. On this day no cab was waiting, and when I called the company's office I could get no information about either why a cab was not there or when one would be available. The train station was a considerable distance from the jail and I almost decided to return to New York. I was tired from working on the appeal and

I estimated that by the time I walked to the prison half the visiting time would have expired. But, for whatever reason, I was determined to see Assata. The sun was hot and my briefcase heavy, and by the time I had climbed the hill leading from the highway to the checkpoint, I was exhausted. Perspiring but pleased at my endurance, I watched Assata come through the sliding doors and greet me indifferently, barely giving me a glance. I wondered what was wrong and didn't open my briefcase as I usually did. And the visit, the last time I was to see her for five years, was almost a disaster as I fought to control my anger. I noticed that during our entire conversation she was strangely preoccupied, talking to me while she looked through the glass partition to the small room on the other side where the soda machines were. We had spent many times together, especially in Middlesex County jail, really saying little, communicating with each other in acquiescent silence. But this was preoccupation, not reflection. She was alert, making purposeful observations, looking at the inner door to the main dormitory behind the bubble, watching each time the door opened to let in or out a messenger or another corrections officer.

I opened my briefcase finally and spread out the notes I had made for her on the progress of the appeal, but she never looked at them. I knew that she believed her food was being poisoned and I had promised to try to conduct an investigation to determine the source. Was she impatient because I had no results to report? I also knew that she had been working as a case aide, a social service position in which she helped inmates with their problems, and sometimes she had asked me to provide minor services for them that they weren't able to do themselves. Was there an overwhelming problem that was bothering her? While Assata was always gracious and pleasant to visitors who came to see her, whether at Alderson or Rikers or Clinton, genuinely pleased and humbled that they would suffer the searches and other personal annoyances necessary to talk to her for an hour or so, she rarely hesitated to communicate her dissatisfactions, pain, or apprehensions to me. I was at least pleased that she had been on a daily exercise regimen and looked fit and healthy.

So I waited for what I believed to be a deeply despondent mood to change. As I reflect now, she was absorbed in measured calculations during the only opportunity she had for them—visiting time. But I should have suspected something when she suddenly held up her arms and put them around me and, just before I embraced her, let large tears fill her eyes and spill silently down her face. Not ever, in the six years of prison, had she cried in my presence. Not even once. We held each other for a long time before the guard told me I had to leave. I was deeply troubled, unable to explain it and not aware that the tears were caused by her anticipation of a very long separation from her child and her family. Or in anticipation of her death while attempting to escape. I blessed each day of her freedom and prepared myself for her death, if she were captured; but death outside of prison walls, somehow, was bearable.

Assata had repeatedly told Kakuya that one day she would be free and that the first thing she would do would be to come to her. So each time the telephone rang or a knock sounded on the door, Kakuya, then five, knew it must be her mother. She flew to the door to answer it, wriggling away from Doris's grasp. She positioned herself near the telephone to grab it before Doris when it rang. And she rejected all of the reasons we gave her that her mother was now in danger and would not expose her to it by coming to the house. As far as Kakuya was concerned, Mommy Assata would come. She had promised.

Except for two occasions, at Christmas, Assata had seen Kakuya only through a glass partition that separated inmates from visitors on Rikers Island. The visits at Middlesex County jail were held in a room on the first floor that was too small for any activity except for Assata to hold Kakuya on her lap, sing freedom songs to her that she had composed, and play impromptu games. Kakuya was always impatient during the wait to see her mother and would crawl across the cement floor to the head of the circular staircase, peering down, angry, bewildered, and squealing in anticipation of her mother's emergence at the bottom of the staircase.

From the beginning, Kakuya had recognized the special meaning of this person, and her gurgles of attempted communication changed to long child-adult conversations during the daily phone calls Assata made during her second stay at Rikers, from June 1977 to May 1978. She also knew that the beautiful, brightly colored blankets that covered her bed and her dolls' bed, as well as the many dresses and coats she wore, were knitted for her by her mother. Assata's paintings and handmade birthday cards decorated Kakuya's room, and a pillowcase on which

Assata had embroidered the words "Break De Chains" was never moved from its special place on her bed.

The week immediately following Assata's escape was a reign of terror for Doris. First, she didn't believe that Assata had really escaped because her assessment was that it was impossible. She theorized that the FBI or some other police agency had murdered Assata and had publicized the escape as a cover-up. Almost destroyed by this theory, she was not prepared for the actions of the Terrorism-Fugitive Squad of the FBI, which began the day after the escape and continued over the next week. On November 3, members of the squad filled the corridor of her apartment, heavily armed, and pounded on her door with such force that Eddie Johnson, her second husband, fearing a break-in, opened it and told them that Doris was too upset at the news of her daughter's escape to talk to them. He told them to contact me, her lawyer, to arrange an appointment. They returned several hours later, yelling over gunpoint blows to the door, "Open up. FBI." This time the door was not opened. Doris told them she would talk to them only in my presence.

I was at home, glued to the radio and in constant telephone contact with her, but they never called me. The next morning, at 7:45, they returned. Through the peephole Doris could see the black mass of bodies crowding the hallway. She repeated her insistence that her lawyer be present, and they told her they had no intention of calling me and demanded she open the door at once. Eddie had gone to work and she had been dressing Kakuya for nursery school, but she hesitated for only a moment before she refused to open the door. Surprisingly, they left, and there was quiet for the next few days. But on November 8, they attempted another tactic. They came to the school where she taught and spoke to the principal, who called her out of the classroom to tell her the FBI was there and would not leave until she talked to them. It was open school week and the parents present in her classroom buzzed about the drama unfolding. The new battleground was particularly disturbing because danger was now manifesting itself everywhere, even stalking her on her job, in the presence of her students and their parents. Not satisfied with her refusal to see them in the school, the FBI agents came back to her house at about 5:00 P M and repeated the thunderous banging on her door, threatening to enter by force. Unsuccessful, they telephoned her throughout the night until, recognizing their voices, she hung up the phone and eventually took it off the hook.

On November 13, 1979, I filed an action in federal court against William H. Webster, director of the FBI, for a preliminary and permanent injunction prohibiting the FBI from attempting to talk to Doris without the presence of her lawyer, from mail and telephone surveillance, and from maintaining electronic surveillance in and around her apartment. An affidavit attached to the assistant U.S. attorney's opposition to my action, sworn to by Thomas Bernard Locke, the Manhattan supervisory special agent for the FBI, stated that a federal warrant was issued for Assata's arrest on November 3 and, further,

> it is standard investigative procedure in fugitive cases for agents to communicate with the immediate family as soon as possible. Such communication had the following aims: (1) to solicit the family's cooperation in the investigation, if possible, and to obtain any relevant information which they possess; and (2) to impress upon them that the FBI wishes to apprehend the fugitive in question without violence and without causing harm to the fugitive or to anyone else. This latter purpose was especially important with respect to Ms. Chesimard, since on the basis of her previous record and her escape it appears likely that she would offer armed resistance to any attempt to recapture her. We thus wanted to advise Mrs. Johnson that while we were intent on apprehending Joanne, we wanted her unharmed and wished to avoid any shoot-out or other violence. . . . We also believed that it was important to communicate this message directly to Mrs. Johnson.

While Locke admitted that the FBI had come to Doris's house, he denied any surveillance at all. On April 15, 1980, Charles E. Steward, Jr., the District Court judge, denied injunctive relief and dismissed the complaint. But no further efforts to see Doris or to talk to her on the telephone were made after the action was filed. I appealed the decision, however, and during a pre-argument conference, scheduled by the Court of Appeals, Second Circuit, on May 19, 1980, I agreed to withdraw my appeal if the FBI assured me that there would be no further efforts to contact Doris. While I received no direct promise from the FBI, I entered into a stipulation that inferred that an agreement had been reached; the appeal was withdrawn with permission to reinstate it by June 15, 1981, if, within that time, further harassment occurred. Also Doris, who had suffered a cardiac infarction in December 1979, forcing her to retire from her job, simply wanted an end to the overt intimidation and threats. But the search of the Joint Terrorist Task Force, the team of FBI agents and state and local police organized to apprehend Assata, continued to be terroristic, illegal, brutal, and in total disregard of innocent lives.

On November 9, 1979, Ronald Boyd Hill, a former Black Panther and a friend of Assata's who had visited her at Clinton, was arrested in his Brooklyn home by forty flak-jacketed New Jersey, New York, and FBI gunmen who stormed his apartment, claiming that the Clinton corrections guards had positively identified him as having aided in the escape. Newspaper headlines heralded the capture and State Police Superintendent Pagano beamed in satisfaction, promising more arrests. One million dollars bail was set. The only problem was that Ron, married with four children, was enrolling one of the children at a day care center in Brooklyn at the time of the escape, a fact testified to by several witnesses and certified by the parking ticket issued to him at the time of the escape. Judge Eve Preminger of the New York Supreme Court reduced his bail to $2,500 on November 29 following a hearing, and on February 24, 1980, all charges against him were dismissed.

A few days after Assata's escape, a white policeman attempted to arrest four Black University of Maryland students in Asbury Park, New Jersey. The officer, who suspected that one of the students was Assata, fired a shot into the air and was quickly surrounded by a jeering crowd that forced him to admit his mistake and retreat to his precinct.

In the early morning hours of April 19, 1980, the Joint Terrorist Task Force cordoned off four blocks of Morningside Avenue in Harlem and a fifty-man army crashed through building number 92. They showed no warrants, despite the April 1980 U.S. Supreme Court ruling that police must have a warrant before entering a suspect's home to make a "routine" arrest. They broke down doors and held women and children hostage as, brandishing shotguns and machine guns, they questioned them about Assata's whereabouts. The police searched apartments, ripped open drawers and closets too small to conceal anyone, and destroyed property in the process. Ebun Adelona, who had two degrees in nursing and was a doctoral candidate in anthropology at Columbia University, was asleep with her five-year-old daughter when the agents burst into her apartment, forced her into the hallway, and ordered her to raise her nightgown so that they could search for gunshot wounds, under the impression that she was Assata. Others terrorized that night included a high school student, a teacher, and a television producer. Harlem congressional representative Charles Rangel demanded a full investigation by Attorney General Benjamin Civiletti and FBI Director William Webster. Neil H. Welsh, head of the New York FBI office, resigned on May 5 with two years remaining before his mandatory retirement, but he denied that his resignation was connected to the 92 Morningside raid. The tenants brought a federal civil action against the FBI through their attorneys, NCBL, and the New York Civil Liberties Union.

In the summer of 1980, a task force of FBI agents and New Jersey state troopers staked out various locations in the Bedford-Stuyvesant section of Brooklyn, where the residents are primarily Black, in the search for Assata. The prime target was the community center and Uhuru Sasa (Freedom Now) school founded in 1975 by Jitu Weusi, chief of operations for the Black United Front and longtime community activist. Pagano said that the New Jersey officials were "reasonably certain" that Assata was hiding in the school but called off the raid because they were afraid it would spark a riot. "That is a very volatile area," he said. "If we were wrong, or if something untoward happened, we could have stimulated a community incident. We were afraid of creating more of a problem than we would have solved by capturing her." Community leaders denied that Assata was ever in Bedford-Stuyvesant but said they would not have turned her in even if they had seen her. Weusi said, "We feel she was tried unfairly and we believe she is innocent."

A pregnant Fulani Sunni Ali's Mississippi house was raided in gestapo-like violence by hundreds of FBI as she lay sleeping with her small children. Her musician husband, Bilal Sunni Ali, was later charged with aiding in Assata's escape in a federal indictment and was acquitted.

On April 14, 1981, two policemen, John Scarangella and Richard Rainey, stopped a van allegedly for a routine license plate check in St. Albans, Queens. A shoot-out ensued during which Scarangella was killed and Rainey wounded. It was reported that the gunmen escaped in a car driven by Assata. A week later, newspapers quoted police department officials' opinion that the gunmen were members of the BLA because "9mm automatic weapons, a BLA trademark," had been used and because fingerprints found on the abandoned van "were those of known members of the BLA." It was further reported that "the gunmen are believed to have opened fire to prevent capture of Joanne Chesimard, the so-called 'soul' of the BLA who had vowed she will never be taken alive. Police suspect that she was being carried from one hideout to another in the white van when it was stopped for a license check by the two policemen." Several days after this pronouncement, Chief of Detectives James Sullivan admitted, "We have no evidence that they were in any way her bodyguards or that she was in the van during the shooting." Abdul Majid (Anthony LaBorde), a member of the Black Panther Party and a paralegal worker, was arrested in Philadelphia in January 1982 and indicted for the shootings, charged with Assata's escape and with committing an October 1981 Brinks armored car robbery in Rockland County. Bashir Hameed (James Dixon York), a former member of the Black Panther Party, was arrested for the shootings in August 1981 in South Carolina. Both were allegedly identified through eyewitness reports. Bill Kunstler and C. Vernon Mason represented them at their trials, the first two of which ended in hung juries. At the third trial the district attorney suddenly uncovered several witnesses who testified that sometime after the second trial both men had confessed their participation in the crimes to them. The two were convicted and sentenced to thirty years to life without parole. An appeal is pending and, in spite of the police-inspired media accusations that Majid had aided in Assata's liberation and was involved in the Brinks robbery, he was never indicted for either.

On October 23, 1981, Sekou Odinga (Nathaniel Burns) and Mtayari Shabaka Sundiata (Samuel Smith), both former Black Panthers, were arrested in Queens while traveling in a van the police claimed was involved in drug transactions. As they approached the van, the police opened fire, killed Mtayari, and arrested Sekou, who they believed was responsible for Assata's escape. He was taken to the precinct where, in an effort to force information from him concerning Assata's whereabouts, they tore his nails off and repeatedly shoved his head into a toilet bowl

full of urine. When he still refused to talk, they kicked him with *179*
such force that his pancreas had to be removed. He was indicted
for the Rockland County Brinks robbery, but the indictment was
dismissed when a federal grand jury in New York filed a RICO*
conspiracy indictment against him and Silvia Baraldini, a member of the May 19 Organization, charging them with a cornucopia
of crimes, including aiding in Assata's escape. Both were found
guilty and sentenced to twenty years in prison on each count
with a recommendation of no parole.

While members of the Black Panther Party and other
militant organizations were special targets, many other individuals and families were attacked, but this harassment was rarely
reported in the media. In response to this massive, government-
sponsored effort to intimidate the larger Black community into
terrified rejection of Assata, posters were plastered on every
available outdoor space in Harlem and Bedford-Stuyvesant, in
New Jersey, and in other areas throughout the country, declaring
in bold letters, ASSATA IS WELCOME HERE. And Mae Jackson, a
longtime Brooklyn community activist, along with others, paid
for a half-page ad in the African American New York weekly *The
Amsterdam News,* proclaiming support for Assata and urging
her to stay strong and stay free. It was entitled "Run, Assata,
Run," reflecting the famous slave song for those who had escaped.

---

*The RICO statute (Racketeer Influenced and Corrupt Organization Act),
enacted in 1976 (18 U.S.C., Section 1962), "a law originally passed to address
organized crime influence in the labor field, has also been turned against
political activists and their organizations. The law has now been applied to
designate as criminal enterprises, organizations with political aims and to try
members of such groups under broad conspiracy rules which allow for up to 40
years in prison" (*International Review of Contemporary Law,* 1990, p. 121).

Chapter 18

Unsubstantiated rumors were my only hint of Assata's whereabouts. Hours merged into days. Days became months. And by April 1980, when Assata still remained free, the legal and emotional stringencies that had consumed me for the last seven years were replaced by a restless calm. Doris, Kakuya, and I visited my parents in North Carolina, and we reminisced about the past and wondered about the future as we sat on the isolated privacy of Freeman's Beach, the sound of the waves insulating our words. Our stubborn hope resisted the reports of Assata's imminent capture and eased the underlying anxiety our brave words offered each other. Bevvie had given birth to Donny in December 1974 and was now living in Doris's building, providing Doris with the comfort of another grandchild and adding a companion to Kakuya's small world. In January 1980 the family's size was again increased when Bevvie had another child, Brad.

I needed to work, but I was undecided about what I wanted to do. Unlike my sister and the rest of my family, I have always been a maverick. Neither money nor economic security had ever seemed a legitimate goal or anything that summoned my passions. I lived simply and, except for the repayment of debts I had accumulated in recent years, salary was not a real consideration. I wanted a job that was both challenging and satisfying. Strangely enough, I did not factor my age into my future. I was now fifty-seven, but I was healthy and had an excess of energy. I still played a good game of tennis and only on occasion did my legs cramp during long swims. I had leaped over middle age without a thought that time was running out for me or that there wasn't enough time left to choose a new direction. I had impatiently dismissed the interminable inconvenience of menopause, and other people's concerns about being old were never mine. It wasn't that I was unmindful of the wrinkles in my face, the sagging skin, or the unfamiliar reflection that confronted me in

180

store windows. It was just that I was never in the tomorrow
syndrome. Today was not a bridge to tomorrow. Today was to be
lived today. And tomorrow was to be lived tomorrow, if reached.
Yesterdays were storehouses of time well spent and never to be
regretted.

One day in April 1980, as I looked through the *New York
Law Journal* employment section, I saw an opening for executive director of Harlem Legal Services and mailed in my résumé.
I had no real hope of being hired, considering the political
favoritism that permeates all small communities, especially
when opportunities are few, and I had never been a part of
Harlem politics. I was shocked when, after several interviews
with the board of directors and staff attorneys, I was appointed.
And I began the job in June 1980 with the zeal of a crusader.

There was no question in my mind that the agency needed
to be completely overhauled, from the evening janitor to the
supervisory staff. And I met this new challenge with enthusiasm
and a brisk broom, stunning the entire staff. For seven months
prior to my appointment, there had been no executive director,
and the result had been confusion and disorganization. Harlem
Legal Services was one of eight delegate corporations throughout
the city under the umbrella of Community Action for Legal
Service, Inc. (CALS), a not-for-profit corporation organized
under the judiciary law of the state of New York and funded by
Legal Services Corporation, created pursuant to the federal
Legal Services Corporation Act and ultimately subject to its
jurisdiction. Our budget was only $573,660, the smallest allo-
cated to any of the delegate corporations, despite the fact that
the needy population in Harlem was the largest.

The staff consisted of one director of litigation, seven
attorneys, one unlicensed VISTA attorney, one administrative
assistant, three administrative secretaries, one bilingual secretary, two intake officers, three paralegals in the government
benefit unit, two tenant organizers, a receptionist, and two
investigators.

The guidelines established by the Legal Services Act narrowly limited the areas in which legal representation could be
extended to the poor. Only civil cases were allowed, and the
most common cases involved evictions, consumer fraud, and
appearances before administrative agencies for grievances concerning the denial of welfare, social security, unemployment

benefits, or Medicaid. There were also a few cases in Family Court relating to custody proceedings and a very few job discrimination and civil rights actions. The agency had never undertaken major civil litigation or federal class action suits, although its mere presence in Harlem was a mandate for such an effort.

I streamlined procedures to enable the attorneys to respond more substantively to eviction notices and prepared forms to be filled in by the intake workers so we could file affirmative defenses and counterclaims of housing code violations, rodent infestation, unmade repairs, and other violations and could force the city to make building inspections and the court to hold trials before evictions could be carried out. But my primary focus was to create an excellent legal resource for Harlem that was visible, dependable, and accessible.

With other staff members who shared my commitments, I began voluntary outreach programs. We supported the struggle to prevent the closing of Sydenham Hospital, and I represented Harlem Legal Services on the board of Harlem Health Services Research and Development Corporation, established to operate a full-service acute-care health facility after Sydenham was closed. We sponsored, together with various community organizations spearheaded by the Milbank Frawley People's Council, a one-day educational conference with community participation. We joined the Abyssinian Baptist Church and Mt. Zion AME Church in a joint effort to remedy the sparsity of preschool educational centers. We organized massive drives with the regional director of Legal Services Corporation to prevent the threatened defunding of the agency and joined forces with the Community Law Office and the National Conference of Black Lawyers to bring a class action suit challenging the forced relocation of long-term occupants of buildings earmarked by private sponsors for destruction in the name of rehabilitation. We also held a monthly operation with community organizations to distribute to residents information concerning legal problems.

I had become increasingly concerned about the erosion of the housing stock in Harlem, the arson-forced abandonment of apartment houses that now stood empty at the corners and down the side streets of beautiful boulevards, windowless and blackened, looking down on the growing number of families forced to leave them. I became convinced that the pattern of destruction was not accidental and began searching the records in City Hall, the City Planning Board, and the Board of Estimate to try to trace the reasons for the city's inertia in rebuilding Harlem, despite the rapid rise of rehabilitated areas elsewhere. In the process, I uncovered the first Urban Renewal Development Plan the city had projected in 1956 for the St. Nicholas Avenue section of Harlem but had never implemented. City-owned properties acquired by tax foreclosure outnumbered the remaining 35,000 buildings that were also in tax default but, pursuant to Mayor Edward I. Koch's plan for Harlem, were not taken over by the city. More than coincidence accounted for the locations and unoccupied status of the buildings the city did own. They were on the corners of the avenues in Harlem, and the buildings adjacent to them formed a solid block of development potential. The families who had been living in them had been forced out either by arson fires or by city proclamations declaring them unsafe. Although the buildings were vacant and non-revenue-producing, the administration refused to sell them to interested Harlem residents. When the city was finally pressured into making some available, eleven brownstones were selected, and the sale was by lottery and offered citywide.

Tax defaults on occupied buildings abandoned by private owners but scattered throughout Harlem on unplanned rehabilitation sites were ignored along with the housing code violations that riddled them. Koch's deputy mayor, Nathan Levanthal, admitted that the administration had intentionally cut back on the number of properties it took over to save the cost of maintaining them. What he did not admit was that the situational violence inflicted by Koch's policies on the families remaining in those buildings was designed to accelerate the vacancy rate.

In 1979, New York Governor Hugh Carey started the decline of services to the city by cutting $3 million of the state contribution to the city's code enforcement program, which handles building complaints. By the start of the winter of 1980, the number of employees in the city's code compliance units had declined from 1,100 in 1975 to 820, and the number of building inspectors had been reduced from 625 to 382. Simultaneously, the city halved its budget for emergency fuel and boiler repairs, from $15 million to $7 million, leaving those tenants still living in the privately owned buildings that had been abandoned by landlords without fuel, repairs, or other services, trapped in a remediless squeeze. The tragic consequences of Koch's policies to human life in the event of a cold winter were predicted by the community-based Task Force on City Owned Property in the summer of 1980. When the coldest weather of the century hit New York in December 1980, *The Village Voice* reported: "The fact is that Ed Koch prepared for this winter by turning off the valves on the city's radiators, continuing the decimation of programs designed to keep the people warm."

Koch's policies set the stage for the disasters that followed the subzero temperatures that gripped the city from the last week in December 1980 to the third week in January 1981. The families living in buildings abandoned by owners to whom they continued to pay rent were devastated. The majority had small children and were employed. Horror story after horror story filled the pages of the daily newspapers. The buildings were without heat. Water froze in pipes in the few buildings that had water at all. It was a common sight to see people opening fire hydrants and lifting pails of water up to their apartments. There were fires from defective kerosene and oil heaters. And when people were discovered frozen to death in their apartments Koch declared that a crisis existed. He offered two solutions to the families. One was to leave their apartments and accept temporary housing in the 369th Regiment Armory, located on Seventh Avenue and 141st Street. The other was to accept city-owned vacant apartments suddenly made available. The problem with these one thousand apartments, however, was that while they had heat, they had no stoves, refrigerators, or toilets, and the large holes in the walls and floors provided easy access for the rats and roaches that invaded the rooms.

Afeni Shakur, who had taken a leave of absence from Mobilization for Youth and had recently joined Harlem Legal Services to head the Housing Data Bank Project, a special program funded by CALS, went with Gloria Cox, one of the housing organizers, and Faye Jackson and Judith Abramson, our two paralegals, a few days after the armory opened to help with food and clothing operations. When they returned, they hurriedly described to me the conditions they had found. And my visit corroborated their observations. The armory was not being occupied only by families who had sought temporary shelter from the cold. Homeless men from all over the city had been admitted. They had not been separated from the small children on the enormous first floor but mixed freely among them. The occupants were permitted to use only two bathrooms of the eight in the armory, and they were not designated by gender. They were filthy, had no hot water, and provided only one shower to be shared by everyone. At one point, more than four hundred men, women, and children were crowded into the unsegregated space. Three of the children had chicken pox but were refused admittance to Harlem Hospital because the hospital feared an epidemic among its confined patients. Harlem State Senator Leon Bogues described the sight of men urinating in the corners of the armory and issued a call for the city to open more shelters and to segregate the single, homeless men and the families. Reverend James S. Robinson of St. Paul's Community Church condemned the lack of privacy and the dirty bathrooms, stating, "People were being treated like they were in concentration camps. Security guards thought they were the gestapo. People were masturbating in the corners." At his request, the City Council representative from Harlem, Fred Samuels, visited and found the conditions "deplorable" and urged the city to find separate facilities for the "derelicts."

Immediate legal action was necessary, but I had a problem. My small staff had neither the time nor the expertise to prepare a class action suit to prevent the city from operating the armory under these conditions. I also anticipated the official wrath that would follow once such an action was filed. And I knew that I was treading the thin line of permissible legal actions established by Legal Services Corporation.

I filed a suit anyway. I prepared and typed it at home, after the working day, photocopied the complaint on commercial machines, hired private process servers to serve Koch and all the city departments named as defendants, and paid the filing fee in the U.S. District Court for the Southern District of New York. But the attorney named in the class action was Harlem Legal Services.

Official reaction was instant and furious. Stanley Brezenoff, the administrator of the Human Resources Administration, issued a press release in which he said, "The filing of this suit should get an Oscar for ridiculous performance. How can there be a violation of constitutional rights of people who choose to come to an emergency shelter?" He added, "Harlem Legal Services might better use the funds it must spend to litigate this suit to redress real violations by others of the rights of the poor."

In describing the suit, the *New York Post* headlined its story "Tenants Bite the Hand That Fed Them." And Koch, interviewed on a local television show, said, "Chutzpah, go to Moscow" as he berated tenant leaders across the city who criticized him for being pro-landlord.

J. J. Gonzalez, a television reporter on the CBS affiliate in New York, refused to accept my disinclination to discuss the situation but successfully cornered me in the library at Harlem Legal Services for an interview. I described the conditions I had seen and the reasons for the class action. That night, when the segment was aired, my undoctored statements were followed by a scene taken in front of the armory where a mother who claimed to have been staying in the armory with her three children praised the city, blessed Koch, and applauded the clean and comfortable conditions she had found there—a typical media misinformation campaign fabricated to serve political interests. Within days after the action was filed, Koch closed the armory precipitously. Still unable to return to their apartments, now with pipes broken from the cold and completely uninhabitable, the families were forced to move to the homeless shelters provided by the city. And most lost their possessions and apartments forever when the city condemned their buildings as constituting a danger and issued vacate orders forcing the last, reluctant ones out into the cold.

Sadie Haynes, a member of the class action and the single occupant of a building at 32 Morningside Avenue, offered a solution to the families evicted from the armory: to rehabilitate the building, which was both abandoned and city-owned, with the labor provided by the families. It had twenty apartments, and an engineer determined that with repairs to electrical wiring, plumbing, and the boiler, the building could be made habitable. I donated the thousand dollars needed to repair the boiler and provide coal, and many other community organizations donated more than a thousand dollars for paint, lumber, and other equipment. The families, including children and fathers, began their sweat labor in the building, and Harlem Legal Services initiated negotiations with the city for a lease arrangement with the families. Harlem congressional representative Charles Rangel supplied blankets, and Reverend Calvin Butts of the Abyssinian Baptist Church began discussions about establishing a school for the children.

But while the community's response was overwhelmingly positive, the majority of the board of directors of Harlem Legal Services was less than enthusiastic, and those members who were dependent on political favor for their jobs, for their agency grants, or for any petty favor bestowed on them by City Hall joined Koch's efforts to contain and destroy the agency, which had now provided an example of what legal activism could accomplish. Koch's plan became obvious on February 17, 1981, when David Jones, a Black personal aide to Koch, suddenly was added to the board. And at the same meeting at which Jones appeared, I was directed "not to take on any other projects other than the ones listed in [my] report until further notice from the Board." The minutes of the meeting further reflected the statement of the chairman that "the Harlem Legal Services Board wants its Executive Director to manage the office and not several other projects."

I interpreted "other projects" to mean special projects I had initiated, like the Housing Data Bank. In 1980, CALS had announced to its delegate corporations that a one-time grant was available for special programs, to be funded after proposals had been submitted and approved. The money was to be used for the proposal program only and was not to be commingled with the legal services annual budget. I submitted a proposal for a Housing Data Bank that would identify every vacant building in Harlem, its owner, the date of conveyance, its size, the number of apartments it had contained, the reason for the vacant condition, whether it was condemned, and the reasons given, and would locate the buildings on large maps to identify the pattern of vacant buildings and city acquisition. My purpose was to provide the statistical foundation for a major legal action, to be jointly prepared by community law firms and bar associations, challenging the city's policy of planned shrinkage. I also visualized, once the data bank had been established, computerizing the information and using it as a central source of instantly available housing information for the Harlem community. After the year's grant ended, I hoped that the project would be continued by one of the housing community agencies in Harlem.

Since the board of directors had been careful not to openly display criticism about the armory suit or to suggest that its action against me was in direct response to the negative publicity Koch and the administration had received, it had narrowly worded its directive, addressing it only to "special projects." I therefore felt no compulsion to limit the agency's involvement in two other important matters that came to my attention.

On February 27, as usual, I was in the office at about 7:30 A M My early arrivals and open door amused the staff, who had become accustomed to the appearance of the executive director at about 11:00 A M, after which he secreted himself behind his closed door until 3:00, when he left for the day. I used the early-morning time before everyday office matters consumed me to review my appointments, check the *Law Journal*, photocopy and distribute cases of significance to the staff, check the previous day's intake for new cases accepted and the attorneys assigned to them, and prepare the next year's budget, statistical evaluations, and reports to the board of directors.

On that day in February I was drinking coffee and looking through the large windows facing 125th Street, contemplating the restrictions laid down by the board and pondering whether I would be able to remain in a job that required only an office manager, hardly the position for which I had submitted my résumé. I thought about approaching some of the board members who seemed amenable to the new challenges for change and to the possibility of an agency different from the previously dormant, invisible agency that had become a means for lethargic and uninterested lawyers to obtain a weekly paycheck and for board members to receive questionable status and petty favors. But I also wondered if my motives in soliciting their support would be perceived as generated by self-interest and a ploy to retain a very well paid job. I was in the midst of this dilemma when Afeni, Gloria Cox, Joyce Ware Thomas, a community activist who was campaigning against the format of the brownstone lottery, and Carolyn Rivers, another community activist who worked at Mobilization for Youth, walked into the office.

I was surprised to see them. It was only 8:20, but as they drank their coffee and ate Danish, they explained their urgency. Funeral services had just been held the week before for the seventeenth Black child found murdered in Atlanta, and the mystery surrounding their deaths was a topic of frequent discussion in Black communities across the country. The murderer had not been apprehended, and the similarities of their deaths, usually by strangulation, their young ages, which ranged from ten to fourteen, and the locations in which their bodies had been

discovered indicated a serial killer. But the fact that all but two   189
females were Black male children stirred even more ominous
overtones and more frightening speculations. Was the KKK
responsible? Another theory posed the possible involvement of
the U.S. government so that blood or other specimens could be
obtained for an experiment in genetic manipulation.

The latest discovered child was Jeffrey L. Mathis, age ten,
and on the weekend the *Daily News*'s center spread had photographs of his funeral and of the inconsolable tearstained face of
his mother, Willie Mae Mathis. By May 1981, five more bodies
would be discovered and five more children would be reported
missing. My staff members' immediate question was whether we
could organize a candlelight vigil for the families in remembrance of the children of Atlanta and in a demonstration of
unified compassion with their grief. Each of the staff members
had small children and their empathy was vivid. The idea was as
exciting as the chances of success seemed remote.

What form should the vigil take? What would be the most
appropriate route? Permits would be required. Speakers would
have to be chosen. A speaker stand would have to be constructed. Time was important. The vigil needed to be held
quickly, but was there time to get the information out to the
public? How could we synthesize our efforts to include as many
organizations as would be interested in participating? Would the
media cover the event? And, the most important factor, would
the mothers from Atlanta be willing to make the trip to New
York?

I wondered whether the board would consider this a "special project" and prevent our involvement. But I made my
decision without hesitation. I gave the go-ahead and agreed to
underwrite the plane fare and other travel expenses, including
hotels, restaurants, and any other miscellaneous monies that
might be needed. The four were a tremendous resource of
information and community associations. Their energy and
competence flushed positively across their faces. They knew we
could do it.

I gave them carte blanche to use my private telephone, and
the first call they made was to the STOP (Save Them Or Perish)
office in Atlanta, an organization started by the mothers of the
murdered children. Camille Bell, whose son Yusuf, age nine, had
been missing since October 1979 and had been discovered in

November 1979, dead of strangulation, was the chairperson. Willie Mathis was the vice president, and Venus Taylor, whose daughter Angel Lanier, age twelve, was found in March 1980, dead of strangulation, was the secretary. When we reached them we learned that they had mounted a national campaign to press for state and federal investigations of the murders and had been making public appearances to bring the murders to the attention of the public outside Atlanta. They were on a tight speaking schedule and could be in New York from March 12 to 16. They agreed to come and the vigil was scheduled for March 13.

The only board member who evidenced any enthusiasm for the plan was Valerie Jordan, a tall, soft-spoken, good-looking woman, genuinely interested in Harlem affairs and a longtime volunteer. Her only comment was to wonder if we could guarantee a crowd on Friday the 13th, a day notorious for its superstitious aura. At the same time, she gave me a list of organizations to invite to participate.

Organizational support came from every segment of the Black population, both in Harlem and throughout the other boroughs. Unions, tenant organizations, churches, health workers, and hospital workers became part of the march. The list of sponsoring organizations included the Coney Island Community Health Center; the Coalition to Save Sydenham Hospital; the Black United Front, Metropolitan and Harlem chapters; the National Black Human Rights Coalition; Black Women's Collective; Black New York Action Committee; National Black Independent Party, New York chapter; Neighborhood Boards 1, 3, and 5; the National Black Students Association; the Coalition of Black Trade Unionists; the West Harlem Community Organization; the Church of the Resurrection; the Abyssinian Baptist Church; the Nation of Islam; Harlem Consumer Educational Council; the Community League; the Jackie Robinson Foundation; Local 420, District 65; Harlem and Bellevue Hospital workers; Wamko Wa Sigsa Community School; United Harlem Growth; the Addicts Rehabilitation Center Gospel Choir; the College Print Shop; the workers at General Motors Corporation in Tarrytown, New York; the New Birth Collective; the Black Acupuncture Association of North America; the Urban League; the Republic of New Afrika; Harlem Health Research and Development Corporation; the Parents Association of P.S. 85; the Patrice Lumumba Coalition; the West Side Community Organization; and many others. More than eight hundred "concerned employees and friends" at Bellevue Hospital contributed $852 to the families, and Rosemari Mealy, a local radio host and longtime community activist, proudly delivered the messages and the checks. The North Star Fund issued a special grant to Harlem Legal Services to be used for transportation and other expenses incurred for the families. Many more hundreds of dollars were donated to the families by other organizations and individuals.

Rosemari obtained the sound permit to operate the loud-speaker at the termination of the march. Bill Lynch, later to become an aide to New York Mayor David Dinkins, provided the platform truck for the stage and set it up. Ahmed Obafemi took responsibility for security, along with other members of the Republic of New Afrika, monitoring the route with walkie-talkies. Community organizations arranged for speakers, who included Florence Rice, director of the Harlem Consumer Educational Council, Father Lawrence Lucas of Resurrection Church, and Pat Wagner, community organizer, along with the Atlanta mothers. Jazzmobile donated music, and the Abyssinian Baptist Church choir and many other dance and vocal companies volunteered their talents. The children of Harlem read poetry they had composed. Fliers, candles, and green ribbons were donated for the vigil, and Harlem children tied the ribbons around every tree along the route.

On the evening of March 13, more than 20,000 people walked in silent remembrance, holding candles and wearing the green ribbons, up Adam Clayton Powell, Jr., Boulevard from 110th Street to the speaker's platform at the Schomburg Library at Malcolm X Boulevard and 135th Street. Traffic had been rerouted, and the glowing lights of the candles moved slowly and ceremoniously through the night, from sidewalk to sidewalk. Mothers and fathers and small children walked, united, resolute, responding to the murders of the Atlanta children, who could have been their own.

The media coverage was all any organizer could have wanted, from the time the families arrived at LaGuardia Airport at 8:30 A.M. on the morning of Thursday, March 12, to the time they left the city the following Monday morning. At the first press conference the day the families arrived at the Harlem State Office Building on 125th Street, the press was represented from as far away as Brazil. I was in charge of arranging the families' many television, radio, and newspaper interviews, which included *Tony Brown's Journal,* Gil Noble's *Like It Is,* NBC's *Live at Five* with Carol Jenkins, Channel 5's Pablo Guzman, radio interviews with Rosemari Mealy on WBAI and Jane Tillman Irving's *Access* on WCBS, and an interview on WLIB. The Black Caucus, politicians in the New York State legislature, and the Coalition of Black Trade Unionists met with the families and promised their continued support. On Saturday, Reverend Calvin Butts held a luncheon with five organizational representatives at the Abyssinian Baptist Church, and the visit ended with a special commemorative service at Reverend Herbert Daughtry's House of the Lord Church in Brooklyn on Sunday.

The five days were exhausting, but I was heartened that they had become a part of Harlem's history that I think its people will never forget.

Chapter 19

Pride about the leadership role Harlem Legal Services had provided in mobilizing the vigil and the weekend's events revived my hopes that it could become a neighborhood entity of substance. But with the exception of Shirley Carter, a Harlem lawyer of inestimable prestige, and Valerie Jordan, the board never mentioned the vigil to me. Instead, restrictive memoranda after restrictive memoranda from the chairman were placed on my desk with increasing frequency.

I had initiated a practice of inviting community organizations to hold their evening meetings in our large library, which was separated from the rest of the office. Doors to the attorneys' offices were locked, and I remained until the meetings ended, along with one of the investigators who volunteered to stay late with me. I received a memorandum: No organizations are to use the library for meetings without prior approval from the chairman.

On occasion, some of the small children of staff members came to the office after school when their mothers worked late. A memorandum was placed on my desk: No children are allowed in the office at any time.

The written reports I submitted to the board describing office procedures, progress reports on the budget, and other matters were so detailed and lengthy that the board passed a resolution that my reports, both written and oral, be shortened. But at each meeting the same questions were asked about the same complete answers I had already given. The board members were especially concerned about the Housing Data Bank, despite the fact that it was directly supervised by CALS, was outside the Harlem Legal Services budget, and was solely within my province to administer. Ignoring the full disclosure of every detail I had given them about it, they continued to ask: What was its budget? What was its purpose? Didn't it duplicate other city services? Was it necessary? Who was hired from the special funds? What expenditures had already been made? How much money was left? The questions were accusatory, as if I were designing a foul plot.

When three staff lawyers resigned, CALS instituted a hiring freeze that prevented me from hiring replacements. Shortly thereafter, the remaining lawyers went on their annual strike for higher wages, leaving the clients they were representing stranded in Landlord Tenant Court. While I supported the strike, my concern for the many clients being represented by the agency far outweighed my sympathy for the lawyers' cause. They refused to accept my recommendation that at least one of them volunteer during the strike to appear in court for their clients, if for no other purpose than to adjourn cases until the strike ended. They not only rejected the suggestion but demanded that intake be closed, even for emergencies, which I refused to do. To my way of thinking, the lawyers had failed to advise their clients of the imminent strike, the legitimate reasons for it, and the fact that the legal services on which their clients had relied would be interrupted. The result was a complete absence of community support. It is my belief that no public or private agency or politician or individual can remain viable without seriously communicating and connecting with the community. David Abramson, a young, white VISTA volunteer who had been assigned to Harlem Legal Services by CALS and whose stipend was paid from federal funds, joined me in Landlord Tenant Court every morning for the month it took to defend cases abandoned by the lawyers. Without David's tireless assistance, many families would have been summarily evicted.

The board knew about the strike and its devastating impact. They responded to the crisis by demanding to know "why more experienced attorneys could not be used in Landlord Tenant Court to represent Harlem Legal Services." The minutes of their May 18, 1981, meeting continue: "The Executive Director stated that Mr. David Abramson, who now represents Harlem Legal Services in the court, and is recently associated with Harlem Legal Services has done a fine job. He has accompanied her on several occasions in court and has built up a tremendous amount of experience." The minutes do not reflect my report to them about the strike. Or that David was a VISTA volunteer and not on the Harlem Legal Services budget. Or that I had not hired him.

Or that there were no other attorneys to represent the clients in court. Or that the families, had they not been represented, would have been evicted. Instead, the board directed me to "hire only experienced lawyers in the future."

They intruded beyond their legal parameters into every aspect of office operations, no matter how automatic or mundane. They invited the staff attorneys to meet with them in secret session to air any grievances they might have with the office and me. At one board meeting, Shirley Carter impatiently reminded them that the matters which were in my sole discretion, as executive director, should remain in my discretion and not be usurped by the board. At that meeting, however, their hidden agenda was revealed. After my report, the board went into executive session and when they returned they charged me with permitting the Black Panther Party to use the photocopying machine. I could not believe the moribund mentality that could resurrect this once great but now extinguished dinosaur for the purpose of tainting me with what they considered to be an undesirable association. I knew of no active branch of the Black Panther Party after its COINTELPRO-engineered demise in 1971. Of course, Afeni Shakur was an acquitted defendant in the Panther 21 trial, but the clumsy, stupid attempt to discredit me was more humorous than threatening. And it bruised my intelligence. Even assuming I was a member of an organization they classified as terrorist, would I be so stupid as to advertise my association in this meaningless, open way?

But a memorandum was placed on my desk following the meeting: The photocopy machine is not to be used without special, prior approval by the chairman. By now all of my questions about quitting were resolved. I would resign. But not before Harlem Legal Services settled one more pending major piece of litigation it had initiated.

On March 2, as plans for the vigil were under way, Susie Grier, a tenant living in a group of city-owned row houses on West 139th Street between Fifth Avenue and Malcolm X Boulevard, came with an urgent problem. When the intake worker called me to evaluate the situation, doubting it was an acceptable case for us, I reviewed the information she had taken. As far as I was concerned, no case was unacceptable unless the client's income exceeded the guidelines or it fell into one of the categories specifically proscribed by the Legal Services Act. Ms. Grier's only income was from social security, and her emergency was a "Forthwith Vacate Order" that had been posted in her building that morning demanding that all tenants immediately vacate the buildings because a condition existed that threatened the health and safety of the residents: the buildings were without water.

Alarmed, I interviewed Ms. Grier and learned that there were 42 tenants of an original 275 living in the buildings, which had been designated for gut rehabilitation by the Rhoden-Sanford Corporation developers. I decided that Harlem Legal Services should represent the tenants, but there were many facts still to be determined to support the allegation of a violation of the constitutional right not to be deprived of property without due process of law. Besides federal violations, what New York State constitutional and statutory violations had occurred? And there was little time. The vacate order meant now! But the city's action taken against these tenants was being duplicated all over Harlem: it was displacing people arbitrarily, in defiance of due process, to make way for unaffordable new buildings to which the tenants could never return. It was a classic application of the marvel of gentrification. And I was leaning toward filing a class action on behalf of all the tenants, not only in Harlem, but citywide, so affected.

I discussed the matter with the director of litigation, Ishmael Lahab, who gave his predictable evaluation: this was not a case for us. When I pressed him for a reason, he said he didn't think we should get involved. I then asked the staff attorneys to work with me on the case. Each one declined, stating that his or her caseload was too large to permit time for additional work. I could simply have assigned it to one of them. To put a case of this degree of importance and legal complexity into inexperienced hands was one thing. But to discard it into resentful and indifferent hands was another. So I filed the class action suit in federal court myself.

The rest of the staff joined me in battle. The tenant organizers blanketed each of the buildings, obtained information and approval for the class action, and documented residency histories. I was also fortunate to have Raymond Machado on staff. I had hired him to head a project I was designing on behalf of prisoners whose civil rights were violated, and Ray, an ex-offender himself, had unparalleled investigatory skills. He spent two entire days at City Hall, the City Planning Commission, and the Board of Estimate searching for the evidence I needed to support the federal action I was contemplating.

Ray's investigation revealed several interesting facts. Simeon Golar was the Black secretary-treasurer of Rhoden-Sanford, the developer, and the president of R.G.S. Realty Corporation, which owned all of the Rhoden-Sanford stock. Golar had been involved in the civil rights movement, had been chairman of the New York City Housing Authority from 1970 to 1973, and had been appointed by Mayor John Lindsay as a Family Court judge from 1973 to 1976. In later years Golar was to run for public office on a platform promising affordable housing for the poor.

In 1979, Golar first approached Housing, Preservation, and Development (HPD) with his plan to gut-rehabilitate the five buildings on West 139th Street. The buildings consisted of six stories of walk-up apartments, with a total of 334 units and 8 stores. His plan was to convert them into two six-story elevator buildings that would contain 214 units, including 6 studio apartments and 94 one-bedroom apartments. At that time, the Harlem Interagency Council for the Aging was competing with Rhoden-Sanford for site development but withdrew its bid in exchange for becoming a co-sponsor and the community adviser group for Rhoden-Sanford with a guaranteed monetary payoff. The plan was subject to the New York Private Housing Finance Law, the New York City charter, and the City Planning Commission's Uniform Land Use Review Procedures (known as ULURP) before final approval could be given by the Board of Estimate. ULURP required full due process, which included a ten-day public notice of hearings to be conducted by community boards in which the site was located, in this case Community Board Number 10, the City Planning Commission, as well as the Board of Estimate. Additionally, ULURP specifically set forth the only way in which the recommendations of a community board would be considered by the City Planning Commission: notice of a public hearing at least ten days before the scheduled date and a legal quorum present at the time the vote was taken. Failure to comply rendered approval of the project null and void, and it could not be submitted to the City Planning Commission for approval by the Board of Estimate.

Ray obtained the minutes of the hearing before Community Board Number 10 at the time it voted to approve the Golar project. There had been no quorum. He further extracted from the *City Record,* in which all city notices are printed, the failure of the City Planning Commission to give a ten-day notice of its hearing, at which time it approved the plan. This information, together with the action HPD had taken in violation of the tenants' statutory and constitutional rights, formed the basis of the action I was prepared to bring against the city and Rhoden-Sanford. The story as told by the tenants and as substantiated by Ray's investigation revealed that after Community Board Number 10 approved the plan on August 12, 1980, the City Planning Commission approved the plan on the following day, finding that ULURP due process procedures had been met. I must point out that elementary due process is violated by the requirement that the "public notice" be placed in the *City Record,* typed in print so small that it must be perused with a magnifying glass to be seen. To say nothing about the reality that no one reads the *City Record,* even city officials.

But in order for Golar to obtain an FHA mortgage, the buildings had to be vacant, and the city used every guerrilla tactic possible to displace the tenants. On March 1, 1980, the city discontinued heat, hot water, and janitorial service, forcing many tenants to move. When some remained, the city posted a notice to vacate in the hallways on August 29, 1980. It stated:

> PLEASE TAKE NOTICE that the City of New York, which is not the owner of the Building, seeks to empty and demolish the Building and demands that you vacate and move out within ninety (90) days after this Notice to Vacate has been served upon you.
>
> IF YOU FAIL TO VACATE AND MOVE OUT OF THE BUILDING within ninety (90) days, the City will commence appropriate judicial proceedings to have you removed from the building.
>
> This action is necessitated in order to implement a plan for the development of the site upon which the building is located.

However, Earle Murray, the area director of the In-Rem Property Management Office in central Harlem, which was responsible for maintaining city-owned properties, proved the vacate order was merely a device to cover up HPD's intention to rid the building of tenants as quickly as possible. Just before the vacate order was issued, Murray wrote to his director, Robert

Moncrief, that although he could install a new boiler needed in the building, "based upon the uncertainty of future plans I would not, in good conscience, spend $20,000 to $25,000 dollars to install a new boiler. Therefore, my decision would be to submit these five buildings to the Consolidation Unit to vacate same. We should advise the sponsor."

This unilateral opinion, which deprived the tenants of essential services for life functions, not only was inhumane but violated the Housing Maintenance Code. That code specifically sets forth a legislative declaration that "the sound enforcement of minimum housing standards is essential to . . . bring about the basic decencies and minimal standards of healthful living in already deteriorated dwellings which, although no longer salvageable, must serve as habitations until they can be replaced. The obligation of the City of New York to maintain minimal standards of healthful living, even in apartments which are designated for site-project development, is clear." Further, HPD violated its own rules and regulations of 1973, which specifically state that until tenants have been relocated, they are entitled to essential services. So the refusal to repair the boiler constituted violation of statutory as well as constitutional rights.

The tenants, particularly the elderly, still resisted relocation to hotels or uninhabitable apartments in neighborhoods far removed from Harlem, unfamiliar and threatening to them. The quality of the apartments to which they were invited by the city was the same as that offered to the families forced to find temporary shelter in the armory that month: no refrigerators, stoves, or toilets and infested with rats and roaches.

At the time the 1980 vacate order was issued, there was a total of 275 tenants in the buildings. But by January 26, 1981, specifically as a result of the threats of the vacate order and the lack of heat, the number had been reduced to 42. Despite the fact that Golar's project, Harlen Houses, was threatened by the city's failure to clear out the buildings, he offered the tenants no alternative plan, money, or other inducements to ease their burden of relocation. Instead, he sent a letter to all of the remaining tenants, including Susie Grier, stating: "May I point out that you must arrange to remove from your present apartment no later than March 15, 1981 or you and your neighbors will be denied urgently needed housing at affordable rents, and, or course, you will not receive from the City of New York relocation benefits to which you are entitled if the project goes through."

This letter was sent in light of the city's clear position that there were no relocation benefits available to the tenants and despite Golar's own representation at Community Board Number 10's hearing that he could make no promises that any of the tenants removed from the site would return to the rehabilitated buildings. I learned further that James Roble of the Community Law Office, a group of volunteer Wall Street lawyers, had met with Willa Van Eaton, a real estate manager in the relocation unit of HPD, and with the tenants who had come to him for legal assistance on November 5, 1980. At that meeting Van Eaton told the tenants that relocation benefits of one month's rent and a month's security to find an apartment could not be offered by the city. I also learned that Robles told Van Eaton that he would not bring an action against the city on behalf of the tenants, negating his promise to the tenants that he would.

On January 28, 1981, the city accelerated its assault against the tenants. It capped the main water lines leading into the buildings from the street and now, in addition to no heat or hot water, they had no heat and no water at all. But the 42 stubborn tenants remained, clinging to familiar, if incredibly uninhabitable, conditions, still hopeful that someone, somewhere would help them correct the situation. They had no idea that help would not come from the Community Law Office. Neighborhood children brought water up to the tenants from the fire hydrants in the street, and they heated it over their gas ranges. And Golar continued to urge the city to evict the remaining tenants, complaining it was not acting quickly enough.

On March 1, 1981, the city responded by issuing the forthwith vacate order. The reason given was that the building constituted a danger to the life, health, and safety of the occupants and was unfit for human habitation because of the following conditions: "No heat. No hot or cold water. Broken water pipes in the rear cellar. No electricity in the public hallways from the 3rd to the 6th stories."

The interaction between Golar and the city reeked of collusion, but I had no way of proving it. I relied on what appeared to be clear constitutional violations and so framed the complaint I filed in federal court.

The first claim for relief charged the defendants—Anthony

Gliedman, commissioner of HPD; Herbert Sturz, chairman of the
City Planning Commission; Edward Koch, chairman of the Board
of Estimate and the mayor of New York City; Lloyd Williams,
chairman of Community Board Number 10; and Rhoden-Sanford
Corporation—in their individual and official capacities with
"improperly using their official powers to terminate vital services, including water supply to the plaintiffs, thereby violating
their property rights, their rights to due process and equal
protection of the law and freedom from cruel and inhuman
treatment as guaranteed by the 5th, 8th and 14th Amendments
to the Constitution of the United States."

The second claim for relief charged that "the acts of the city
defendants, in illegally using their official powers, under color of
state law, to terminate vital services by issuance of a Vacate
Order, which was predicated upon their own intentional failure
to make a simple repair, constituted a collusory effort with the
other defendants to force plaintiff-occupants to move from their
apartments in violation of plaintiffs' rights under 42 U.S.C. 1983,
and represents a conspiracy to deprive plaintiffs of the equal
protection of the law, in violation of 42 U.S.C. 1985."

And the third claim for relief charged that "the city defendants approved the application for rehabilitation of the West
139th Street site submitted by Rhoden-Sanford, without com-
plying with Section 197-c (ULURP) of the New York City Charter, which acts constituted a violation of plaintiffs' civil rights
under 42 U.S.C. 1983."

Judge Kevin Duffy signed the order directing all the defendants to show cause on March 6 why an injunction should not be
issued prohibiting the city from forcibly removing the tenants,
prohibiting the implementation of the site development, and
ordering the city to restore water to the tenants.

During the hearing, the city presented its main argument:
that Harlen Houses would provide 214 completely rehabilitated
apartments in a fifteen-block tract "which has been one of the
great achievements in the renaissance of Harlem . . . that Harlen
Houses would have to be abandoned if the site is not cleared
immediately, and the City would lose its entitlement to the
twelve million dollars of federally insured moneys which are to
pay for the development." The judge turned to me angrily and
said, "Is this what you want? Don't you want Harlem to be
rehabilitated?" And he abruptly left the courtroom after dismiss-

ing the complaint and refusing to issue the injunction. Duffy had given no reason for his decision, but I filed an appeal nevertheless. I was without hope that, even if the appeal was successful, there was time to avoid the evictions. Had there been time, we could have gone up to the Supreme Court of the United States.

I consoled myself with the thought that at least the tenants had received a five-day reprieve, during which time the tenant organizers had been communicating with other organizations in an attempt to relocate them. Unless water and other services were restored, relocation was the only realistic alternative for them now.

I visited the tenants in their apartments. They were so helpless—old residents of Harlem who had been living in the buildings for thirty-five to forty-five years. They had seen Harlem in its renaissance heyday and all were active members of the local churches, their main sustenance in their old age. Their children had married and lived elsewhere. Some, like Susie Grier, took care of sickly relatives who were close to their own ages. Their apartments were as clean and as attractive as any I had ever seen, and they pointed with pride to the various certificates awarded them from Harlem organizations and churches over the years for their volunteer work. They had hope for Harlem's eventual emergence from the degradation into which it had plummeted, and they wanted it to be redeveloped. So they had not been opposed to the rehab project, they simply did not want to leave their apartments permanently and move into the hotels the city offered. They would have had to move out of Harlem, their home for so many years, and break ties with neighbors, friends, churches, and organizations that had been a solid part of their lives. Additionally, they feared that, despite Golar's letter promising to return them to their former buildings, once the project was completed the rent would be too high for them to pay out of their small pensions and social security. And they did not believe that the promise would be kept.

Those who had accepted the city's offers of relocation returned to tell horror stories of cramped single-occupancy hotel rooms in dangerous neighborhoods, of furniture damaged in transport to storage warehouses, where other items had been stolen and long-cherished possessions lost. The tenants had offered an alternative plan: to remain where they were in one of

the last buildings scheduled for rehab and to be returned to the
first one when it was completed. I also knew that the tenants'
helpless situation was not their fault. They had incorporated
their tenant organization and attempted to enter into an interim
lease program with the city for the maintenance of the buildings,
but the city refused their proposal. They had attempted to obtain
legal help through the Community Law Office and had not been
helped. They were now left with only the certainty that the
dignity of their lives was not to be ground into the dirt of
indifference with their consent. And with each defeat they
became stronger. If relocation was inevitable, it would be a move
into decent apartments.

On March 17, I met with Frederick Samuel, Myles Matthews
from Representative Rangel's office, and officials of HPD. They
urged me to communicate to the tenants that the survival of the
project depended on their leaving the site. I did. And they
refused. On March 18, I tried a different legal approach and filed
an Article 78 proceeding against the city's administrative bodies
in the New York Supreme Court for an order canceling the
forthwith vacate order and requiring the city to restore water
and heat to the buildings, based on the illegalities that nullified
the order.

The city's response was that an Article 78 proceeding,
which challenges city administrative decisions, must be brought
against the city within four months of the action complained of.
The ULURP illegalities occurred in August 1980, seven months
earlier. The forthwith vacate order, however, was within the
time frame, and the petition set forth the fact that the vacate
order was in violation of the Housing Maintenance Code because
the city itself had disconnected the water without just cause and
then used the resulting health hazard to justify its condemnation
of the building as unsafe.

The city further replied that the tenants "were in no way
harmed by any technical irregularities in ULURP." The city then
made its final argument: "If petitioners [tenants] do not relocate
immediately, Harlen Houses will have to be abandoned . . . and
where a party demands that the Court exercise its equitable
injunctive power, the Court must weigh the relative harm that
will be caused to the parties by the granting or denial of the
injunction. . . . Here, of course, the harm to the City is enormous

and irrevocable: a twelve million dollar project that would provide rehabilitated housing for over 600 needy New Yorkers will be lost; an area of blight will threaten the security and integrity of a fifteen block renewed neighborhood in Harlem."

On April 10, 1981, Judge Louis Okin gave his decision: he refused to cancel the vacate order and he ordered that all tenants leave their apartments by noon the following day.

Duffy had given his decision from the bench without opinion, and Okin repeated the precedent on April 10, without addressing the issues raised in the petition or the legal argument presented in the lengthy memorandum I had submitted. Rather, it would appear that he did in fact respond to the letter sent to him by Karen Shatzkin, assistant corporation counsel for the city, mailed to him before the case was argued and dated April 1, a reprehensible interference with legal process. In the letter Shatzkin stated:

> Although I fully understand that it is not ordinary procedure to address a matter to Your Honor's attention before it is submitted to you in Special Term Part I, this matter is of such urgency that extraordinary measures are imperative.
>
> The $12 million rehabilitation project scheduled for the site that petitioners wrongfully occupy will have to be permanently abandoned if they do not vacate the buildings immediately. The delay that is normally incident to court proceedings can kill this project—in which event, a victory for respondents on the merits will be an empty one indeed.
>
> I am therefore writing to bring to Your Honor's attention the need for an expeditious determination of this matter. I am enclosing a set of papers submitted to date by both sides.

I filed the appeal I had already prepared, called Ms. Grier, and told her the decision. She was not surprised and asked me to meet with the tenants that evening to explain the decision to them. They grouped together in her living room, the walls of which were covered with family photographs, and we talked. They were calm. They thanked Harlem Legal Services. And then they left to complete the packing they had already begun.

As I took a cab home, I experienced burnout for the first time in my life. I was hollow, dissociated, and very tired. The next day, Saturday, was a rainy, cold day, and Ruth Whitted of the Harlem Interagency for the Aging, who had my home telephone number, called to tell me that the marshals had arrived and that she was facilitating the tenants' relocation to hotels. I had neither the heart nor the energy to go to the building. I sat home, without moving, staring at the rain storming across the windowpanes, dry and inside an apartment I had called home for a very long time. And I suffered with them.

Chapter 20

When I submitted my resignation, the board held a special meeting to dissuade me and suggested I take my month's vacation to reconsider. Valerie Jordan came into my office several times in June, as I completed the next year's budget, and pleaded with me not to leave because she felt that I had made a difference and because "only a coward walks away from a fight when the going gets rough." All of the staff members, except Lahab, the director of litigation, and some of the lawyers, asked me to change my mind. I listened wearily, no longer willing to spend any more of my remaining productive years in a job that was funded by city, state, or federal monies, to effect changes those bureaucracies were dedicated to resist. And I knew that the government's repressive containment of any legal action to force implementation of elementary human rights would continue.

In September 1981, I opened my own office on West 106th Street, renamed Duke Ellington Boulevard, in New York City. I transformed a large street-level store into an attractive office. Walls were paneled, rugs covered the floors, and the four offices I had built to accommodate the lawyers I expected to hire for the law firm I anticipated creating were decorated with Assata's and Kakuya's paintings. From 1981 until 1984, I successfully represented clients in civil actions, including job discrimination and human rights violations, and appeals in criminal cases. I also defended tenants in Landlord Tenant Court pro bono.

Glenda Robinson, a green card holder from Suriname, whom I had known as an active member of many Harlem community organizations, was an excellent receptionist and secretary, the only full-time employee I had despite my ambitious plans to add at least three young, bright Black lawyers. But with the help of temporary secretaries, hired as I needed them for briefs and other major typing services, paralegals who answered the calendar in court, investigators, and process servers,

I was able to manage easily. The only problem was that I was constantly in court, and Glenda became my right arm. I was totally dependent on her to make appointments for both new and old cases, to keep the office running smoothly, to open it on time, and to close it at the end of the day.

Glenda's ability to manage without my constant supervision made it possible for me to represent Solomon Brown, a defendant in the Brinks case. On October 20, 1981, two Nyack, New York, state policemen and one Brinks guard were killed during a Brinks armored car robbery in Rockland County, New York. Judith Clark, Samuel (Solomon) Brown, Katherine Boudin, and David Gilbert were arrested at the scene. Various militant organizations were linked and charged with interconnected terrorist acts. David Gilbert and Kathy Boudin were identified as members of the Weather Underground and Judith Clark as a member of the May 19 Movement. Samuel Brown was unclassified but was called an ex-convict member of the BLA. Alleged BLA members Sekou Odinga, Kwesi Balagoon, and Mutulu Shakur were indicted later, along with Marilyn Buck, a white anti-imperialist.

Sol, the only Black captured at the scene, was beaten into unconsciousness by the Nyack police at the police station. He was taken to Nyack Hospital, where he remained for one day, and then was discharged to Rockland County jail, where the other defendants had been incarcerated. The Rockland County sheriffs picked up where the Nyack policemen left off. The beatings occurred three times a day for the next six days as each new shift was given an opportunity to blackjack and kick him unmercifully. David, in an adjacent cell, witnessed the assaults, tried to ease the bruised areas with cold water, and fed Sol. Sol didn't know that his neck had been broken until he was transferred to Otisville Correctional Facility, a federal institution, on October 27. At that time his attorney, Chokwe Lumumba, a militant attorney from Detroit and counsel for the New African People's Organization, obtained permission for a private doctor to examine him and determine the source of his dizziness, blurred vision, and constant pain. He underwent a spinal operation at the Westchester Medical Center and on January 26, 1982, was transferred to Woodbourne Correctional Facility with the other defendants, his neck in a brace. Chokwe filed a civil action for damages.

But while Sol was at Otisville, the other defendants had no knowledge that he had been visited by FBI agents Kenneth Maxwell and Robert Cordier. The agents had met him in secret, in a separate, concealed part of the prison, entering and leaving the facility by hidden entrances. Nor were the others aware that the two agents had visited him at Woodbourne. Unlike the others, Sol had no friends or relatives, and the other defendants collected around him, giving him money for cigarettes and other commissary items.

It was David Gilbert who, on March 26, telephoned his own lawyer, Lynne Stewart, to say that Sol was no longer at Woodbourne. The suspicions of the defendants had been aroused when, that day, for an hour or so prior to his removal, they all had been locked in their cells, an unprecedented act. And it was on that day that I was asked to try to locate him. During the next four days, the FBI, Woodbourne corrections personnel, and the Metropolitan Correctional Center (MCC) denied knowledge of Sol's whereabouts. But on the next day, their fears that he had been abducted by the FBI were confirmed by Kenneth Walton, the deputy assistant director in charge of the New York division of the FBI, who announced at a press conference the capture of two additional suspects alleged to have been involved in the Brinks robbery. Walton also announced that the details of the robbery had been obtained from two defendants already in custody, with the clear implication that one of them was Sol.

On March 29, federal Judge Morris Lasker granted my petition for a writ of habeas corpus, directed to the U.S. marshal and Walton, to "produce Samuel Brown to the end that this court may inquire into the cause of his present detention and that he be ordered returned to Woodbourne Correctional Facility." Immediately after the writ was signed, I learned that he was in Manhattan's Metropolitan Correctional Center, on the third floor in the federal protective custody section reserved for government informers. I saw him there, and he told me that his first visits from Maxwell and Cordier had come shortly after his arrival at Otisville, before his operation. They questioned him, beat him, and told him that if he refused to give them the information they wanted, they would kill him. He said that he refused to talk the first time, but on their second visit, December 31, 1981, Maxwell beat him, slapping him across the head, while Cordier wrote a statement and told him to copy it down on a pad

they provided. He said he was in pain and frightened and did
what he was told. They visited him again on January 29, 1982, to
show him photographs to identify, but he said he had not been
able to do so because his vision was still blurred.

While he denied that he had testified before the grand jury,
an order had been signed by Judge Lloyd F. MacMahon on March
26 for his appearance before the grand jury. The affidavit that
supported MacMahon's order was made by Kenneth Maxwell and
John S. Martin, the U.S. attorney for the Southern District, and
attached to the writ. It stated that Sol had told them that "the
attorneys appearing in his behalf in the Rockland county proceedings were not chosen by him and that he believes his safety
would be in jeopardy if those attorneys were made aware of his
cooperation with the FBI." The attorneys in question were Susan
Tipograph, Sol's attorney in a Brooklyn criminal case at the time
of the Brinks robbery, and Chokwe. Susan was now the attorney
for Judith Clark.

The writ was public information, but Sol's affidavit, the
alleged source of the FBI affidavit, was sealed. I had never seen
Sol before, and, as he talked to me in a rather unconnected way
that was just short of incoherence, twisting his head partially to
see me above the high neck brace, wincing and still in pain,
somehow his memory of dates and circumstances was so vivid
that their clarity gave credibility to his statements: that he had
never said he was fearful of his attorneys; that he had written an
eighteen-page statement for the FBI, but under duress and not
voluntarily; that he had not testified before the grand jury; that
he did not want to be in protective custody; that he was being
held at MCC against his will; and that he wanted to return to
Woodbourne.

He made an affidavit incorporating all of the information he
had given me, and I attached it to an amended writ of habeas
corpus. Judge Lasker granted it and directed the U.S. marshals
and the FBI to produce him. I had also petitioned that all
statements made by Sol to the FBI be disclosed, but that part of
the motion was denied. After a hearing, at which Sol testified, he
was released from federal custody and returned to Woodbourne.
And I found myself with a client who, while he denied collabora-
tion with the FBI, nevertheless had made a statement, as yet
unrevealed, that was responsible for the arrest of two additional
defendants in the Brinks case, both of whose indictments were

later dismissed for lack of evidence. And then there was the ultimate question: Was he being returned to Woodbourne as a spy for the government to entrap the other defendants?

His fragile health was of concern to me, and I could not help but sympathize with the suffering he had endured at the hands of the Nyack police and the FBI. But it is my feeling that once a person collaborates with the FBI, for whatever reason—whether inducement, fear, or the hope of assistance—that person can never again be trusted. I knew Sol did not have the discipline of an ideologue like Sekou, into whose tortured body the police had burned tattoos with lit cigarettes but who had steadfastly refused to relinquish any information to them. And Sol had no history of militant resistance to the police or to societal brutality against African Americans. Nevertheless, I was his lawyer now and, for the record, I put my doubts aside about his integrity, although I always talked to him as if he were wired.

After Sol returned to Woodbourne, the other defendants and their lawyers distanced themselves from him, refusing to discuss trial strategy during joint conferences that had previously included him. The problem was that, with the exception of Chokwe, they also distanced themselves from me. The loneliness of the long bus ride to and from a hostile Rockland County was not diminished by the lunches I ate alone in that town. I felt like a pariah, under suspicion by the activist attorneys with whom I had felt a camaraderie and because of whom I had agreed to represent Sol in the first place. After all, I was not a Robert Bloom. And sympathy with their position did not ease my resentment. In addition, I was spending months away from my office and sacrificing my only source of income. Although I had filed a notice of appearance for Sol as a privately retained lawyer in March 1982, I represented him pro bono. When the pretrial hearings began in September, it was necessary for me to apply to be assigned to the case to obtain a free daily copy of the transcripts. I didn't even know what the hourly rate was for assigned representation because I had never filed a list of expenditures with the court for reimbursement, which would have included the bus fare and other out-of-pocket expenses, as well as trial time.

When pretrial hearings began, only Kathy Boudin, represented by Martin Garbus, Leonard Weinglass, Leonard Boudin (her father, who made occasional courtroom appearances but who was not involved in the daily trial preparation), and Linda Bectiel (who researched legal issues for them and prepared their written motions), and Sol participated. The other defendants declared their prisoner of war status, refused to submit to the court's jurisdiction, and participated in no court proceedings. I conversed with Sol every day during the hearings, discussing the evidence introduced, and gave him the daily transcripts to read. Because he was isolated from the others, I provided him with cigarettes, candy, money, and other small items he asked for.

But immediately after the completion of the pretrial hearings, on December 15, 1982, Sol called me to say that he had telephoned the U.S. attorney's office, that he was going to testify against the other Brinks defendants, and that he was being transported to MCC the following day. Given his obvious mental fragility, compounded by both the beatings he had received and the rejection by the other defendants, I was not surprised. But neither could I continue to represent him. And the last time I saw Sol was on December 22, 1982, in Rockland County jail, when he confirmed that he was voluntarily collaborating with the government and I told him I could no longer be his lawyer. The worst fears of the defense had been confirmed. Even though the still undisclosed statement Sol had made to the FBI was a haunting reality, his frequent disclaimers as to the voluntariness of the statements, as well as his repeated assurances to the others that he would never testify against them, if not entirely convincing, at least permitted them to be nervously hopeful that he would no longer be a government collaborator.

I made a motion to be relieved as his lawyer, stating that when I began representing him I believed that his statement was involuntary, the result of beatings by the FBI, and that he had repudiated its contents. I said that to continue to represent a defendant who had participated in joint meetings with co-defendants and shared trial strategy and thereafter agreed to be a government witness against them was repugnant to me and precluded me from offering even a modicum of representation to him. I further stated that, in the interests of justice and to avoid violating Sol's constitutional right to effective assistance of counsel, which I could not guarantee, the court should grant my motion to withdraw. Judge Stolarik not only refused to permit me to withdraw, pointing out that I had been assigned, but threatened me with contempt if I did not continue representing

Sol. Contempt was a familiar term to me, and I told him to exercise his option. But I would not be Sol's lawyer.

Robert Litt, the assistant U.S. attorney prosecuting the federal RICO indictment, which included conspiracies in the Brinks robbery and in the liberation of Assata, at which Sol was expected to testify, called me and reminded me that I was still Sol's attorney, and he wanted to let me know that neither the U.S. attorney's office nor the FBI would interfere with me in any way and would actually facilitate my visits with Sol. Incredible! Sol also telephoned my office frequently. He wanted to know whether I was still his lawyer and said he wanted to see me desperately. Would I please visit him? Incredible! I taped all of my conversations, both at home and in the office, and when I reviewed them several years later, I was amazed. The government was just as clumsy and stupid as was the board of directors of Harlem Legal Services.

It was not until June 3, 1983, when the venue had been changed to Goshen, New York, that the new judge, Ritter, granted my motion to withdraw. He had directed me to appear in court and I did so reluctantly, prepared for a contempt citation. I sat in the first row among the spectators, demonstrating my separation from Sol. Under those circumstances, I suppose Ritter had no choice but to accept my decision. I later learned, during the federal RICO trial in which Sekou and Silvia Baraldini were charged with aiding in Assata's escape and, along with Chui (Cecil Ferguson), Jamal (Edward Joseph), Illiana Robinson, and Bilal Sunni Ali, with conspiracy in the Brinks case, that Sol did not testify for the government. He did, however, on the appeal of his conviction in the Rockland County case, cite the allegation that I had failed to adequately represent him because I was a "movement" lawyer, and my loyalties were not to him but to the other defendants, thereby denying him his constitutional right to effective counsel under the Sixth Amendment. The Appellate Division of the Supreme Court of the State of New York dismissed his argument, stating that I had in fact represented him more than adequately. Their opinion, published in the March 16, 1988, *Law Journal*, said in part, "Though Ms. Williams's request to withdraw as counsel upon learning that the defendant provided information to Federal Agents may be an indication that she was interested in the success of the 'Movement,' there had

been no showing that this interest created a conflict which bore
a relationship to the defense. The law and the circumstances of
this case, viewed together, reveal that meaningful representation
was provided the defendant . . . that she vigorously represented
the defendant's interests and conducted his defense appropri-
ately."

had spent months away from the office working on Sol's case in Rockland County, calling Glenda at lunch break every day to check cases and emergencies, arranging evening appointments, and spending weekends at the office catching up. So it was not until May 18, 1983, when I had received at least twenty wrong numbers and no calls to my usually busy phone lines that I first became aware that intercepts had been placed on the phones. I called the telephone company that day to report the interference after I had dialed the office number from a pay phone and received the message "There is trouble on the line. Call again." When I called again I heard, "I'm sorry, this phone has been disconnected." I reported what I believed to be cross-wiring and the lines appeared to clear up.

By the end of December there had been a sharp drop in new cases, but overall 1983 had been my most financially successful year, and I made allowance for the seasonal slump, assuming I would be able to weather the lull. But by February 1984, I still had no new cases, and although I was as busy as I ever had been, my time was spent on matters I had already been paid for. On Monday, February 27, 1984, Glenda told me that her grandmother had died in Suriname and she was taking the 2:00 P M flight from Kennedy Airport the next day. She needed money for the trip and I wrote her a check, which she took to the bank to cash. She had made an appointment for me at 3:00 P M. with a longstanding client and asked if she could leave when he came so that she could get ready. I suggested that she leave as soon as she returned from the bank, but she insisted on staying until the client arrived. I had spent the night completing a brief and, telling her to call me at home when the client came, I left the office. When she hadn't telephoned by 4:00 P M , I called her. She told me that the client hadn't kept the appointment and that she was closing up. Despite the fact that I told her to keep the keys for the few days she would be gone, she insisted on coming to my

apartment to return them. I noticed that she was extremely
nervous and agitated, but I attributed her anxiety to her grandmother's sudden death.

She never returned. After two weeks, when I looked into her
desk, I realized that she never intended to return because the
drawers had been emptied of all of her personal possessions. I
knew something was drastically wrong, but the true circumstances of her departure were not revealed to me until two weeks
later by the client with whom I had had the appointment the day
she left. And I was shaken by what he told me. Glenda had been
trafficking cocaine from the office during my absences. When I
was present, she would nod customers away after they knocked
on the upper glass door to determine whether I was there. My
office was in the back, concealed by a folding door that I always
kept closed, so it was impossible to tell by looking through the
door whether I was in the office. My client told me he had made
cocaine purchases from Glenda and had heard her make many
drug deals over the phone. On that Monday he was to be the
intermediary between her and a major drug supplier. She had
asked for an exceptionally large number of kilos to be delivered
to the office at exactly 3:00 P.M., and my client was to make the
delivery and pick up the money from her. Glenda knew the
supplier, but his suspicions were aroused by the unusually large
order and her insistence that delivery be made at the office at
exactly 3:00 P.M. Unknown to Glenda, the supplier refused to
complete the transaction, telling my client either that I was
being set up by the FBI for a major drug bust or that he was, and
he ordered my client to stay away from the office that day. Not
only had he not made an appointment with me, but he said that
Glenda had assured him I would be in court and he was surprised
to see his name in my appointment diary.

As he talked, the pieces fell into place and I realized that I
had been the target of a major FBI sting operation, saved only by
the street smarts of the supplier. As I analyzed it, my dwindling
bank account reflected my depleted business, and clearly I
needed money to continue my practice. Between the phone
intercepts and Glenda steering new business away, I was in the
kind of financial situation in which selling drugs to extricate
myself would be an acceptable explanation to the public. I could
see the headlines, the exorbitant bail that I could not have
posted, the lengthy trial, the guilty verdict, and the endless

appeals while I was, win or lose, eternally discredited as a lawyer. I asked my client why he was telling me now, and he said that Glenda was still in the city and might return for her job and, somehow, his sense of decency compelled him to tell me in the event she did. I didn't ask why he hadn't told me about Glenda before because it wasn't necessary: she had once been useful to him, and she no longer was.

After my conversation with him, my neighbors in the stores adjoining the office told me tale after tale of drug traffic in the office during my absences, especially on Friday afternoons, when I was rarely there. I had made it easy for Glenda because I always called several times a day to check for messages and she always knew where I was, when I planned to return to the office after court, and when I was going directly home. I learned that there was a lookout to spot me coming up the block in the event I returned unexpectedly. In the days that followed Glenda's departure, her customers continued to call, asking for her, pretending to be relatives or friends. One actually blurted out, "Did that bitch blow that gig?" I'm embarrassed to reveal the extent of my stupidity. And my trust. And my carelessness in the face of what I knew the government was capable of doing. But despite trusting Glenda, I had never breached the confidence of any of my clients.

By July I knew I would not be able to continue much longer. When the phone rang it was always the wrong number and for days, even weeks, it simply didn't ring at all. I hired new secretaries who left after a few weeks despite their enthusiasm for the job, and it was obvious to me that their sudden, unexplained departures were the result of government pressure. I spent more time in the office, only because I no longer had the volume of cases that had kept me in court almost daily. A former client came in to tell me that she had just called the office four times, and a man's voice had answered, saying no one was in the office and asking her to leave a message. When she called the operator, knowing I had never had a male secretary, she was told the line was being checked for trouble. She came to tell me that something was drastically wrong and to warn me to be careful. Another client had been directed by an intercept to a number in Florida where I could be reached, another to a Michigan number. I kept reporting the intercepts to the telephone company, who denied that any existed, until I played a recording I had made.

Then the "This line is being checked for trouble" tape was disconnected. But others replaced it. And I was finally forced to accept the fact that I was no match for this electronically sophisticated assault and closed the office.

Had it not been for the comfort and support I received from my family and Doe I think I would have been as shattered as my dreams for a neighborhood law firm had been. Doe, who had successfully operated the real estate business her father had started in Richmond, Virginia, came from a long tradition of breakthrough Black legal achievements and knew the heart-breaking roller coaster journey it was. Her father, Spottswood Robinson, Jr., had been the dean of Virginia Union University Law School, then a Black, segregated institution, had founded the Virginia Mutual Benefit Life Insurance Company of Richmond, and was vice chairman of its board of trustees and general counsel, as well as one of the vice presidents, directors, and attorneys for the Consolidated Bank and Trust Company in Richmond. And her brother, Spottswood Robinson III, had been a longtime civil rights lawyer, working closely with Thurgood Marshall and Robert Carter in preparing the *Brown v. Board of Education* Supreme Court case before he was appointed the presiding justice of the U.S. Court of Appeals for the Washington, D.C., Circuit.

As I had throughout the years in times of trouble, I went to Wilmington and walked for hours on the beach, picking up shells and driftwood, examining them as closely as I did my life. Old memories flooded through me, but only briefly. They were like old friends in old photographs, to be looked at occasionally and remembered warmly, but no longer relevant to the exigencies of present-day crises. I replayed the tape of my recent experiences and forced myself to keep my finger on the forward button when it threatened to slip to rewind, but I couldn't. I was in disorder, no longer able to keep the many compartments of my life separate from each other. Now they were colliding, spilling their diverse contents, forcing me to relive the whole of my existence in one piece instead of within the selected segments I had previously chosen to live them.

I questioned the choices I had made during the long distance of my life. How many had been mistakes? Had I been unintentionally reckless or intentionally courageous? It was only after I had forced myself to reassess each of my choices that I was able to reaffirm them. And it was only after I had carefully examined that self-evaluation inventory that I was able to release the explosive anger I had been withholding. My mother reminded me of her lifelong advice not to accept blame for consequences that I bore no responsibility for creating, and only then was I able to leave Wilmington and return to New York to begin again.

Chapter 22

Shortly after my return to New York, on August 30, 1984, I received the phone call I had been anticipating for five years. Assata called me from Cuba to tell me she had been granted political asylum, her usually quiet voice pitched to unprecedented height above the telephone static. But before I let myself believe it really was Assata, I kept my voice cold and distant, asking her to tell me something only she and I knew, not permitting the flood of relief and happiness to envelop me until I was sure.

I had received many telephone calls throughout the years from people who claimed to have messages from Assata, who asked me to meet them on unlit corners in unoccupied sections of the city, but I had believed none of them. I even had some telephone calls from unidentified voices that sounded like Assata's, and Doris had received calls from Assata-sounding voices telling her to meet her and bring money. There had been rumors she was in Cuba, but there were also newspaper articles pinpointing her alleged presence in the United States. On February 14, 1980, the *New York Post* headlined a story about Florida bank robberies with "Chesimard Hunted in Fla. Bank Heists," reporting, "The FBI says escaped cop-killer JoAnne Chesimard may be responsible for a recent crime spree here, in two South Florida bank robberies," although it added, "no one has identified her yet positively," and it also reported that she had robbed banks in Georgia. In 1981 Assata was called the "mastermind" behind the Brinks armed robbery and was identified by several eyewitnesses as a participant but was never indicted. The entire front page of the November 22, 1982, *New York Post* was covered with the words "Hunted Girl Cop-Killer Gets New Look," and a blown-up photograph of Assata, allegedly uncovered in a safe house in Pennsylvania, adorned the second page, along with the caption "Lovely but deadly." The suggestion was that the photo represented a passport picture, but no postulation was made that she had left the country. On the same day a federal RICO indictment charged Silvia Baraldini, Mutulu Shakur, Susan Rosenberg (against whom charges were later dropped), Sekou Odinga, and three others with planning Assata's escape.

In 1984, when a New Jersey state trooper was killed by a Black man, the *Daily News* headlined its article "Probe Killer's Links to Joanne," while the body of the article quoted both Clinton Pagano, the New Jersey state police superintendent, and FBI spokesmen disclaiming her involvement. On May 10, 1984, the *Daily News* warned, "Chesimard May Be Hiding in New York," and on June 6, 1984, a task force of the FBI and state police in the northeastern states was formed to apprehend Assata and ten other fugitives, among them Susan Rosenberg and Timothy Blunk, who were arrested on December 1, 1984, in New Jersey for possession of explosives. Newspapers roared, "Terror Suspects Nabbed in Jersey. Pair Linked to Joanne Chesimard." The *Daily News* featured a story, "They're Down to a Fearsome Foursome," accompanied by pictures of Assata and three others: Marilyn Buck, wanted in connection with the Brinks case, called the "quartermaster" and the "only white member of the BLA, providing getaway cars, safehouses, false documents and weapons," and later convicted of aiding in Assata's escape; Thomas Manning, who with Raymond Luc Levasseur was being sought in connection with the December 21, 1981, shooting of Philip Lamonaco, a New Jersey state trooper, both believed to be members of the Sam Melville–Jonathan Jackson Unit, which had taken responsibility for bombing several buildings in Boston; and Mutulu Shakur, called the strategist for both Assata's escape and the Rockland County Brinks robbery.

So when Assata called me, I had to be sure it was she, and that she was in Cuba. She convinced me by repeating a singsong ditty she always teased me with as a child: "Anty, Panty, Jack O'Stanty." And, barely coherent, I gave her Doris's new unlisted phone number and immediately began making plans for Doris, Kakuya, and me to visit her in Cuba.

The most difficult part of my planning was having Kakuya certified as having been born. I had attempted to obtain a copy of Kakuya's birth certificate shortly after she left Elmhurst Hospital, where she was born, and had been told by the Department of Health's Bureau of Vital Statistics that none was on record, although filing a birth certificate is an automatic procedure required by all hospitals. But since we had the hospital's official custodial release, and a birth certificate had not been needed when we enrolled Kakuya in nursery school and Hunter College's Campus School, I had attended to more urgent demands on my time. But now we needed it to have a passport issued, and I shifted into high gear, spending days at the Manhattan, Bronx, Queens, and Brooklyn Departments of Vital Statistics, although it should have been on file at central headquarters in Manhattan. No one could explain why it had not been filed. I even went to New Jersey and obtained an affidavit from Dr. Garrett attesting to the fact that he had delivered the baby at Elmhurst Hospital. I was finally told that the only way a "delayed" birth certificate could be filed was if her mother signed an affidavit requesting one. When I said that her mother was out of the country and not available, I was told that the only other way was for Kakuya's court-appointed guardian to apply. When I went to Surrogate's Court to file a petition for Doris to be appointed Kakuya's legal guardian, I was told I needed her birth certificate. And the passport office told me that they needed both her birth certificate and letters of guardianship before they would issue a passport.

Several months had passed by this time, and my temper had reached fever pitch. I stormed into Manhattan's Department of Health and demanded to see the supervisor, who told me the only other way a birth certificate could be issued was if the director of Elmhurst Hospital requested one, so I took the subway to Queens to speak to the director. I think I must have explained the situation to about five uninterested people at Elmhurst Hospital, all of whom told me that they couldn't help and that the director didn't do that sort of thing. One indifferently motioned me over to the office of the director of hospital records, who was out to lunch. I waited for the director to return and was shocked when a tall, attractive, red-tinted and straightened-haired, fashionably dressed Black woman waved her long, fingernail-polished hands in aloof disbelief and said, "Of course the child was born here. And of course I'll prepare the application." I have told this story a million times because it demonstrates the falseness of many Black militants' belief that the courage to fight our battles is clothed only in Afro hairdos and African dresses. Although I would not ever again straighten my hair because I consider it unworthy of my heritage and admit that I too perceive these bourgeois Black people with a certain unconscious disdain, this woman was an example of the way in which outside appearances can conceal true identity. As I left, she smiled for the first time and said matter-of-factly: "Of course, we won't be surprised if the Department of Health refuses to accept this."

I arrived back in Manhattan just before closing time, prepared for the worst, already planning the legal action I knew I would have to take, but the supervisor, while shocked and disbelieving, had some hurried consultations with her superiors and issued Kakuya's birth certificate then and there. I filed the petition for Doris's letters of administration in Surrogate's Court and waited two months before they were granted—and then only after I had been to the clerk's office several times asking why they were delayed and had written a letter to the surrogate, Bertram R. Gelfand. Perhaps the easiest phase of the process was receiving the passport, which arrived a few days after we sent in the application, and within weeks all of us were on the plane to Cuba and Assata.

But during this period before Kakuya's papers were in order, I decided to visit Assata first and squeezed out a five-day weekend for the trip. Number one, I couldn't wait to see her, but, number two, a decision had to be made whether Kakuya would remain with her and I had to be satisfied that the person I had known so well hadn't been negatively altered before Doris and I would be willing to relinquish Kakuya. The flight to Miami was short compared with the endless wait in the Miami airport until check-in time for the chartered plane to Havana. I waited alongside the crowd of Miami Cubans lugging enormous suitcases and duffel bags of food and other household articles and listened to the excited language I barely understood even though I had hurriedly begun playing my beginner's Spanish records. At every checkpoint through which I was permitted to pass before boarding the plane to Havana, I wondered if I would be stopped. Would the U.S. government let me through? My determination to reach Assata quelled all my anxiety as I vigilantly watched for disguised FBI agents.

Over and over I thought, What changes had five years made? Was she the same person or, at least, was she an acceptable modification? I was filled with both joy and apprehension, unable to separate one from the other. When the

plane landed at José Martí Airport in Havana to the noisy 223 applause of the passengers, I stepped out of the plane and paused halfway down the steps leading from it. I watched the passengers scurry into the buses waiting to take them to the terminal, took a deep breath, and lowered my eyes to continue down the stairs when I saw Assata, smiling and yelling "Anty," waiting at the foot of the steps with a Cuban official to drive me to the hotel room the government had reserved for me.

She was Joey and Assata all at the same time and as we hugged and talked and hugged and talked, it was as if no intervening years had separated us. We slept very little over the next three days and I visited her apartment and toured the school Kakuya would attend if the decision was made for her to stay with her mother. I was pleased with this country that had provided a haven for Assata, who was still energetic and still committed and who was enrolled in the political economics master's program at the university and was writing her autobiography. She was full of anticipation at the prospect of seeing the child she had so seldom even held in her arms and at the same time fearful of the long-awaited meeting.

In April 1985, Kakuya, Doris, and I made the first of many trips to Cuba, and while we were there we all decided that Kakuya would remain with Assata.

Kakuya was two weeks old when we had brought her home from Elmhurst Hospital. One room of Doris's three-bedroom apartment had been easily converted into a nursery and Doris had taken a year's leave of absence to care for the baby. And it was fortunate she did, because when Kakuya was about six weeks old, Doris noticed an almost imperceptible inward turn of her left foot. Dissatisfied with the diagnosis of several podiatrists, which ranged from a perfect foot to an untreatable condition, she found Dr. Lloyd Sears, a nationally acclaimed Black podiatrist with an office in Queens, who found the embryonic deformity and put her leg in a cast from the knee down for several months. When it was removed, he prescribed massages three times a day and an orthopedic corrective bar that held both ankles stiffly distanced from each other and that she wore at night. At the end of a year, the foot was completely corrected, although she still has to wear light acrylic inserts in her shoes.

Because Kamau had a sickle-cell trait, a condition common to many Black people, Doris had Kakuya's blood analyzed soon after she left the hospital. At the time, the tests were negative, but when she was retested at an older age, it was discovered that she too has the trait. The doctor explained that for the first six months of life, Kakuya retained her mother's antibodies, which accounted for the original negative results. While the disease is dormant and will not affect her life span or health in any way, should she have a child by a person with the same trait, their children will have a one in four chance of full-blown sickle-cell disease.

Except for these two conditions, Kakuya was a bright, eager, fast-moving, inquisitive, and perceptive child who both walked and talked at an early age. She has her mother's large eyes and her father's forehead, and she was a beautiful child, blessed with superior intelligence, which we were quick to notice. Doris read the poems of Claude McKay, James Weldon Johnson, and Langston Hughes to her every night after she was tucked in bed and, if on some occasions she was a little late, Kakuya loudly reminded her that she was waiting. As she grew older, they read together, Kakuya imitating the Black dialogue, which she loved, with ease. She was also a fearless child and climbed the highest monkey bars at the playground long before other children her age.

But her physical and emotional environment was circumscribed by the danger posed to her by Assata's public image and the possible retaliation that loomed from many sources. It was difficult to explain to her why her nursery school friends never invited her to their houses or why none of them visited hers, although she had the companionship of Bevvie's son, Donny, who was the same age and lived in the same building. Doris and Kakuya vacationed to all of the Caribbean islands during the summers, as well as EPCOT Center in Florida and the Sea Islands in South Carolina. When Kakuya was four, Doris had her tested and applied to the Hunter College Campus School for gifted children, where she was accepted. Before she was admitted I advised Dr. Alan Seidman, the principal, that she was Assata's daughter because I wanted to avoid the negative impact any sudden revelation might have had in relation to her admission to the school or her continuance there once accepted. He said, "Thank you for telling me, but it makes no difference. Kakuya is our kind of student. We want her here. She belongs."

We were fortunate that all of her first-grade teachers were

Black and understood that Kakuya was special because she was 　　*225*
Assata's child. Any question about the "special" nature of her
presence in the school was quickly dispelled when, shortly after
she was admitted, television monitors were placed throughout
the school, the number of uniformed guards was doubled, and
they carried walkie-talkies. But her teachers provided their own
special brand of security around her, quietly and unnoticed.
Kakuya lived with me during her first year at Hunter, and her
teachers would not let her out of their presence at the end of the
day until I came to get her. They would stay late, if necessary,
and would relinquish her to no one except my sister or me.
Kakuya also had a code word to be used in case of emergencies if
a stranger offered to bring her home on the pretext that one of us
was ill. The word was *Amala,* Kakuya's middle name, which
means "hope for the future," and the person would have had to
know the name as well as its meaning. In her later years, when
she remained with Doris, she took the express bus from the
Bronx and I met her at the first bus stop and we walked to school
together. Even when she was ten, Doris paid a very responsible
Hunter High School student, who lived nearby, to accompany
her home on the express bus.

Kakuya was so bright, hardworking, and charming, in the
same rather quiet way typical of her mother, that everyone took
a personal interest in her. The math teacher scolded her for
preparing projects for other students, giving her an A and
explaining that the others would get the marks their own efforts
had earned. The science teacher awarded her a certificate of
achievement. The social studies teacher marveled at her research paper about the Trail of Tears journey of the Cherokee
Indians, and the English teacher knew that the play she had
written, dictated to me over a long, arduous weekend and typed
by me, was in fact written by no one else but Kakuya. And she
was so talkatively inquisitive that I nicknamed her "Running
Mouth" and had a sweatshirt made for her with the words printed
on the back.

As she grew older, we enrolled her in the Alvin Ailey Dance
School and she performed in their annual benefits at City
Center. We bought her a piano and hired a piano teacher, and
Kakuya played so well that she was one of the recitalists who
appeared in a special concert for beginning students in Brooklyn.
All of her many talents were encouraged, both to expose her to

an environment of people with broad perspectives and to wrap Kakuya in the traditions and culture of her people. African books filled the bookshelves, and African paintings decorated the walls. Countee Cullen's and Langston Hughes's poems of struggle were extended to the wider African struggle, and Doris took her to community meetings and cultural events of significance to Black people. We supplemented her small family birthday parties by renting the Roxy Roller Skating Rink off the West Side Drive, to which all of her school friends were invited and came.

When Kakuya went to Cuba to live with Assata, we were both bereft, and Doris grieved for months, barely able to remain in the apartment filled with Kakuya's mementos. But we were both comforted by her reunion with Assata and the fact that Kakuya was not living in the drug-infested, death-driven racist country that might claim her life. In Cuba she was protected. And safe from physical harm.

Afterword

In 1984, after Assata's phone call, Doris and I visited our parents with Kakuya to tell them the good news. We noticed that our mother's usually sharp perceptions and memory were becoming dulled, and our father, who initially denied the possibility, was finally forced to acknowledge the debilitating disease, later diagnosed as Alzheimer's, which took her life on her birthday, November 9, 1986. But while she was still alert she knew that her "Piggy," Assata, was safe in Cuba. After her death my father spent his days on the beach, driving the four-wheel-drive Subaru over the sand that his eighty-six-year-old legs could no longer travel. But God failed to fulfill the contract my father said had been made with him—to live until he was at least one hundred years old—and on July 21, 1991, at the age of ninety, he died after a few days' illness.

During 1987, 1988, and 1989, I taught a seminar in family law at the Urban Legal Studies Program at CCNY and, since then, I have been associated with the firm of Stevens, Hinds and White, Lennox's office. International in both its composition and its legal interests, the firm has lawyers from Africa, the Caribbean, Europe, and the States and three secretaries, Felicia, Joyce, and Rosetta, who provide exceptional expertise. While the daily practice of law is no longer part of my life, I still accept especially challenging cases, but I spend equal time reading African history, relearning African art, and painting the seashells and driftwood I collect from Freeman's Beach with Black liberations colors (black, red, and green) and with Horus's eye. And I have come to the conclusion that Assata reached a long time ago: direct action by the people is the only hope for change.

I avoid meetings where rhetoric mimics the great Black orators of long ago. Nothing is new or newly said. Ideas only sound new because they are applied to the old realities experienced by a new generation while the conditions of Black people remain fixed in the stagnation created by white racism in the United States.

227

Unfortunately, centuries of Black efforts have led to a perverse analysis by some of today's African American youth of the reasons for our collective failure to attain equality. This analysis has turned blame inward and directed misplaced accusations at our heroic past leaders, with no recognition that historical distance should not be permitted to obscure historical reality. Unless our young people remember that legal barriers to full participation first had to be removed; that legal slavery and then legal segregation had to be abolished; and that the right to vote had to become the law of the land before the unrelenting extralegal restrictions on our lives could be attacked, their analysis of the reasons for our present condition remains defective. Our collective effort for survival must move forward as it looks backward. To blame our past leaders because they were able to achieve only partial success during their lifetimes is to dismiss generation-framed limitations and to minimize the tenacity of the racist restrictions the dominant society has imposed on our lives. It is true that past gains are not enough; each generation must continue whatever struggle is required by the changing nuances of the racism they face. But we can no more charge any one person or generation with the responsibility for our past fate and our future direction than we can implant future vision into every eye.

Whites continue to criticize us because every Black person does not emerge "bloody but unbowed" from that deep abyss of containment into which they have lowered us. But their criticism is hypocritical; it is a self-congratulatory appraisal of their own success that allows them to deny the helping hand they have received from white society. If history has a lesson to demonstrate, it is that repression of an entire segment of society will backfire. White society cannot continue to fasten the consequences of its own selfish, destructive design on its victims in order to escape its own responsibility. If there is ever to be change, white society must first recognize and accept the fact that the Black condition was intentionally fashioned by whites and that if there is no change in that circumstance, whites too will suffer.

I have examined the various theories advanced by Black pundits for bringing about change in this country. But barring total restructuring of this society, I remain unconvinced that any of them are workable formulas. I believe that equal opportunity to equally produce and share in the wealth of a country is the political and economic framework that provides the only fair system. The U.S. government's failure to give assistance to the health, employment, housing, and other basic needs of its citizenry has not created a just system, and I expect no real changes to occur until the masses decide that change must come and pressure for that change.

I believe in what I like to call the verticalization of the horizontal. The horizontal base would contain the bedrock of self-knowledge and self-worth. Its ferment would hold upright upon it every Black person: the laborers and the professionals; the teachers and the students; the preachers and their congregations; the elderly and the children; the businesspeople and the customers. Together we would move upward into a realization pinnacle, one solid apex, where Black aspirations would be attained and Blacks would be empowered to pierce myths and shatter obstacles. How should we proceed?

What if all African American children learned that their history did not start in America, after slavery? What if they learned that long before their ancestors were enslaved by Europeans, Europeans had enslaved other Europeans by the hundreds of thousands? What if they learned that Europeans were imported as slaves to the Americas before Africans were? What if they learned that we did not leave our greatness on the shores of Africa? What if they knew that our homeland had provided the genesis for all human culture?

What if recent Black college graduates upgraded their knowledge of African history and entered the teaching profession, especially in cities where the majority of schoolchildren are Black? What if they changed the curriculum to include history as it happened? What if the books the African American scholars have written about the primogeniture status of Africa in world culture were required reading for every student? What if, after twenty years of teaching in public schools, at say the age of forty-two or forty-five, the teachers broke away from their boards of education and, with the money they had saved in collective accounts for just such a purpose, began schools across the country to teach Black children their history? What if wave after wave of young college graduates earned their living in this fashion?

What if.

AUTHORS GUILD BACKINPRINT.COM EDITIONS are fiction and nonfiction works that were originally brought to the reading public by established United States publishers but have fallen out of print. The economics of traditional publishing methods force tens of thousands of works out of print each year, eventually claiming many, if not most, award-winning and one-time best-selling titles. With improvements in print-on-demand technology, authors and their estates, in cooperation with the Authors Guild, are making some of these works available again to readers in quality paperback editions. Authors Guild Backinprint.com Editions may be found at nearly all online bookstores and are also available from traditional booksellers. For further information or to purchase any Backinprint.com title please visit www.backinprint.com.

Except as noted on their copyright pages, Authors Guild Backinprint.com Editions are presented in their original form. Some authors have chosen to revise or update their works with new information. The Authors Guild is not the editor or publisher of these works and is not responsible for any of the content of these editions.

THE AUTHORS GUILD is the nation's largest society of published book authors. Since 1912 it has been the leading writers' advocate for fair compensation, effective copyright protection, and free expression. Further information is available at www.authorsguild.org.

Please direct inquiries about the Authors Guild and Backinprint.com Editions to the Authors Guild offices in New York City, or e-mail staff@backinprint.com.

LaVergne, TN USA
18 November 2010

205464LV00007B/103/A

9 780595 141708